ISBN 978-0-483-26949-1
PIBN 10167619

TRACTS AND ESSAYS,

MORAL AND THEOLOGICAL;

INCLUDING,

A DEFENCE

OF THE

DOCTRINE OF THE DIVINITY OF CHRIST,

AND OF THE

DOCTRINE OF THE ATONEMENT;

WITH

OBITUARIES,

ETC. ETC.

BY THE LATE

WILLIAM HEY, Esq. F.R.S.

MEMBER OF THE ROYAL COLLEGE OF SURGEONS IN LONDON;
HONORARY MEMBER OF THE ROYAL COLLEGE OF SURGEONS IN IRELAND,
OF THE ROYAL MEDICAL SOCIETY OF EDINBURGH,
OF THE LITERARY AND PHILOSOPHICAL SOCIETY OF MANCHESTER;
AND LATE SENIOR SURGEON OF THE GENERAL INFIRMARY
AT LEEDS.

LONDON:

PRINTED FOR HURST, ROBINSON, AND CO., LONDON;
ARCHIBALD CONSTABLE AND CO., EDINBURGH;
AND ROBINSON AND HERNAMAN, LEEDS.

1822.

J. Watts de Peyster

Rose Hill, Tivoli P. O., Duchess Co.,
1st *January*, 1868.

Member of the Netherlandish Literary As[sociation] [*Maatschappij der Nederlandsche Letterkunde*] [Ley]den, Holland.

Honorary Member of the Minnesota Historical So[ciety] and of the Phrenokosmian Society of Pennsylva[ni]a College, *Gettysburg;* of the Philosophian Society, *Missionary Institute, Selins Grove*, and of the Euterpian Society, *Muhlenberg College, Allentown, Pennsylvania.*

Member of the New York and of the Pennsylvania Historical Societies; Member, Third Class, (Honorary) of the Military Order of the Loyal Legion of the United States.

Life Member of the Historical Society of Michigan, and of the Numismatic and Archæological Society of New York.

Corresponding Member of the State Historical Societies of Maine, of Vermont, and of Wisconsin; of the Long Island, and of the Buffalo Historical Societies; of the New England Historic-Genealogical Society; of the Quebec Literary and Historical Society; etc., etc., etc.

CONTENTS.

THE

EDITOR'S PREFACE.

OF the Tracts, Essays, &c. which are now presented to the public,—the two first, on the Divinity of Christ, and the Atonement, were published separately, many years ago, in reply to Dr. Priestley and others, who were engaged in writing and circulating small popular Tracts in opposition to these important doctrines of Christianity. Some account of the controversy, and of the success of these "short defences" has been given in the Life of Mr. Hey, which was published in the early part of the present year.

The Moral Essays, Obituaries, &c. to page 487, appeared, at different periods, in "The Christian Observer;" the papers which follow these pages are now printed for the first time. Mr. Hey, during the course of a long and active life, frequently committed his thoughts on various subjects in divinity to paper; but he destroyed a considerable portion of these writings long before his death; not from any settled distrust of the soundness of his reasonings, but from a fear lest the freedom with which he had discussed some popular tenets, might be misunderstood, or misused, by any into whose hands the manuscripts might fall.

Truth in the understanding, and charity in the heart, are, perhaps, the most precious gifts which can be conferred upon the sons of men in their present state and condition; but although absolutely denied to none, they are found to exist with much inequality, both in their measure and in their relative proportions. Knowledge and grace are not inseparable; for genuine piety may subsist with obscure and inadequate conceptions, and much confusion of thought; but where that is conjoined with modesty and due humility, it is more to be valued than all the treasures of natural science, or the most learned and profound speculations in theology itself. Ill-founded pretensions, however, are not to be acquiesced in, whatever be the character of the assumer; for, when it can be shown that conclusions are not warranted by the premises, or that the premises themselves are highly disputable, to offer as a reply, the fact of his being a good man, is as little satisfactory as if the same answer were returned to refute a charge of his ignorance of the classics, or of philosophy. Correct and definite conceptions of revealed truth are highly desirable; and it is not less our duty, than conducive to our happiness, to cherish no notions as evangelical verities which are not distinctly reflected on the mind from the Sacred Scriptures. But the duty which a man owes to himself, in this particular, is not always the exact measure of that which may be due from him to his fellow Christians. A man should be cheerfully willing to resign any idols* which have been set up in his own mind; yet it may not always be either wise, or expedient, to engage in ejecting them from the minds of others. Many a

* In the sense of Lord Bacon.

Christian adopts a safe and useful course of practice, whose creed might not bear a strict examination; who could not produce sufficient reasons for what he believes, nor analyze and clearly exhibit the principles by which he is conducted; yet, it might be neither kind nor beneficial to inject suspicions, and create perplexities, where the predominant bias of the heart is favourable to the gospel of Christ, and the life is not inconsistent with this profession. Our Saviour gave a lesson of caution and moderation, when he said to his disciples; "I have many things to say unto you, but ye cannot bear them now."

The doctrines defended in the two Tracts which stand first in this volume, are acknowledged by Christians in general to be highly important. These small publications had become scarce; and, as in the opinion of capable judges, Mr. Hey had succeeded in treating the subjects with great strength of argument, in a plain and perspicuous manner, it was conceived, that the reprinting of them would be an acceptable service to the public. As the doctrines of the incarnation and atonement are matters of pure revelation, conveyed to us only by inspired writers, nothing more is incumbent on their advocate than to show that, they are clearly taught in the Holy Scriptures. This the Author has been thought to have accomplished in a manner decisive and unanswerable. Those who demand something more than scriptural evidence, — who require explanations satisfactory to their reason, and consonant with their experience, are in quest of a sort of knowledge which the Bible no where professes to give. The wisdom of God has judged it proper to communicate information to us, on certain subjects, in part only, and this is probably as much as it may concern us to know; for mysteries are not presented to us to be wholly understood, but to be received and believed. To prove that any particular doctrine is contained in the Bible, --to maintain its credibility, and to defend it against opposers, ought never to be confounded with a full comprehension of the subject, and a capacity of explaining it; yet these very different undertakings have not always been sufficiently distinguished, even by persons of much penetration and ability. That "we know but in part," is a position not less applicable to natural science, than to theology. Our acquaintance with the qualities and properties of organized and unorganized substances is partial and imperfect; few physical phenomena admit of complete explanation; yet all this is very consistent with much real information, and with that measure of practical knowledge which is sufficient for the purposes of human life. To reject what is cognizable, because it is conjoined with something that is obscure and inaccessible, is just as rational, as if a man should close his eye-lids in the evening, because he has not the light of the sun.

The several Essays on sacred and moral subjects, with the Obituaries, &c. were published, as hath been remarked, at different intervals, in the "Christian Observer." It is not certainly known whether Mr. Hey had prepared those which follow page 487 for the press; but, as they all appear to have been the result of serious inquiry and reflection, his friends conceive, that they may not prove unacceptable to those who knew and respected the writer. The considerations on natural and moral ability and inability were principally designed to remove some of the objections, which have been occasionally proposed, against the scriptural doctrines of moral depravity and of divine grace. Those who have directed much of their attention to the abstruse questions connected with the free agency of man, will be aware that the principles assumed in this discourse have been employed for similar purposes, but with various degrees of confidence and success, since the days of Augustine to the present time. In the controversies of the Jansenists, the professed disciples of Augustine, with the Molinists, the discussions on grace were conducted with a subtlety, refinement, and copiousness of argumentation, that has scarcely left room for any addition. The substance of these disputations is exhibited, with much precision and ability, in a posthumous work ascribed to Fenelon, comprised in twenty-four dialogues; these, with a dialogue, composed, as it has been thought, by Nicole, and annexed to the last volume of "Les Provinciales," which were published under the fictitious name of Montalte, unfold the nature of the controversy, in which the able and animated polemics of that period were involved, with sufficient detail and amplitude. It would be uncandid and unjust to withhold all praise and admiration from the laborious efforts of many of those great men, who, with the best intentions, have endeavoured to remove the veil which is thrown over these profound and difficult subjects; of their success it may be proper to speak less confidently.

If, to the numerous and acute metaphysicians, to whom we have alluded, be added the names of Thomas Aquinas, Bradwardine, Baxter, Bayle, Hobbes, Bramhall, Crousaz, Placette, Leibnitz, Jurieu, Bossuet, Locke, Collins, Clarke, Butler, Jonathan Edwards, Reid, &c. men of comprehensive intellect, deep penetration, superior powers of reasoning, and unwearied diligence; if men, gifted as these, have been found unequal to the task of clearing away the difficulties, and dispelling the shades which encumber and darken the subject of human liberty and divine influence, a lesson of modesty and humility, at least, is bequeathed to those who may be tempted to resolve the questions with little distrust of their own sufficiency. The lively agency of a passionate curiosity has frequently stimulated its subject to enter upon high and arduous undertakings, and to pursue them with a vigour and steadiness not surpassed in cases where the lust of ambition, or the avidity of gain, have awakened and impelled the exertions of others. The magical power of the imagination readily swells a favourite object beyond its true dimensions, and confers a dignity and importance upon it, which a chastised reason, measuring by a more correct standard, reduces and disallows; nor can the mind, when importuned by a restless inquisitiveness, be easily restrained from expatiating in regions where there is neither path nor guide; where effort is eluded by tenuity, and progress mocked by circuition.

It seems to have been the opinion of Mr. Hey, that the only substantial difference which subsists between moderate Calvinists and Arminians, is in the doctrine of final perseverance; whether, for instance, the influences of the Holy Spirit are ever finally withdrawn from any of those persons to whom they have been once communicated. If this be so, it is greatly to be regretted, that so much time and labour should have been misemployed, and so much improper feeling excited and cherished, upon a curious and doubtful speculation; and one which, to a fair and upright mind, cannot be of much practical importance. But the questions how, and in what manner, the human will is determined, whether grace be irresistible, as well as indefectible, have been agitated with still greater copiousness and assiduity. It may admit of considerable doubt, whether we, standing in the capacity of accountable beings, are greatly concerned in inquiries of this kind. The Holy Scriptures address men as moral agents and responsible creatures, who possess dispositions, and perform actions, deserving praise or blame, punishment or reward; and we are accustomed to treat each other as if we were thus constituted. To engage in a laborious perquisition after the mode in which our volitions are produced, is of much the same consequence to us, as how the perceptions of the mind are excited, whether through the medium of an external world, or by the immediate agency of the Deity; we must, under the admission of either hypothesis, conduct ourselves as if matter were in contact with us, and human actions were spontaneous.

We are subjects under the government of God, and have received those laws and statutes from our supreme Legislator, by which we are now to be ruled, and finally judged. The matter of our duty lies with sufficient clearness before us, for all useful and practical purposes; but it is surely no important part of it to ascertain how, and in what manner, the Divine Providence conducts the affairs, and superintends the actions and thoughts of men, so as to accomplish his wise and holy purposes. That it highly concerns us to be found in the exercise of obedience to the revealed will of God, is unquestionable; but to inquire how the free agency of moral beings is compatible with their absolute dependance upon the Creator; whether there be a self-determining power in the mind by which its elections are effected, or the soul must be always influenced by extrinsic causes in its volitions; whether, in short, there be any medium interposed between the Creator and his creatures, are matters with which our moral improvement and happiness have little connexion. What the force of prejudice, the seduction of sophistry, or a subtle and disingenuous casuistry, may induce a man *to say*, is of little moment, while we see the same person form his purposes, and manage his commerce with his fellow-creatures, as if neither he, nor they, entertained any doubt that a man could bind himself by his promises, and be truly and properly responsible for his engagements. If, then, those who acknowledge the natural government of the world to be under the immediate influence and control of the Deity, never permit metaphysical difficulties to impede them, when transacting the business of life; they ought to be furnished with very satisfactory reasons, if they adopt a different language and mode of conduct in those concerns which more immediately regard the moral administration of the Supreme Being, or the dispensation of grace. We know as little of the proximate cause of volition in the one case as in the other; nor is it either wise or becoming, in creatures of our scanty measure, to permit any speculations on the attributes of God, to lessen our sense of entire dependance upon Him, or diminish our gratitude for mercies received; or, on the other hand, to impair our impressions of responsibility, and weaken the motives to a sincere and unlimited obedience. "This is His commandment, that we believe on the name of his Son Jesus Christ, and love one another."

POSTSCRIPT.

THE late pious and learned President Edwards, in his Treatise on the Freedom of the Will, has discussed the subject of natural and moral inability, with much acuteness and perspicuity; and Mr. Hey, by pursuing a similar mode of reasoning, appears to have been persuaded of its conclusiveness and utility. It is highly probable, that neither Mr. Edwards nor Mr. Hey were aware, that "A Discourse on Natural and Moral Impotency" had been published by a Joseph Truman, B. D. in 1671, a second edition of which appeared, after his death, in 1675. His different writings show him to have been a man of piety, of considerable reading and research, of great moderation, and in sentiment, on theological subjects, approaching nearly to his contemporary, Richard Baxter.

The definitions and illustrations given by Mr. Hey and Mr. Edwards tend to correct much of the improper language that has been introduced in treating on these subjects, and to reform the mode of thinking and speaking on the doctrine of human ability in morals. How far any of the real difficulties, connected with these abstruse questions, are elucidated, or removed, may be left to the judgment of the reader. When it is maintained that every man has the power, ability, &c. of keeping all the divine commandments, and of complying with the requisitions of the gospel, this can only be properly meant of his physical capacity of willing; for, if he have not the natural power of volition, he is not a capable subject of either civil or moral government; he is not a man. But it may admit of inquiry, whether the term power, implying a physical attribute, can be applied, when predicated of the soul, with perfect propriety and in the same sense, to physical acts, and to the moral qualities of the mind. That a man is responsible for his voluntary actions, will be easily admitted, because the terms imply, that they are under his immediate control and direction; but it may not be quite so clear, that the internal dispositions of the soul are equally subjected to the physical power of volition. Can a man, in the proper sense of the word, change his love of sin into a love of holiness, as he can change the direction of his eye or his hand?* To reply that he can, if he will, is somewhat like saying that his power of willing, not being impeded by any natural, necessitating cause, nothing is wanting to correct its moral obliquity but his own good pleasure: in other words, subdue an evil moral habit by a physical act of volition, and you will be a good man. If a man be denominated virtuous, or vicious, according to the determination of his will, then, to will and to do, may be represented as identical in morals, since the terms merit and demerit refer to the purpose of the mind, whether an external act be consequent, or not. But something more than the mere physical power of volition seems to be included in the inquiry;—perhaps it may be a question of this kind, Has the mind a power of imparting a good moral quality to any, or every exercise of volition? Should this be doubted, then it would seem probable, that something is required beyond the mere phy-

* In the production of voluntary motion, by the agency of the mind upon the body, something resembling impulse seems to be in operation; but are we warranted to conclude, that this is analogous to the mode in which mutations take place in the mind when it acts upon itself, so that the character and disposition may be changed by simple volition, as it can alter the direction of corporeal motions?

sical act of willing to change a vicious into a virtuous mind.* If this suggestion be admitted, the solution offered by Truman, Edwards, &c. would have only removed the difficulty one step higher, and we should seem to end where we began.

There is no difficulty in employing the terms can, and will, agreeably to the definitions given by Mr. Hey, when they are applied to physical acts; but when they are applied to the generation of new moral qualities in the mind, there is something of the air of a paradox about them. That the existence of evil dispositions in the mind denotes a culpable state; that God has provided certain means for the changing of these, and renovating the soul; that the honest and diligent use of the means prescribed will be accompanied by the divine blessing, and issue in success, are propositions to which every Christian must assent. But when a wicked man is told that he has the power of becoming

* If any one should suppose, that the moral quality of the volition may receive an immediate impression from the object of the election, so as to determine its character, he may be reminded, that this superinduced quality must, in that case, be posterior in its existence to the act of willing; whereas, the moral quality ought to be coetaneous with, and inseparable from, the physical act, in order to our denominating it virtuous or vicious.

a good man, he will allow this as it respects his overt acts; but he will perceive, or think that he perceives, a something ambiguous, when it is further affirmed, that nothing is wanting to his delighting in the laws of God, but his own choice. If it can be proved, either from Scripture, or experience, that the soul has, in the proper sense of the words, the same control and dominion over love and hatred, complacency and aversion, in morals, that it has over the voluntary motions of the body, there must be an end to the controversy. But till it be shown that terms, implying physical power, may be applied, with strict propriety, to the production of moral dispositions, by the agency of the will, in the same sense as voluntary motions are connected with the exercise of volition, a man may be puzzled, without being persuaded, by such a course of reasoning. The doctrine of the two delectations has been ingeniously supported by the followers of Augustine; but it may be doubted, whether it has shed new light upon this difficult question; for, after all that has been offered, a man seems to be left in the situation of him who feels no conviction, although he may not be furnished with a conclusive answer.

London, October 1, 1822.

SHORT DEFENCE

OF

THE DOCTRINE

OF THE

DIVINITY OF CHRIST;

WITH SOME

REMARKS UPON A LATE "APPEAL TO THE SERIOUS AND CANDID PROFESSORS OF CHRISTIANITY."

TO WHICH IS ADDED,

A SUPPLEMENT,

CONTAINING

OBSERVATIONS UPON A LATE "FAMILIAR ILLUSTRATION OF CERTAIN PASSAGES OF SCRIPTURE."

"I will also shew mine opinion." JOB xxii. 10.
"Speaking the truth in love." EPHESIANS iv. 15

THE

PREFACE.

To write in defence of a doctrine, which has been so repeatedly and ably defended by many learned men; or to make any remarks upon a pamphlet, which has been already answered, may appear to some a very unnecessary employment. It may be proper, therefore, to inform the reader, that the following observations were written chiefly for the sake of the common people, who have not time to read, or money to purchase many books; and that no reflection is intended upon the gentlemen, who have already published their remarks upon the "Appeal." The writer of these observations, imagining that the multiplicity of the subjects handled together in that pamphlet, tends rather to confound than instruct those who have not read or thought much upon the subjects it contains, has chosen to fix the attention of his readers to one point, which certainly deserves the most deliberate consideration.

It is allowed on all hands, that the truth respecting this doctrine is *fundamental* in religion. If the Lord Jesus Christ is but a *mere man*, then the doctrine which attributes *divinity* to him, is undoubtedly "a *radical corruption*" of the Scriptures: but if he is so one with the Father as to be, with him, the *true God*, then to reject his divinity is a *radical error*. The reader, therefore, should consider well, that the subject before him is not of a trifling nature, and such as he may either embrace or reject with safety. This is by no means the case. If he is wrong in this matter, he is *fundamentally* wrong.

The first and great commandment is, that we should worship the Lord God, and him only. If, therefore, we either withhold divine honour from him who is God, or give it to him who is not, we are breaking that commandment, on which all the rest depend; we are either *blasphemers*, or *idolaters*; and we are assured, that none such shall inherit the kingdom of God. Let me then beg of my reader to keep in view the importance of the subject, and to remember what is required of us in order to our preservation from fundamental errors. There are two things absolutely necessary: 1. That we pray earnestly to God for divine wisdom: "If any of you lack wisdom, let him ask of God." James i. 5. 2. That we be sincerely desirous to do the will of God when known: "If any man will *do* his will, he shall know of the doctrine whether it be of God." John vii. 17. Without these we have no reason to expect to be guided into all truth.

In the following observations I have referred the reader to the word of God only, and to that as we have it in our native tongue; for to me there seems to be a great impropriety in appealing to the unlearned about any doctrine, and then entertaining them with criticisms upon the learned languages, which they cannot understand. If the persons appealed to are those who only know the English language, no reference ought to be made but to the *English* Bible. The Author of the "Appeal," thinks the lower class of people are as capable of judging concerning the important truths of revealed religion as the most learned;* which can only be true on supposition that the Bible, as we have it in our own language, is sufficient "for doctrine, and instruction in righteousness."

The Writer of this Tract conceals his name for the reason mentioned by the Author of the

* Preface to Mr. Elwall's Trial.

"Appeal," viz. "To give what he has written, a better chance of being read without prejudice."* And as he claims no assent to any thing he has said, upon his own credit or authority, his name would be of no service to the reader. The Bible, to which alone he refers, is open to every one; and he desires the reader to judge for himself, whether the sense in which he quotes any Scripture be agreeable to the context, and to other passages or not. He is not, however, ashamed of the doctrine he defends, for it is that upon which (after the most mature deliberation) he can cheerfully venture his eternal salvation. He is free to acknowledge, that he daily "calls upon the name" of Christ, that he may be saved; that he "honours the Son even as he honours the Father;" and looks for "grace, mercy, and peace, not only from God the Father," but also "from the Lord Jesus Christ." Wishing the reader every spiritual blessing through Him, he begs leave to subscribe himself,

A LOVER OF THE BIBLE.

* Dr. Priestley has acknowledged himself to be the Author of the "Appeal," since this was written.

A SHORT DEFENCE,

&c.

I. It has been objected to the doctrine of the *Divinity of Christ*, that it is *incomprehensible*, and *contrary to our reason*. On the former account, not the proper object of our faith, though it were true; and on the latter, not to be believed on any testimony whatever. Both these objections appear to me to be without foundation, though constantly insisted on by those who oppose this doctrine.

The thing proposed to our belief in this doctrine is this; "That the glorious person, whom the Evangelist St. John styles, The *Word*, who was in the beginning with God, and was God, was made flesh, and dwelt among us; thus uniting in his own person, in an inexplicable manner, the divine and human nature."

"We believe this fact," I say, "as a doctrine of revealed religion," that the divine and human nature are united in the person of Christ; "but as to the *manner*" in which they are united, "we *believe nothing*, because we *know nothing* about it; the sacred writers not having *explained*, that is, not having *revealed*, or made it known unto us."* We are, therefore, unjustly charged with making a thing *incomprehensible* the object of our faith; for the proposition which we believe is perfectly clear and intelligible; it is a plain *fact*, received upon divine testimony, which is the best evidence in the world.

And as this proposition is not *unintelligible*, so neither is it contrary to reason: for who can prove, that it is impossible in the nature of things, that the divine and human nature should be united in the same person? Yet good proof should be given of this before it be asserted, that the *Divinity of Christ* is a thing contrary to our reason, and such proof I am persuaded can never be given.

But here it may be said, that this doctrine, being founded upon that of the *Trinity*, is absurd and irrational, since it is impossible

* See Dr. Priestley's Queries to the Anonymous Answerer, page 19.

that three should be one, and one three. To this it hath often been replied, that the objection is full of ambiguity, and is either true or false as the terms are explained. If it mean, that three cannot be one, and one three, precisely in the same sense, the assertion is true; but it does not affect those who believe there is but one God, though subsisting in three *persons;* (as they are usually called;) and if it be asserted, that what is *three* in one respect cannot be *one* in another, the objection is without foundation. The plain state of the case is this; The same Scriptures, which constantly assure us that there is but one Supreme Being, whom we call God, do repeatedly ascribe the peculiar attributes and acts of God to "the Father, the Son or Word," and "the Holy Ghost;" and lest we should thence imagine that there are three Gods, they likewise inform us that these *three* are *one*. "There are three that bear record in heaven, the Father, the Word, and the Holy Ghost, and these three are *one*." 1 John v. 7. So the Apostles were commanded to "teach all nations, baptizing them in the name of the Father, and of the Son, and of the Holy Ghost." Matthew xxviii. 19. And since it has pleased "the one only true God" to speak of himself as if he were three distinct *persons*, although we cannot conceive what there is in the divine essence to render this the fittest representation of himself, we are bound to believe it upon his testimony who cannot lie, and who alone knoweth his own glorious and incomprehensible manner of existence. We have abundant evidence in the Scriptures, that there *are* three who bear record in heaven, and that these three *are* one, and therefore we believe that *it is so*; though *how* it is so we *know not*, and therefore do not *believe* any thing about it.

Those who deny the *divinity* of our Lord Jesus Christ, bring us many passages of Scripture to prove, that he was a man, and inferior to the Father; but these passages are really nothing to their purpose, for they do but prove what we ourselves contend for. We believe that the Eternal *Word* not only took our nature upon him, but also, that he sustained the office of *Mediator* on our account: that, through his own voluntary condescension, he was sent by the Father into the world; fulfilled all righteousness in our nature, and became obedient even unto death; that in consequence of this humiliation, he was highly exalted, made head over all things to the church, and constituted the judge of quick and dead; and that, finally, when the work for which he undertook the office of

Mediator shall be fully accomplished, he will then lay aside the peculiar dignities of his office or *mediatorial kingdom*, and reign in the preceding dignity of his nature for ever and ever.

There is not, therefore, the least contradiction in representing Christ as inferior to the Father with respect to his human nature, yet equal to him with respect to the divine; for the different representations and *seeming* contradictions in the scriptural character of our Saviour plainly prove, that his *compound person* partook of natures essentially different from each other. We use a similar manner of speaking with regard to ourselves, and on a similar account. When a writer calls mankind sometimes mortal, sometimes immortal; at one time corruptible, at another incorruptible; instead of charging him with contradictions, we immediately perceive, that he has a reference to those totally different substances, a material body and immaterial soul, which are, in an inexplicable manner, united in us. Let us use the same degree of common sense with regard to the Scriptures, and all the difficulties concerning the character of Christ will vanish. There will then appear no contrariety in calling him the "Son of man," and yet the "Lord of

Glory." Luke xix. 10. 1 Corinthians ii. 8. But it lies upon those who deny the *divinity* of Christ, to reconcile those passages of Scripture, which attribute divine perfections to Christ, and speak of him as God, with those that are expressive of his inferiority to the Father; and till this is satisfactorily done, they must give us leave to think, that the former refer to his original nature, and the latter to his assumed manhood, and mediatorial character; which is the only way of reconciling those Scriptures that otherwise would be *quite contradictory*.

The Author of the "Appeal" says, page 12; "You have been taught to believe, that Jesus Christ was not *man*, but very and eternal *God*, without considering, that, by thus making more Gods than one, you are guilty of a breach of the first commandment." If he means to say, that the divines, usually called *orthodox*, teach that Jesus was not man, the assertion is not true. Whether they are consistent in teaching this together with his divinity, is another question; but that they do teach both is a matter of undoubted notoriety. They do not, however, by such doctrine, set aside that fundamental article of all religious truth, the Unity of the Divine Being; but they speak of God as he is pleased to speak of himself, and think they cannot follow a better example.

II. There are certain attributes or perfections which solely belong to, and characterize, the Supreme Being. These cannot be ascribed to any creature. Wherever we find these perfections ascribed to any being in the Scriptures, we have the fullest assurance that such being is God; both because they are incommunicable in their own nature, and because God hath declared he will not give his glory to another. Isaiah xlii. 8. But these perfections are ascribed to our Lord Jesus Christ in the Scriptures, therefore he is very and eternal God. This I shall prove by the most clear testimony of God's word, and then take notice of the principal objections which are made to this doctrine in the "Appeal."

1. The *eternal existence* of the Supreme Being is one of those incommunicable perfections, which can be ascribed to no creature whatever. "Thus saith the Lord, the King of Israel, and his Redeemer the Lord of Hosts, I am the First, and I am the Last, and besides me there is no God." Isaiah xliv. 6.

This glorious attribute of the Deity is repeatedly ascribed to Christ: "When I saw him," says the beloved disciple, "I fell at his feet as dead; and he laid his right hand upon me, saying unto me, Fear not, *I am the First and the Last.*" Revelations i. 17. Again, I am Alpha and Omega, the Beginning and the End, *the First and the Last;* chapter xxii. 13.

It is the character of the immutable and self-existent God, that "he was, and is, and is to come." Revelations i. 4. And this is the true character of Jesus Christ, who "is the same yesterday, and to-day, and for ever." Hebrews xiii. 8. He who, in the fulness of time, was to take our nature upon him, is thus described from the Prophet Micah. "Thou Bethlehem Ephratah, though thou be little among the thousands of Judah, yet out of thee shall *he* come forth unto me, that is to be Ruler in Israel; whose goings forth have been from of old, from *everlasting;*" chapter v. 2. Hence our blessed Lord speaks of "the glory which he had with the Father before the world was." John xvii. 5. And claims to himself that awful name I AM, which belongs only to the Supreme Being; "Before Abraham was, I AM;" chapter viii. 58. "Had our Saviour only said, 'Before Abraham was, I was;'

thus much at least would have been the consequence, that he had an existence before Abraham.—But now that he says, 'Before Abraham was, I am;' something more is implied; something that peculiarly belongs to the expression I AM, and what that is we may learn from the original use of the words. They are the words which God made choice of to express his own *eternity* and *power*, when Moses inquired after the name of God: he answered him, 'I AM THAT I AM.' 'Thus shalt thou say to the children of Israel, I AM hath sent me unto you.' Exodus iii. 14. What now could tempt our Saviour to use and apply this expression to himself? He knew it never had been applied to any but God, and would have been in the man so applying it, in the highest degree committing *the robbery* of making himself *equal with God*. Besides, according to analogy of language, the words, without this construction, express nothing; no idea belongs to them; for a man cannot in his mind carry the present time back, and make it antecedent to the time already past; and therefore to say, Before a thing was, I am, is shuffling ideas together, which can have no place in the understanding. If, therefore, you admit the expression to have any meaning, you must allow the

I am to belong to Christ, in its proper and peculiar use, as signifying eternity and permanency of duration."* It is plain the Jews understood our Lord in this sense, for they immediately "took up stones to cast at him" for his blasphemy, as they thought it; and our Lord, instead of attempting to show them that they misunderstood him, confirmed their apprehension, by escaping out of their hands.

The eternal existence of Christ is likewise pointed out to us in that eminent type of him Melchisedek; who, in order that he might prefigure him in this, as he did in other respects, had no beginning of days recorded of him; "Without father, without mother, without descent, having neither beginning of days, nor end of life; but *made like unto the Son of God*, abideth a Priest continually." Hebrews vii. 3. Our Lord was the "root," as well as the "offspring" of David. Revelations xxii. 16. "David's Lord," as well as "David's Son." Matthew xxii. 45. Which clearly shows, that whatever the Jews *did*, they *ought* to have "expected more than a man for their Messiah." It was owing to their ignorance of the Scriptures in this respect,

* Bishop Sherlock's Discourses, vol. iv. Discourse 1.

that they were not able to answer our Lord's question, which he put to them with a view, no doubt, to lead them to the knowledge of his true character.

2. "He that built," or created "all things is God." Hebrews iii. 4.* But the Word, who was made flesh, and dwelt among us in the person of Jesus Christ, created all things. We are assured that the Almighty did not make use of any inferior being, as an instrument in the great work of creation. "I am the *Lord* that maketh all things, that stretcheth forth the heavens *alone*, that spreadeth abroad the earth *by myself*." Isaiah xliv. 24. "I have made the earth, and man upon it: I, even *my hands*, have stretched out the heavens," &c. Isaiah xlv. 12. "And, therefore, when the Apostle says, that God "created all things by Jesus Christ," Ephesians iii. 9. it is the same as if he had said, He created all things by *himself*, by *his word*, or with *his own hands*. The solemn address which the Psalmist makes to the Almighty, Psalm cii.

* If the reader will compare this passage with its context, he will find, that these very words are spoken of Christ; though they are introduced here in that sense only, in which no one will dispute their meaning.

"Of old hast thou laid the foundation of the earth: and the heavens are the work of thy hands," &c. belongs to Christ. "Unto the Son he saith, *Thou*, Lord, in the beginning hast laid the foundation of the earth; and the heavens are the work of *thine* hands. They shall perish, but *thou* remainest: and they all shall wax old as doth a garment; but *thou* art the same, and *thy* years shall not fail." Hebrews i. 10, &c.

"In the beginning," says the Evangelist, "was the Word, and the Word was with God, and the Word was God. All things were made by *Him*, and without *Him* was not any thing made that was made. He was in the world, and the world was made by *Him*, and the world knew *Him* not." John i. 1, 3, 10.

The chapter from whence this passage is taken, so clearly sets forth the divinity of Christ, that the greatest force must be put upon it, and the most unnatural construction made use of, to evade its testimony to this important truth. The Evangelist assures us, that by the *Word* is meant God himself, and it is plain that the *Word* was Christ, for it was he of whom John the Baptist was sent to bear witness, and whose glory the Evangelist saw, as the "only begotten of the Father;" from whence it necessarily follows, that Christ is

God; and, therefore, this glorious person, whose messenger and forerunner John was, is called by the Prophet Isaiah, "the *Lord* our God;" chapter xl. 3. which is the incommunicable name of the Supreme Being.

The work of creation, which indubitably characterizes the Deity, is likewise, in Colossians i. 16. ascribed to our Lord Jesus Christ: "By him were all things created that are in heaven, and that are in earth, visible and invisible, whether they be thrones, or dominions, or principalities, or powers: all things were created *by* him, and *for* him. The last clause assures us, that he was, in the most proper sense of the word, the Creator: all things were created "*by* him," and "*for* him:" "*by* him," as their cause, and "*for* him," as their end. By the same language is the Almighty described in other passages of Scripture, as Hebrews ii. 10. "It became him, *for* whom are all things, and *by* whom are all things." And in Revelations iv. 11. "Thou art worthy, O Lord, to receive glory; for thou hast created all things, and *for thy pleasure* they are, and were created."

Can human language express any thing more clearly, than these passages of Scripture express this great truth; that our blessed Redeemer, the Lord Jesus Christ, is also the

Almighty Creator, and, consequently, Very and Eternal God? If they do not prove this, it signifies nothing attempting to prove any thing by Scripture; words can convey no meaning, but upon all language rests impenetrable darkness and confusion.

All the other attributes of God necessarily follow this of creating power. He who created all things must uphold all things, for this is equivalent to a continued creation; he must be every where, and know every thing; and he is the proper object of worship to all his intelligent creatures. These attributes are not only applicable to Christ by way of inference, but they are directly applied to him in the Holy Scriptures.

3. "He upholdeth all things by the word of his power:" Hebrews i. 3. and "by him all things consist." Colossians i. 17.

4. He is *omnipresent*, otherwise he could not be in heaven and earth at the same time, which he assured Nicodemus was the case, in that memorable conversation which he condescended to hold with him. "No man hath ascended up to heaven, but he that came down from heaven, even the Son of man who *is* in heaven." John iii. 13. The same truth is

evinced from the promises, which our Lord hath made to all his true disciples: "Where two or three are gathered together in my name, there am I in the midst of them." Matthew xviii. 20. And, "Lo, I am with you alway, even unto the end of the world;" chapter xxviii. 20. Whereas, on the supposition that he is a *mere* man, it is not only impossible for him to be with all his disciples, but he cannot be with any one of them, for he will remain in heaven till "the times of restitution of all things." Acts iii. 21. But he is truly always in every place, for he can attend to the prayers of all that "call upon him." 1 Corinthians i. 2. "He is able to succour them that are tempted." Hebrews ii. 18. And to defend his sheep, "that none shall pluck them out of his hands." John x. 28.

5. The Lord Jesus is likewise *omniscient*. Thus the Apostle Peter addressed him; "Thou, Lord, knowest *all* things." John xxi. 17. The Almighty claims it as his prerogative to know the hearts of men. "Thou *only* knowest the hearts of the children of men." 2 Chronicles vi. 30. And this prerogative belongs to Christ. "Jesus knew from the beginning who they were that believed not." John vi. 64. "Certain of the scribes said

within themselves, This man blasphemeth; and Jesus, *knowing their thoughts*, said, Wherefore think ye evil in your hearts?" Matthew ix. 34. Jesus did not commit himself unto "them, because he *knew all men*, and needed not that any should testify of man, for he knew *what was in man*." John ii. 25. "There were certain of the scribes sitting there, and reasoning in their hearts; and immediately, when Jesus *perceived in his spirit* that they so reasoned within themselves, he said," &c. Mark ii. 6, 8. "And Jesus immediately *knowing in himself*, said," &c. chapter v. 30. It cannot here be justly said, that Christ might know the hearts of men by revelation from the Father, for the texts themselves guard against this perversion of their meaning, by attributing this perfection precisely and absolutely to Christ himself. "He knew *in himself*; and needed not that *any should testify*;" which is not true, if Christ knew what was in men only by revelation, and not by his own inherent knowledge. This perfection of God is thus expressed in the prophecy of Jeremiah; "The heart is deceitful above all things, and desperately wicked, who can know it? I the Lord search the heart, and try the reins;" chapter xvii. 9, 10. "And this our blessed Saviour claims as his own attribute. " All the churches shall know that I am *he which searcheth the reins and the heart.*" Revelations ii. 24.

It is proper to be remarked here, that, notwithstanding this, our Lord assures us he did not know all things; for, speaking of the day of judgment, he says, " of that day and hour knoweth no man, no not the angels which are in heaven, neither the Son, but the Father." Mark xiii. 32. This is as strong a proof of his real manhood, as the passages above-mentioned are of his real Godhead; and therefore, when connected, they show that our Lord Jesus Christ is God and man. Let but the reader attentively compare this Scripture with those just before quoted, and he will find, that the application of those to the divine, and of this to the human nature of Christ, is the only method of making them consistent with each other. For as Christ is " *He* who searcheth the reins and the heart," which we see is the distinguishing character of God, he could have been ignorant of nothing had his nature been simple, or of one kind only; or if he had known " all things" by revelation from the Father, there would have remained nothing which he did not know, on the same supposition. But now that *perfect* and *imperfect* knowledge are both ascribed to him, it proves him to have been partaker of natures essentially different from each other. With respect to his *divine* nature, he "needeth not that any should testify," for he himself "knew all things." With regard to his *human* nature, he was capable of growth "in wisdom as well as stature." Luke ii. 52. And thus, by comparing one Scripture with another, we find an easy solution of the difficulty.

6. The blessed Jesus is likewise the *object of divine worship;* for, in the days of his flesh, he suffered himself to be worshipped by his disciples; after his resurrection, and ascension into heaven, he was worshipped by his Apostles, who acted under immediate inspiration, and by the first christians; and he is now worshipped in heaven by the glorified hosts of saints and angels.

"And, behold, there came a leper and worshipped him, saying, Lord, if thou wilt, thou canst make me clean. And Jesus put forth his hand and touched him, saying, *I will*, be thou clean." Matthew viii. 23. "Then came she and worshipped, saying, Lord, help me; Jesus answered, O woman, great is thy faith;" chapter xv. 25, 28. The blind man whom he had restored to sight, said, "Lord,

I believe, and worshipped him." John ix. 38. "The Apostles said unto the Lord, Increase our faith." Luke xvii. 5. And Thomas, when his unbelief was removed by Christ's condescension, cried out, "MY LORD AND MY GOD." John xx. 28. Yet none of them received the least reproof for mistaking the object of their worship.* It is true, the word *worship* is sometimes, though very rarely, used in Scripture for the respect which is due from man to man; but in the instances above-mentioned, it is used in its proper sense, because it was accompanied with a confession of faith in him who was worshipped, and an express avowal of his being the proper object of divine honour. If we compare the behaviour of the Apostles, under like circumstances, with that of our blessed Saviour, the contrast throws great light upon this matter. When the people at Lystra were going to pay divine honours to them, "they rent their clothes, and ran in among the people, crying out, We also are *men*." Acts xiv. 14. And Peter, when Cornelius fell down at his feet and worshipped him, "took him up, saying, Stand up, I myself also am a *man*." Acts x. 25. It was not, therefore, "more *common* homage and

* See also Matthew xiv. 33. xxviii. 9, and 17.

respect than the Apostles approved of," which they rejected, but such as was not due to *men*. The angel who was employed in giving John the emblematical history of the church, rejected with abhorrence the adoration which that disciple was about to pay him, overcome with the grandeur of the scenes he had beheld: "See thou do it not; I am thy fellow-servant, and of thy brethren that have the testimony of Jesus; *worship God*." Revelations xix. 10. If Christ, therefore, was not God, he was not only much inferior to this angel, but even to his own disciples, in his regard for the glory of God, and the due conduct of his followers. Christ, indeed, rejected the honour which the young ruler paid him; because (as appears from the history) he had no knowledge of his true character; at the same time, our Lord gave him such an answer, as would directly lead him, if he was sincere, to make the proper inquiry; for the question, "Why callest thou me good," was doubtless put to him with the same design as that proposed to the Pharisees, "How then doth David in spirit call him Lord?" to try whether they were able to account for it, and to lead them to the true knowledge of himself.

St. Paul makes the worshipping of Christ, the characteristic of a Christian; which clearly proves that all such did worship him, and were instructed to do so by the Apostles. "Unto the church of God, which is at Corinth, to them that are sanctified in Christ Jesus, called to be saints, with all that in every place *call upon the name* of Jesus Christ our Lord, both their's and our's; Grace be unto you," &c. 1 Corinthians i. 2. It appears from the inspired history of the primitive church, that Christians had their name not only on account of their adhering to the doctrine of Christ, but also from their worshipping him, or "calling upon his name." Thus Ananias, addressing himself to the Lord concerning Saul, says, "Here he hath authority from the chief priests to bind all that *call on thy name*." Acts ix. 14. And again, in the same chapter, "all that heard him were amazed, and said, Is not this he that destroyed them which *called on this name* in Jerusalem?" Acts v. 21. Here there can be no reason to suspect that any "common homage or respect" is meant, because the object of the respect was absent in body, and therefore "calling upon him" must imply a spiritual omnipresence in the person *called upon*.

That our Lord Jesus Christ is the object of divine worship, in the most proper sense of the words, appears likewise from Romans

x. 13. "Whosoever shall call upon the name of the Lord, shall be saved." Which passage, compared with its context, abundantly confirms the truth I am defending; it is quoted from the Prophet Joel, and is applied by the Apostle unto Christ, who is therefore the Lord over all, upon whom we are to call for salvation. "If thou shalt confess with thy mouth the *Lord Jesus*, and shalt believe in thine heart, that God raised *him*, thou shalt be saved. For the Scripture saith, Whosoever believeth on *him* shall not be ashamed; the same Lord over all is rich unto all that call upon *him:* for, whosoever shall call upon the name of the *Lord* shall be saved. How then shall they call on *him* in whom they have not believed? And how shall they believe in *him* of whom they have not heard?" The same person is spoken of through the whole passage, viz. the Lord *Jesus*, and the Apostle applies to *him* the words of Joel, which are applicable to none but *God*.

It is evident that St. Paul himself made Christ the object of his worship, for he prays to him as well as to the Father, in almost every Epistle, for spiritual blessings upon those to whom he writes: "Grace be unto you, and peace from God our Father, and the Lord Jesus Christ." So he prays particularly for the Thessalonians. "Now the Lord Jesus Christ himself, and God, even our Father—comfort your hearts, and stablish you in every good word and work." 2 Thessalonians ii. 16, 17. And in 2 Corinthians xii. 8, 9, we have an instance of the Apostle's praying to Christ on his own account likewise. "For this I besought the Lord thrice, that it might depart from me. And he said, *My grace* is sufficient for thee: for *my strength* is made perfect in weakness. Most gladly, therefore, will I rather glory in my infirmities, that the *power of Christ* may rest upon me." The blessing which the Apostle here received in answer to his prayer, was the *power*, *strength*, or *grace* of *Christ*, to whom he addressed his prayer, as the answer shows, "*My grace* is sufficient."

The holy martyr Stephen employed his last moments in praying to this adorable Saviour of the world. "They stoned Stephen, calling upon God,* and saying, Lord Jesus, receive my spirit." Acts vii. 59.

The angels are commanded to worship

* The Translators of the New Testament have intimated to us, that the word *God*, which they here inserted, is not in the original, by causing it to be printed in the Italic character.

Christ; "When he bringeth in the first begotten into the world, he saith, And let all the angels of God worship him." Hebrews i. 6. *Worship* must here signify proper adoration; because, in the passage (Psalm xcvii. 7.) to which these words refer, it is expressly distinguished from false worship. "Confounded be all they that serve graven images, that boast themselves of idols: worship *him* all ye gods." "What invention could contrive a more positive and incontrovertible manner of calling the *Son*, *God;* than to say, 'Let all the angels of God,' or, 'let other gods worship *him*?' What is this but to call him the *Supreme God?* And manifestly to make the distinction betwixt God by *nature*, and by *office?* All these *gods* by *office*, are to worship the *God* by *nature*. 'Worship *him* all ye gods;' and this the Apostle applies to Christ, and says, that it was spoken of him; and how to call him *God* more directly cannot be imagined."*

Lastly; in the Revelations, the heavenly hosts are represented as paying equal honour and worship to "him that sitteth upon the throne, and to the Lamb." For unto Christ

* Leslie's Socinian Controversy discussed. Dialogue 2. page 45.

every knee shall bow, of things in heaven as well as things on earth.* "The four beasts and four and twenty elders *fell down* before the Lamb." Revelations v. 8. And again, "Every creature, heard I saying, Blessing, and honour, and glory, and power, be unto him that sitteth upon the throne, and unto the *Lamb* for ever and ever. And the four beasts said, Amen. And the four and twenty elders fell down and worshipped him that liveth for ever and ever;" verse xi. &c. which is the attribute of Christ mentioned just before the opening of the vision; chapter i. 18.

Thus we see, that the distinguishing characters of the Supreme Being belong to our Lord and Saviour Jesus Christ; and to me it appears not more unreasonable to deny *humanity* to ONE that has the essential qualities and properties of a *man*, than it is to deny *divinity* to HIM who has the essential perfections and properties of GOD.

III. 1. In the "Appeal," page 13., the following text is produced, to prove that our

* Compare Philippians ii. 10, 11, with Isaiah xlv. 23. and Romans xiv. 11.

Lord Jesus Christ is not God. "To us there is but one God, the Father, of whom are all things; and one Lord Jesus Christ, by whom are all things." 1 Corinthians viii. 6. But in the sense wherein this passage is there introduced, it would prove, that God the Father is not *Lord*, though it is his title through the whole Bible; for the text says, there is but *one* Lord. See also Ephesians iv. 5, 6. The truth is, the Apostle is here opposing the *one* true God to the *many* idols of the heathens, which, says he, are "nothing in the world," possessed of no power or life, much less of those glorious powers, which distinguish the Supreme Being. He could not here be opposing the Father to Christ, because he ascribes to them a joint possession of the Divine Attribute of creating power. The Almighty is thus described by the same Apostle. "*Of* him and *through* (or *by*) him are all things. Romans xi. 36. Here this character is equally given to the Father and to Christ. But who is he to whom the incommunicable attributes of God can be thus ascribed? Not a "mere man," but he who "was with God in the beginning, and was God."

2. A like argument is drawn by the same

author,* from that similar passage of Scripture, John xvii. 2. "This is life eternal to know thee the only true God, and Jesus Christ whom thou hast sent." The sense of which, as of all other passages, must be fixed by comparing Scripture with Scripture. Now the title of "only true God," does not exclude our Lord Jesus Christ, because we are assured, that he is the "true God, and eternal life." "We are in him that is true, even in his Son Jesus Christ; *This* is the *true God*, and eternal life." 1 John v. 20.

3. The Writer of the "Appeal" tells us, that Christ was far from thinking of such an *impious robbery* as that of being equal with God; and refers us for the proof of this, to Philippians ii. 6. where we are assured, that he thought it *no robbery* at all. Here we are informed, that the translation is wrong, and that the words in the original mean quite the reverse of the sense given in our English Bible. A little attention, however, to the scope of the passage will enable us to discern, that the translation is very agreeable to the context, and design of the Apostle. The Apostle is here exhorting to unity and

* "Triumph of Truth," page 17.

brotherly love, to abhor pride and vain-glory, which are the sources of strife and contention; "Let nothing be done through strife or vain-glory, but in lowliness of mind let each esteem other better than themselves:" and to have a tender concern for the welfare of others; "Look not every man on his own things, but every man also on the things of others." To engage our obedience he sets before us the example of Christ, and shews us how great he was, and yet how low he descended for our sakes; "Let this mind be in you, which was also in Christ Jesus: who, being in the form of God, thought it not robbery to be equal with God: but made himself of no reputation, and took upon him the form of a servant, and was made in the likeness of men," &c. And as a further encouragement to us, he reminds us of the exaltation of our Redeemer as the consequence and reward of his profound humiliation; "Wherefore God also hath highly exalted him, and hath given him a name which is above every name; that at the name of Jesus every knee should bow," &c. In this passage there are evidently three different states of Christ pointed out to us. The first, his state of dignity from which he descended; "Who, being in the form of God:" the second, his state of humiliation, which he voluntarily took upon him; "And took upon him the form of a servant:" and thirdly, his subsequent state of exaltation; "Wherefore God hath highly exalted him." These three states or conditions of Christ are essential to the Apostle's argument: take away any one of them, and the example which the Apostle would propose is lost; the force of the argument is not only weakened, but the argument itself entirely destroyed.* If we set aside the first state, that of his natural dignity, the second will be no longer a state of voluntary humiliation. For if he was not more than a man, it was not owing to his humility, but the order of nature, that he was "made in the likeness of men;" and if he was but a creature, "the form of a servant" was as much dignity as belonged to him, for the highest of God's creatures are his servants. But it is plain, that he was "in the form of God" before he was made "in the likeness of men," because this is mentioned as one instance of his humility. On the contrary, if it would have been an *impious robbery* in Christ to have claimed an equality with the Father in the Godhead, where was his singular humility in

* See Bishop Sherlock's Sermons, vol. 4. Discourse 1.

relinquishing this claim? To abstain from the highest insolence does not surely constitute any one a *pattern* of humility. Can a man be looked upon as *very* humble, so humble as to deserve to be *highly exalted*, because he is not as proud as Satan himself? Common sense will not allow us to suppose the Apostle would argue thus: 'Let this mind be in you which was also in Christ Jesus; who, having no pre-existence, humbled himself to be made in the likeness of men; and, being but a mere man, was so very condescending as not to pretend to be equal with God.'

This important passage of Scripture is illustrated by 2 Corinthians viii. 9. "Ye know the grace of our Lord Jesus Christ, that though he was rich, yet for your sakes he became poor, that ye, through his poverty, might be rich." In this text is implied, 1. That Christ was rich previously to his becoming poor. 2. That his poverty was voluntary, the effect of his grace. And, 3. That his riches and poverty refer to the same thing; to something which he had, and might have possessed, but which he willingly relinquished for our sakes, otherwise there was no humility, nothing worthy of imitation, in his example. But what were the riches which he possessed previously to his becoming poor? He had certainly none, unless we allow him to have existed before his incarnation. Nor can his poverty have any reference to his low condition on earth, which yet the Apostle's argument requires, if we deny either his pre-existence, or his natural greatness and dignity. The plain meaning is, that he was rich in glory before his incarnation, of which he emptied himself, when he took upon him the form of a servant, and was made in the likeness of men.

4. In the "Appeal" we are informed, that although Christ says, "he and his Father are one," "he sufficiently explains himself, when he prays, that all his disciples may be 'one with him and his Father, even as they two are one.'" page 14.

Our Lord's words are, "That they may be one, even as we are one;" not one *with* us, but one *in* us, as the context explains it, verse 21; or "made perfect in one," verse 23; which, I apprehend, refers chiefly to that union, so often mentioned in Scripture, subsisting between the true disciples of Christ, whereby they are one body, of which he is the head. I would observe here, that the expression *even as*, does not always denote *equality* in the sacred writings, but sometimes *similitude* only: as, "Be ye perfect, even as your Father which is in heaven is perfect." Matthew v. 48. The Scriptures speak sufficiently of our sinful and imperfect condition, to show us in what sense we are to understand these words. The Writer of the "Appeal" will agree with me, I am persuaded, that the expression, *even as*, does not always imply *equality*; because there is another Scripture, in which, if he allows it to have this signification, (as I believe it has, because of the concurrent testimony of other Scriptures,) he will invalidate all he has said upon the doctrine of Christ's divinity.* The Scriptures frequently speak of the union which subsists between Christ and his true disciples; but not in the same terms as of that which subsists between the Father and Christ: nor is the glory which Christ gave his disciples, all the glory which he had with the Father. What he gave them may be learnt from what they received, which is thus described by the Evangelist; "Of his fulness have all we received, and grace for grace." John i. 16. But he had a glory with

* "For the Father judgeth no man; but hath committed all judgment unto the Son. That all men should honour the Son, *even as* they honour the Father." John v. 22, 23.

the Father "before the world was;" chapter xvii. 5. which certainly was not the glory which he received as man from the Father, and gave to his disciples. He had likewise such an union with the Father, that he could say with propriety, "All things that the Father hath are mine;" chapter xvi. 15. And, "He that hath seen me hath seen the Father;" chapter xiv. 9. But can every true Christian use, with propriety, the same language?

Again; the union which Christ had with the Father, was such, that he might justly be called the Almighty's fellow: "Awake, O sword, against my shepherd, and against the *man* that is my *fellow*, saith the Lord of Hosts." Zechariah xiii. 7. But who, except the *man* Christ Jesus, dares claim this title? And, the *nature* of this union appears in the strongest light from hence, that the Holy Spirit is indifferently called the "Spirit of God," and the "Spirit of Christ" in the New Testament. "Holy men of God," says St. Peter, "spake as they were moved by the Holy Ghost." 2 Peter i. 21. But this inspiration, as the same Apostle informs us, was from the Spirit of Christ. "Of which salvation the prophets have inquired and searched diligently, who prophesied of the grace that should come unto you; searching what, or what manner of time the *Spirit of Christ*, which was in them, did signify, when it testified before-hand the sufferings of Christ, and the glory that should follow." 1 Peter i. 10, &c. So the Holy Ghost, who dwells in the saints, is, in one and the same passage, called the Spirit of God, and the Spirit of Christ; "Ye are not in the flesh, but in the Spirit, if so be that the *Spirit of God* dwell in you. Now, if any man have not the *Spirit of Christ*, he is none of his." Romans xvi. 9. Our Lord assured his disciples, when he was going to leave the world, that *He* would send the Holy Ghost to them, who should receive of *his*, and show it unto them. John xvi. 7, 14, 15. ut shall we ascribe unto a *creature*, the power of sending the Holy Spirit, who is God himself? 'A *creature* to send *God!* And to give him something of a creature's to carry! A creature to call God his messenger, and to say, 'he shall receive of *mine*, and show it unto you!' A creature to say that 'all things which are God's, are *his!*' This would be strange indeed! He is surely more than a creature who can use such language with propriety.

5. "The term *God*," as is justly observed

in the "Appeal," "is sometimes used in an inferior sense in the Scriptures; but always in such a manner, that there can be no danger of our mistaking the sense" of it in such passages, which, by the way, are very few. In these, there is never any divine attribute connected with it; but it is either in the plural number, as, "I have said ye are gods;" or, by its connexion, evidences an inferior meaning, as, "I will make Moses a God to Pharaoh." On the contrary, when the word *God* is used without any such connexion, and especially when any divine attribute is added to it, we are certain that the Supreme Being alone is spoken of. Thus the most clear testimony is given in Scripture to the divinity of our blessed Saviour. He that, according to the flesh, was a "*child born*," and a "*son given*," is also the "*mighty God*," Isaiah ix. 6. The "*true God*," 1 John v. 20. The "*only wise God*." Jude 25. "Emmanuel, *God with us*," Matthew i. 23. "*God manifest in the flesh*," 1 Timothy iii. 16. "*God blessed for ever*," Romans ix. 5. whom the inspired Psalmist thus addresses; "Thy throne, *O God*, is for ever and ever." Psalm xlv. 6; and whom Isaiah saw in his awful vision as the *Lord of Hosts*, adored by all the glorious company of heaven, chapter vi. compared with John xii. 41.

6. The Writer of the "Appeal" thinks our Lord disclaimed all title to the Godhead, in the answer he gave to the Jews when they accused him of blasphemy. John x. 33. They to whom that answer was given, thought otherwise, for they immediately attempted to apprehend him, that they might punish him for persisting in his blasphemy, as they judged it to be, "but he escaped out of their hand;" verse 39. When our Lord called himself the "Son of God," the Jews understood him as claiming a divine character, such as could belong to no *mere man* whatever: and their behaviour upon such occasions shewed, that they looked upon this language of Christ as blasphemy, and probably as "an attempt to seduce them into idolatry; a thing which they durst not entertain the most distant thought of." "Therefore the Jews sought the more to kill him, because he not only had broken the Sabbath, but said also that God was his Father, making himself *equal with God*." John v. 18. And in the place above referred to, "We stone thee,—for blasphemy, because that thou, being a *man*, makest thyself *God*,"

chapter x. 33. 'It should be observed here, that the Jews had just before been requesting our Lord to give them a *plain* account of his real character: "If thou be the Christ, (or Son of God,) tell us *plainly*;" verse 24. To this he answers, "I told you, and ye believed not;" verse 25. Now, can it be supposed, that he had told them he was but a *mere man*, and yet could not persuade them to believe it? No; he had expressed himself in such terms, as amounted to a declaration, in their apprehension, that he was "equal with God;" see chapter v. 18. To refer them, therefore, to his former answer, if he knew they misunderstood it, was "putting them off" indeed; and gives us no high idea of his integrity, or of the propriety of that title which is given him, "The faithful Witness." But it is evident that they understood our Lord according to his own meaning; viz. as claiming an equality with the Father, for in that sense it was that they *disbelieved* his assertion. Again; if the Jews really misunderstood our Lord, then he persisted in deceiving them to his death; for he declared himself to be the "Son of God" before the Sanhedrim, as is recorded by all the Evangelists, though he knew what idea the expression conveyed to them, and suffered himself to be condemned to death on this very account, without giving the least intimation that they mistook him, and that he meant to say he was but a *mere man*. So that if Christ was not God, equal with the Father, he was accessary to his own death, and therefore guilty of self-murder, since there needed no testimony but his own to clear him from the crime laid to his charge; and, in this case, the Sanhedrim did an act of justice in "condemning him to be guilty of death." Mark xiv. 64.

7. In the great work of *mediation*, our blessed Saviour condescended to take upon him the form of a servant, and as the reward of his humiliation, has all authority and power over the church committed to him. In this "mediatorial kingdom," he must reign till all things are put under his feet.* But when "the end cometh," and "the last enemy is destroyed; then shall he deliver up" this "kingdom to God, even the Father, and be himself also subject to him that put all things under him, that God may be all in all." 1 Corinthians xv. 24, &c. Although the authority which he received from the Father as *Mediator* shall then cease, the work of *mediation*

* Compare 1 Corinthians xv. 27, with Philippians iii. 21.

being fully accomplished; yet he shall still "reign" in "the glory which he had with the Father before the world was," and that "for ever and ever." Revelations xi. 15. He shall be, with the Father, the source of eternal bliss to the saints; and, with him, constitute the very glory of heaven. "The Lamb which is in the midst of the throne shall feed them, (*the redeemed*,) and shall lead them unto living fountains of waters; and God shall wipe away all tears from their eyes." Revelations vii. 17. And again; "I saw no temple therein," says the favoured disciple, "for the Lord God Almighty, and the *Lamb*, are the temple of it. And the city had no need of the sun, neither of the moon, to shine in it; for the glory of God did lighten it, and the *Lamb* is the light thereof." chapter xxi. 22, 23.

The Author of the "Appeal" thinks, that till the doctrine of Christ's divinity, which he styles, by way of eminence, "the great ruption of Christianity," be removed, it will be in vain to preach the gospel to Jews, Mahometans, &c. page 17. I have shewn from the word of God, that they, both Jews and Gentiles, which were converted in the Apostle's days, were brought to "call upon the name of Christ, that they might be saved;" and I doubt not, but that the preaching of the gospel, wherever it is successful, will now produce the same effect. Instead, therefore, of adapting the gospel to the corrupt prejudices of mankind, let us join with the Psalmist in addressing our great Messiah, that, by the power of his grace, all nations may become obedient to the faith. "Gird thy sword upon thy thigh, *O most Mighty*; with thy glory and thy majesty. And in thy majesty ride prosperously, because of truth, and meekness, and righteousness; and thy right hand shall teach thee terrible things: thine arrows are sharp in the heart of the king's enemies, whereby the people fall under thee." Psalm xlv. 3—5. AMEN.

SUPPLEMENT.

SINCE the publication of the preceding little Tract, the Author of the "Appeal" has published an "Illustration of certain passages of Scripture," relating to the subjects of the "Appeal," which, he says, may be considered as a reply to all the answers he had seen to that Essay. I shall now take notice of that "Illustration," so far as relates to the doctrine I have been defending, especially where a reply seems more immediately to have been intended to any argument contained in my "Short Defence."

A few general observations have occurred to me in reading over this "Illustration," and comparing it with his "Appeal," and "Triumph of Truth," which I shall lay before the reader, and then proceed to examine what is said upon particular passages of Scripture.

1. In the preface to Mr. Elwall's trial, &c. our Author declares it to be his opinion, that "the lower class of people are as capable of judging concerning the important truths of religion, as the most learned;" which, as I have already observed, supposes, that the English translation of the Bible is sufficient for instruction in these important truths. Mr. Elwall, who is looked upon by our Author as an eminent defender of the truth, gives not the least hint that our English Bible is likely to mislead us in the doctrine of Christ's divinity; on the contrary, this doctrine is spoken of as being *clearly* repugnant to the Bible, and as a matter which any man of common sense may determine upon with the greatest certainty, provided he be sincere in his search of truth. "Nothing is more plain," says Mr. Elwall, "than that a deceived *heart* hath turned them (who hold this doctrine) aside, because they will not make use of those rational faculties which God has given them." page 12. Accordingly he tells us, page 15, that the doctrine of Christ's divinity is the "master-piece of all the absurdities that ever were invented:" and page 16, that it is one of "the most odious and absurd doctrines that ever was imposed on mankind, directly contrary to natural and revealed religion, and to

all the rational faculties God has given us." In the "Appeal" page 22, it is asserted, that "men of plain understandings never do believe any such thing;" and that so far is the Bible from giving the least countenance to this doctrine, that "it requires much *acuteness* to give it even a *plausible* colour." Upon this allowed sufficiency of the English Bible, I undertook my "Short Defence;" not because I judged that our translation gave any advantage to the doctrine I defended, but that by appealing only to the Scriptures as we have them in our own language, the controversy might be of more general use, and afford less room for vague and unsatisfactory criticisms. However, it appears that our Author does not chuse to stand upon this ground, for, in the preface to his "Illustration," he contradicts the sentiments he had before espoused. He there tells us, that, "though the inspired writings were very intelligible when first published, a long course of years has rendered them *extremely difficult* to us, who use a different language, and whose manners and customs are so exceedingly unlike the Jews:" that on this account, "the *unlearned* are *very liable* to wrest the Scriptures:" and that the passages of Scripture which he has attempted to explain, are, for the most part, "highly figurative, and *peculiarly difficult* to understand." Besides, "one unfavourable circumstance," he says, "occurs with respect to the right understanding of the Scriptures in this country, that the English translation of them was made at a time when the christian world was but just emerged from the darkness of popery, and while the belief of all those opinions which are combated in the 'Appeal,' (and which he repeatedly calls the most absurd and impious,) were almost universally retained. Our translators, therefore, having been educated in the belief of, and in a reverence for, those opinions, and not having had their minds sufficiently enlightened to call them in question, it is no wonder that without any ill design, they should, in many places of their version, have expressed their own sentiments, and not those of the Apostles." If this be really the case, the condition of the generality of people in this nation is truly deplorable. We are to receive the Bible as the word of God upon pain of damnation, and yet we are quite uncertain where it speaks the language of inspiration, and where the sentiments of the translators; so that the gospel, which was intended, as this Author speaks, "to be the solid foundation of the faith, hope, and joy of *common* people,"* is become, according to him, quite insufficient to any but those who understand the Greek and Hebrew languages, and the common people have yet a solid foundation of their faith to seek. I am far from thinking that the knowledge of the original language of Scripture is useless, or that our translation is not in some places capable of amendment; but I am persuaded, that there is not one doctrine of revelation destroyed by our translation, or which may not be made out by comparing one Scripture with another, without having recourse either to the Greek or Hebrew. I shall, therefore, continue to appeal only to the English Bible, and leave to the learned those criticisms upon the original languages which they may think needful.

2. I have already shown the consistency there is in sometimes speaking of Christ as inferior to the Father, and sometimes as equal with him.† The Author of the "Illustration" has not discovered the impropriety of such language, and yet continues to make use of

* "Appeal," page 22.

† "Short Defence," page 9 and 10.

the acknowledged inferiority of Christ, as Man and Mediator, to prove that he is in no sense equal with the Father. When several passages in the Revelations were brought to evince the divinity of Christ, because the incommunicable attributes of God are there ascribed to him, and he is there represented as receiving the same worship as the Father; the *illustrator* answers, "It is plain, the Author of that book considered Christ as a person subordinate to the Father, and the minister of his will, and therefore no single expression should be interpreted in such a manner as to make it imply the contrary," page 25, *i. e.* that Christ, as to his divine nature, is equal with the Father, for this is what he means by the *contrary*.* Now, let any man of common understanding judge, who it is that reasons inconclusively in this debate. We assert that Christ is God and man; the latter is allowed; we prove the former from the ascription of the divine attributes to him, &c. To this our Author replies; "Those Scriptures cannot mean what they seem to express; Christ cannot be God, because he is man." Surely they who could argue thus,

* Arguments of the same kind are used, page 29, 31, 35, 37, and 40.

should not think those who oppose them err, "because they will not make use of the rational faculties which God has given them." Had this Author made it appear that it is impossible the divine and human nature should be united in one person, his arguing would have been conclusive; but till then it is just as weighty as to say, that man cannot be endued with an immaterial soul, because he has a material body.

3. I have before taken notice of the misrepresentation which this Author makes of the doctrine of Christ's divinity;* and am sorry to find he still insinuates that we espouse the senseless notion of a plurality of Gods; whereas, he must very well know, that it is as much our belief there is one Supreme *Being*, as that there are three *persons* (as they are usually called) in the Godhead. The "Illustration" of texts relating to the divinity of Christ is introduced with this observation, "Nothing can be more evident, from the whole tenor of the New Testament, than that the person who is distinguished by the name of the *Father*, is the only true God, exclusive of the *Son*, or any *other being* what-

* See "Short Defence," page 10.

ever. Nevertheless, there are some single and unconnected passages, especially in our translation of the Bible, which seem to favour the contrary opinion, namely, that of the divinity of Christ." page 21. This opinion, that there are more *beings* than one who are *supreme*, is no less contrary to our doctrine, than it is to common sense; and therefore, ought not to be charged upon us. Whoever would prove that our doctrine is contrary to reason must show, that it is impossible the Divine Being can subsist in such a manner, as to make it proper that he should represent himself as *Father, Son, and Holy Ghost*; which we, on account of the distinct agency ascribed to each in the Scriptures, call by the name of *persons*; hereby not pretending to explain the precise manner of this subsistence, but only using the fittest term, which human language will afford, to express this inexplicable mystery. It is not candid to misrepresent a doctrine which we oppose; but this is continually done by those who deny the doctrine of the Trinity. If they would oppose us by rational arguments, let them not go about to prove that the existence of three Gods (a doctrine we abhor) is contrary to reason, but that the existence of a triune God is so. If they are conscious that they cannot demonstrate the doctrine, as we profess it, to be absurd, let them candidly acknowledge this inability; and let them not persist in misrepresenting our belief, and then triumph in refuting what we never asserted. It is easy to avail themselves of the obscurity with which, in our present state of imperfect knowledge, we are obliged to speak of this mystery, and thence to argue that we believe we know not what; but arguments of this kind may with equal force be used with respect to the very *being* of a God, his *eternity*, *self-existence*, and *omnipresence*, of which we cannot form more adequate ideas, than of his existence in a trinity of *persons*, as set forth in divine revelation.

4. In my "Short Defence," it was not my intention to consider the doctrine of the Trinity any further than was necessary in speaking to that of Christ's divinity, and, therefore, I did but quote two passages of Scripture expressly upon that head. The first was, 1 John v. 7, the authenticity of which has, indeed, been called in question, and concerning which the *illustrator* asserts, that "it is not to be found in any ancient manuscript;" page 38. This assertion is not trne; but as it would take up too much room

in this "Short Defence" to give a fair statement of the controversy relative to this text, I must refer my reader to Mr. Travis's letters to Mr. Gibbon, in which he will find it satisfactorily proved, that this passage had a place in the authentic Epistles of St. John. The *illustrator* adds, that allowing this text to be genuine, it is but *supposed to contain* the doctrine of the Trinity; because, in fact, it expresses no more than that "three agree in giving the same testimony." If "the Father, the Word, and the Holy Ghost," are *three* that bear record in heaven, then the doctrine of the Trinity is *certainly contained* in this text. For since the inspired writers inform us, that "the Father, the Word, and the Holy Ghost" is *God*, it must necessarily follow, either that there are three Gods, or that these three are *one*.

5. The other Scripture which I quoted as teaching the doctrine of the Trinity, was the appointed form of baptism. Matthew xxviii. 19. "Go ye therefore, and teach all nations, baptizing them in the name of the Father, and of the Son, and of the Holy Ghost." Allowing the terms Father, Son, and Holy Ghost to be expressive of the only true God, the meaning of this passage is most obvious and natural;

but with a Socinian interpretation it will be difficult to make any sense of it; for according to this we are to be baptized into the name of God, the name of a mere man, and the name of the power of God, an interpretation which sufficiently refutes itself. In the "Illustration," it is said, "This form of baptism seems to be intended to remind Christians of the different parts which God and Christ, and the Holy Ghost, acted in the scheme of man's redemption," page 36. What this Author means by the Holy Ghost as distinguished from God, I am at a loss to conceive. After having informed us,* that by the Holy Ghost no distinct person is meant, but only the power and energy of God, or God himself considered as exerting his power, it is as unintelligible to talk of the different parts which God, and the Holy Ghost, acted in the scheme of man's redemption, as it would be to tell us of the different parts which God, and the power of God, acted in the work of creation.

Our Author thinks himself vindicated in supposing that this text does not imply an equality of the Father, Son, and Holy Ghost, because the Apostle Paul says, 1 Corinthians

* "Triumph of Truth," page 12.

x. 2. that "the children of Israel were baptized unto Moses;" "but he certainly did not mean that Moses was their God." Here, I think it plain, the Apostle uses the term *baptized* merely in a figurative sense, or by way of allusion, and not in that proper manner in which it is used in the passage under consideration; for it was "in the cloud, and in the sea," that the children of Israel are said to have been "baptized unto Moses," and not by an ordinance expressive of any dedication of themselves to him; which shows that the being "baptized unto Moses," as the Apostle phrases it, was a very different thing from that solemn institution of Christ we are now considering. Besides, it is not said, that they were baptized *in the name of Moses*, but only *unto Moses*; whereas, we are to be baptized *in the name of the Son*, as well as of the *Father*.* The Apostle, who is certainly the best interpreter of his own words, shows us that these expressions are far from being synonymous; for he asks the Corinthians with an evident abhorrence of the thought, "Were ye baptized *in the name of* Paul?" 1 Corin-

* We read likewise of some who were baptized *unto John's baptism*, but it is never said that any were baptized *in the name of John*. See Acts xix. 3—5.

thians i. 15; and rejoices that he had baptized so few christian converts at Corinth, "lest any should say he had baptized *in his own name*;" verse 15. But surely, if this expression had only implied the being baptized into the profession of his doctrine, he would not have shown such an abhorrence of it; for in this sense they might have been baptized *unto Paul*, as well as *unto Moses*. Whereas, if the appointed form of this sacred ordinance intimates the solemn dedication of ourselves to him in whose name we are baptized, as I doubt not it does, the propriety of the Apostle's abhorrence is evident; for no creature must be joined with God as the object of that dedication which we make of ourselves to God in baptism.

6. I might urge many other Scriptures which contain the doctrine drawn from these I have already quoted; but at present, I shall add but one more, and this is the sixth chapter of Isaiah, as expounded by the inspired writers of the New Testament. The Prophet says, "I saw the *Lord* sitting upon a throne, high and lifted up; above it stood the Seraphim,—and one cried unto another and said, Holy, holy, holy, is the *Lord* of Hosts." Here the heavenly host are represented as giving

glory to the only true God; but this God is Father, Son, and Holy Ghost, if the language of inspiration is to be regarded. That the Father is here spoken of, is allowed on all hands: that the Son is likewise here intended, appears from St. John's exposition of this passage, who, having mentioned the unbelief of the Jews, notwithstanding Jesus had done so many miracles before them, chapter xii. 37, gives the reason of it in the words of the Prophet taken from this chapter. "He hath blinded their eyes, and hardened their hearts," &c., and then adds, verse 41; "These things said Esaias, when he saw his glory and spake of him," viz. of Christ, as the context requires, who is therefore Lord of Hosts: and in the Acts, chapter xxviii. St. Paul informs us that the words which the Prophet received from the Lord of Hosts, recorded in this chapter, were spoken by the Holy Ghost. "Well spake the Holy Ghost by Esaias the Prophet, saying, Go unto this people," &c. The Holy Ghost, therefore, with the Father and Christ, is the *Lord* of Hosts whom the Seraphim adore.

7. In proving the *eternal existence* of our blessed Redeemer, I compared Isaiah xliv. 6. with Revelations i. 17. and xxii. 13. In the

former passage, the Almighty declares in the strongest terms, that he *alone* is "*the First and the Last*," and that this attribute belongs to no other being but the true God. "Thus saith the *Lord* of Hosts, *I am the First*, and *I am the Last*, and *besides me there is no God*." Yet with what solemnity does the blessed Jesus claim this glorious attribute of Deity, when his beloved disciple lay as dead at his feet, astonished at the majesty of his appearance: "Fear not," says he, "*I am the First and the Last*." Now, by what means could our Lord more clearly declare himself to be (as to his divine nature) the self-existent Jehovah, than by assuming this title? It is that which the Creator has chosen to distinguish himself from every creature of whatever rank or office. I appeal to the unprejudiced reader, whether it be a sufficient answer to this argument, to say, 1. "That St. John elsewhere speaks of Christ as subordinate to the Father, and the minister of his will;" which, as I have before observed, is only declaring him to be likewise man, and does not in the least invalidate the proof of his being God-man. Or, 2. "That this high title is attributed to Christ with respect to the state of glory to which he is exalted by the Father," when God had told us that this title points out the distinction between him and every creature. Or, 3. "That Christ is likewise called, *The Amen, the faithful and true Witness, the Beginning of the creation of God;*" page 25, 26.

8. If the reader will attend to the argument drawn from our Lord's use of the expression, I AM,* he will find, that it does not rest upon the *mere use* of those words, as the Author of the "Illustration" supposes, page 41, but upon the *manner* in which they are used. I very readily allow, that our Lord might have said "I am," or, "I am he," to any question respecting his identity, without claiming an equality with the Father, any more than the blind man, mentioned in John ix. made such a claim, when he said, "I am," or "I am he," to those who inquired whether he was the person who before sat and begged; verse 8, 9. On the contrary, supposing the Greek words here translated "I am," to have been rendered "I am he," the eternal existence of Christ stands as clearly evinced from his use of them, compared with the context, as if he had used that similar declaration of the self-existent God; "Before the day was, I am he." Isaiah xliii. 13. The *illustrator* says;

* "Short Defence," page 12.

"The meaning of the passage clearly is, that Abraham foresaw the day of Christ, and that Christ was the subject of prophecy before the times of Abraham;" page 40. This I grant is the meaning of the 56th verse; "Your father Abraham rejoiced to see my day; and he saw it, and was glad." As the writer to the Hebrews explains it; "He saw the promises afar off, and was persuaded of them, and embraced them;" chapter xi. 13. Upon this declaration the Jews propose a question to our Lord concerning his existence; "Thou art not yet fifty years old, and hast thou seen Abraham?" verse 57. To this our Lord answers; "Verily, verily, I say unto you, Before Abraham was, I am;" verse 58. He does not, in this verse, repeat what he had just declared to them in the 56th verse, but answers a question respecting his existence in the words of the self-existent Jehovah; and when they understood this well-known language in its usual sense, our Lord confirms their interpretation by his silence, and by escaping out of their hands.

9. Upon this passage in our Lord's prayer, (recorded, John xvii.) "And now, O Father, glorify thou me with thine own self, with the glory which I had with thee before the world

was;" (verse 5;) the Author of the "Illustration" says; "this must necessarily mean the glory which was intended for him in the councils of God before all time; since in many other places the power and glory which were conferred upon Christ are expressly said to be the reward of his obedience; and to be subsequent to his resurrection;" page 40. Supposing what this last clause asserts to be true, that all the glory which was *conferred* on Christ was subsequent to his resurrection; how will this prove that the glory which was *not conferred* upon him was so too? Or, because power and glory were conferred upon Christ, as the reward of his obedience unto death; how does it *necessarily* follow, that he had no glory with the Father before the world was? I confess I can see no necessity of such conclusion from such premises. The Scriptures are as express in declaring that Christ had glory with the Father "in the beginning, before the world was," as that glory was conferred upon him in consequence of his obedience unto death, and therefore we ought to believe both these declarations; nor should any one presume to deny the one, because he acknowledges the other, until he has shewn that they are incompatible. It is readily granted, that Christ had not *that* glory before his incarnation, which was the reward of his obedience unto death, and was subsequent to his resurrection, viz. the glory of his *mediatorial kingdom*, which glory will be laid aside when the work of mediation is fully accomplished. 1 Corinthians xv. 24: but the glory here spoken of is that which he had when he was in the form of God. Philippians ii. 6. and which preceded his taking upon him the form of a servant, and his being made in the likeness of men; verse 7.

10. We are not told in the "Illustration," how Melchizedek was "made like unto the Son of God," in having no beginning of days recorded of him, Hebrews vii. 3; nor how our Lord was the *root* as well as the *offspring* of David. Revelations xxii. 16. I shall therefore leave the reader to his own reflections on these passages.

11. I was not a little surprized to find it asserted in the "Illustration," that the address to God, quoted from Psalm cii. in the Epistle to the Hebrews, chapter i. 10. "Thou, Lord, in the beginning hast laid the foundation of the earth," &c. is mentioned, "without any hint of its being applied to Christ;" page 35. This Scripture is as clearly applied to

Christ as any in the whole passage, which consists of texts from the Old Testament relative to the glory of Christ, except the seventh verse, wherein the angels are described to shew their great inferiority to him. The manner in which these quotations are connected, puts this, I apprehend, beyond doubt.

"Unto which of the angels said he at any time, Thou art my Son, this day have I begotten thee?" verse 5.

"*And again*, I will be to him a Father, and he shall be to me a Son;" *ib.*

"*And again*, he saith, and let all the angels of God worship him;" verse 6.

"*And of the angels*, he saith, who maketh his angels spirits, and his ministers a flame of fire;" verse 7.

"*But unto the Son* he saith, Thy throne, O God, is for ever and ever;* a sceptre of righteousness is the sceptre of thy kingdom," &c. verse 8.

"*And*, Thou, Lord, in the beginning hast

* "These words," our Author says, "may be rendered, *God is thy throne for ever and ever*; that is, God will establish the authority of Christ till time shall be no more."

This way of translating and expounding the text, appears to me very unnatural. The inspired writers often use the laid the foundation of the earth, and the heavens are the works of thine hands," &c. verse 10.

"*But to which of the angels* said he at any time, Sit on my right hand, until I make thine enemies thy footstool," &c. verse 11.

The conjunction, *and*, prefixed to the quotation from the one hundred and second Psalm, in the tenth verse, refers to the applicatory expression, "unto the Son he saith," prefixed to the preceding quotation in the eighth verse, and therefore has just the same force as if it had been said, "*And unto the Son he saith*, Thou, Lord, in the beginning," &c.

12. I have already observed, that the first chapter of St. John's Gospel sets forth the divinity of Christ so clearly, that the greatest force must be put upon it, and the most unnatural construction made use of, to evade its testimony to this important truth. The "Illustration" of the fourteen first verses evidences

word *throne* in a figurative sense for the possession and display of glory, majesty, or dominion, but never in the sense here supposed. We often read of God's throne, but never of God being any one's throne. Christ is said to sit on the throne of God, and on his own throne, but not to sit upon God as his throne.

the truth of this remark. "In the beginning was the word, and the word was with God, and the word was God. The same was in the beginning with God. All things were made by him; and without him was not any thing made that was made. In him was life, and the life was the light of men. And the light shineth in darkness, and the darkness comprehended it not. There was a man sent from God, whose name was John. The same came for a witness, to bear witness of the light, that all men through him might believe. He was not that light, but was sent to bear witness of that light. That was the true light, which lighteth every man that cometh into the world. He was in the world, and the world was made by him, and the world knew him not. He came unto his own, and his own received him not. But as many as received him, to them gave he power to become the sons of God, even to them that believe on his name: and the word was made flesh, and dwelt among us, (and we beheld his glory, the glory as of the only begotten of the Father,) full of grace and truth."

Our Author introduces this passage of Scripture by observing, that "many of the texts, which are usually alleged in proof of the divinity of Christ, relate to God the Father only;" of which this is "one of the most remarkable." page 30. Yet immediately after the quotation he says, "These words, interpreted in the most literal manner, only imply that *the Word*, or Christ, had a being before the creation of the world, that he had the title of *God*, or a God, and was the instrument by whom the supreme God made all things; but they by no means imply that he was true and very God; for magistrates and others are sometimes called *Gods* on account of their power and dominion, in which they resemble God." page 31. Now, if by *the Word* is meant Christ, as the *illustrator* here allows, how is it that this text relates to God the Father only? Nothing can be more arbitrary than such an assertion, when the Evangelist expressly tells us, that the person concerning whom he wrote, was the "only begotten of the Father;" verse 14. It is granted, that magistrates are sometimes called *Gods*, on account of their power and dominion, which they are appointed to exercise over others as God's vicegerents: but the Evangelist intimates that *the Word*, or Christ, was God previously to the existence of any creatures, with relation to whom he might be a *God* by office; "in the *beginning*," or from "everlasting," as this term is used in Proverbs viii. 22, 23, "the word was with God, and was God; and, therefore, he is *God* by nature. This important truth is repeated, verse 2, "The same was in the beginning with God: and then we are informed that "all things were made by him, and without him was not any thing made that was made;" verse 3. Our Author thinks, "the derivation of Christ from the Father, and consequently his dependance upon him, is sufficiently expressed by his being called, in the last of these verses, 'the only begotten of the Father.'" I have elsewhere shewn in what sense our Lord is called the "Son of God,"* and therefore shall not now enlarge on this subject. I would here only observe, that the appellation used in this passage shows, that Christ is not called the "Son of God," in the same sense as holy men are in Scripture, but in a sense peculiar to himself, otherwise he could not be styled the "*only* begotten of the Father."

The most literal interpretation of this passage does not, however, exactly suit our Author's sentiments; for he adds, "to me it appears, that the Apostle does not speak of the pre-existence of Christ in this place; but only of the power and wisdom of God, which

* "Short Defence," page 29.

dwelled, or tabernacled in his flesh." And again, by "the word of God," we are not to understand any being distinct from God; but only the *power* or *energy of God*, which is so much *with God*, that it properly belongs to his nature, and is not at all distinct from God himself; and that the same power which produced all things was manifest to men in the person of Jesus Christ." This "Illustration" is more distant from the evident scope of the passage than the former; and disfigures this plain and connected discourse of the Apostle with a most unaccountable repetition of something quite foreign to his purpose.—According to the *illustrator* we are to suppose, that the Evangelist introduces his account of the incarnation of Christ, and of his solemn inauguration into his prophetic office on earth, by repeatedly telling us, that power was with God from the beginning, and that power was so much with God, that it properly belonged to his nature; that all things were made by power, and that without power was not any thing made that was made. Now, can any man, who will make use of the rational faculties which God has given him, believe that this is the Apostle's meaning? I am sure if it is, the art of criticism must be racked to discover the connexion of his discourse. Whereas, allowing the doctrine of Christ's divinity, nothing can be more intelligible than the sense of the three first verses, or more natural than their connexion with the subsequent part of the chapter.

Besides, the Evangelist says several things of *the Word*, which are not applicable to power, wisdom, or any *quality*, but evidently belong to a *person;* which demonstrates that he is not speaking of a *quality*, but of a *person*. "John came for a witness, to bear witness of the light, that all men through him might believe: He was not that light, but was sent to bear witness of that light." Surely the Evangelist did not mean to inform us, that John was not wisdom, or that wisdom did not reside in John; but that he was not *the Christ*, that *person* of whom he is speaking throughout the passage.—Again, "*He* was in the world, and the world was made by *him*, and the world knew *him* not. He came unto *his* own, and *his* own received him not. But as many as received *him*, to them gave *he* power to become the sons of God, even to them that believe on *his name*." It is plain, that the relatives in this sentence refer to the same antecedent, and that the antecedent referred to is he on whose name we are to believe for salvation, the Lord Jesus Christ. Again, "The word was made flesh, and dwelt among us, and we beheld *his* glory, the glory as of the only begotten of the Father, full of grace and truth." The Evangelist in this verse likewise, puts beyond doubt what he means by *the Word*, for he calls him "the only begotten of the Father," a title appropriated to Christ.

13. An exposition equally strange with the preceding, does this Author give of Colossians i. 16. "For by him were all things created that are in heaven, and that are in earth, visible and invisible, whether they be thrones, or dominions, or principalities, or powers; all things were created by him, and for him." "In this passage," he says, "we have a view given us of the great and happy change that was made in the world by the gospel; for, by *creation*, we are to understand the *new creation*, or *renovation*, in which sense, the same word is used by the Apostle." Ephesians ii. 10. page 44. It is very true, that the words generally rendered *to create*, or *creation*, are used in Scripture to express the great change produced in the tempers and conduct of men by the gospel: as, "If any man be in Christ, he is a new creature." 2 Corinthians v. 17. And, "We are his workmanship created in Christ Jesus unto good works." Ephe-

sians ii. 10. But because the word *creation* is sometimes used to express the renovation of men's minds, it will by no means follow, that it must have the same signification in this passage; for it is not *men* only who are here said to have been created by Christ, but *all things;* things *invisible*, as well as visible; things *in heaven*, as well as things on earth. And is this giving us a view of the change produced in the world by the gospel? Were things in heaven depraved, that they needed any change of temper? Or was the gospel sent to things invisible, to thrones, dominions, principalities, and powers, to engage them to change their conduct? If the words of Scripture have so little connexion with the sense, as this "Illustration" supposes, it will be no hard matter to make them prove any thing. The change produced in the minds of men by divine grace through the gospel, is very fitly called a *renovation*, or *new creation*, because it really is so; it is the making of that which did not exist before, the creation of new principles of action, new tempers, and dispositions; but that the invisible powers in heaven need any such renovation, is contradicted by all the accounts we have of them in Scripture. The glory of Christ as head of the church, mentioned in the eighteenth verse, and in Ephesians i. 20—23, is distinguished from that which he has as Creator of all things, as I have already observed,* and as appears from comparing the sixteenth and eighteenth verses of this chapter.

14. In my proof of Christ's *omnipresence* I mentioned that conversation with Nicodemus, in which our Lord speaks of himself, as being in heaven, and on earth, at the same time. The author of the "Illustration," thinks this mode of expression to signify only "a state of intimate communication with God," and asserts, that "the notion of a local heaven above the clouds is altogether fanciful;" page 42. I shall not enter into a debate with him about the locality of heaven, but thus much I would observe by the way, that since the word of God, in its least figurative expressions concerning heaven, intimates a locality, we have not sufficient ground from Scripture to treat such a notion as a mere fancy. Many mere men have enjoyed very intimate communication with God, as Moses, with whom God spake "face to face, as a man speaketh unto his friend;" Exodus xxxiii. 11. Yet, neither of him, nor of any other, is it said, that he

* "Short Defence," page 9 and 25.

was in heaven and earth at the same time; but the being in heaven is spoken of in Scripture as inconsistent with a state of mere humanity on earth: as, 2 Corinthians v. 6, 8: "While we are at home in the body, we are absent from the Lord." I do not pretend to form any idea of the manner in which St. Paul was caught up into the third heaven, since he himself has declared he was ignorant of it, and knew not whether he was in the body, or out of the body. 2 Corinthians xii. 2.

15. That our blessed Redeemer is really present, as to his divine nature, with all his disciples, at all times, and in all places, is evident from the Scriptures I have quoted in the "Defence;" page 15 and 16. Our Author has commented upon those taken from St. Matthew's Gospel. In *illustrating* that promise of our Lord, mentioned chapter xxviii. 29, "Lo, I am with you alway, even unto the end of the world;" he says, "Christ, who is constituted *head over all things* to his church, undoubtedly takes care of its interests, and attends to whatever concerns his disciples; and *being with* a person, and *taking care* of him are, in the language of Scripture, equivalent expressions;" page 26; to prove which, we are referred to some texts in Genesis,

where God is said to have *been with* Ishmael, Abraham, Jacob, and Joseph. See Genesis xxi. 20, 22. xxviii. 15. xxxix. 2. But these passages make against our Author's "Illustration:" for, from them we learn, that, when God promises to *be with* any one, he means that he will be really present with him to do him good: and so we are to understand our Lord when he makes the same promise; that he will not only be present with his disciples, but present with them to bless, and guide, and preserve them. Because, *being with* a person, in the language of the Old Testament, implies a *favourable presence;* it can surely never be concluded, that the same phrase in the New Testament implies no presence at all, but only the favour of an absent person. The "Illustrator" adds, that "Christ may even be *personally present* with his disciples when they little think of it. But it is by no means necessary that he be personally present every where at the same time; since God may communicate to him a power of knowing distant events;" *ibidem.* I have given a reason, in my "Short Defence," page 16, why I think our Lord is not present *in body* with any of his disciples; for this is the *personal presence* our Author speaks of; but if he was, this would not fulfil the promise, which is general, and belongs as much to one disciple as another; yet he cannot be present always in body with two distant disciples. We cannot doubt of God's power to communicate the knowledge of distant events to any man, but this knowledge, though attended with a concern in the events made known, is a very different thing from the matter of the promise we are now considering.

16. The meaning of that similar passage, Matthew xviii. 20: " Where two or three are gathered together in my name, there am I in the midst of them;" our Author thinks to be only a representation of the great efficacy of the Apostles' prayers; so that when praying assembled, as became the disciples of Christ, their power with God was the same as his power. " That our Lord could not intend to speak of himself as ' the God who heareth prayer,' is evident," he says, " from his speaking of the Father, in this very place, as the person who was to grant their petitions, verse 19: " Again, I say unto you, that, if two of you shall agree on earth, touching any thing that they shall ask, it shall be done for them of my Father who is in heaven;" page 27. That the efficacy of social prayer is represented in this passage is indeed evident; but that our

Lord is really present with his faithful disciples, when engaged in this solemn exercise, is equally evident from his own plain declaration, " there am I in the midst of them."

Whether in this passage he intended, or not, to speak of himself " as the God that heareth prayer," does not alter the argument: he speaks of himself as being present in various places at the same time, which is sufficient for the proof of his *omnipresence*, and that was all I brought this text to prove. However, it is probable that he meant to speak of himself here, as it is certain he doth elsewhere, as the favourable answerer of humble prayer: " If ye shall ask any thing in my name, *I will do it.*" John xiv. 14.

17. I do not find in the " Illustration," any direct answer to what I have advanced on the article of Christ's omniscience; I shall not, therefore, at present, add any thing upon that head.

18. No reply is likewise given to several of the arguments I have brought in proof of *divine worship* being paid to Christ;* and some of the

* As those taken from Rom. x. 13—15. 2 Cor. xii. 8, 9. 2 Thess. ii. 16. Heb. i. 6. Rev. v. 8—11. " Short Defence," page 18—22.

arguments urged in the "Appeal" are repeated in the "Illustration,"* without any notice taken of the answers to them.

In order to *illustrate* 1 Corinthians i. 2. where the Apostle addresses the whole body of Christians, as those that "call upon the name of Jesus Christ our Lord," our Author says, "That adoration, such as is due to the one living and true God, was not meant by the Apostle in this place, is evident from the very next words; 'Grace be with you, and peace from God our Father, and from the Lord Jesus Christ;' where Christ is evidently spoken of as distinct from God;" page 37. Now, in my apprehension, the very reverse is the conclusion which these words require: for, if the Apostle prays for "grace and peace," which include all spiritual blessings, from the Lord Jesus Christ, as well as from God the Father, it necessarily follows, that he makes Christ the object of the same worship as the Father. The distinct mention of Christ in this place, can only prove that Christ is not the Father: but the joining of Christ with the Father in the same address can never prove, that Christ is not God as well as the Father.

* As that drawn from the different senses of the word *worship* under this head; and others elsewhere.

With equal appearance of reason might it be urged, that, because the Holy Ghost is distinctly mentioned with God, in that apostolic benediction, "The grace of our Lord Jesus Christ, and the love of God, and the fellowship of the Holy Ghost, be with you all," therefore the Holy Ghost is not God: yet our Author thinks this no objection to his believing that the Holy Ghost is not distinct from God at all.

19. The address of the expiring martyr St. Stephen to the Lord Jesus, Acts vii. 59, is thus commented upon in the "Illustration," page 37. "This text by no means implies that Stephen acknowledged Christ to be God, but only informs us, that Stephen addressed himself to Christ, whom he had just seen in person, in a state of great exaltation and glory." The text informs us that Stephen called upon, or invoked Christ, and gives us the very words of his invocation; "They stoned Stephen, calling upon," or invocating, "and saying, Lord Jesus, receive my spirit." He recommends his soul into the hands of Christ, and implores of him a reception into glory; and if this be not praying to him, I know not what is. An address made by an inspired person, in a time of the greatest distress, when

none but God could help him, containing a supplication for the greatest blessing, and the crown of all others, a reception into glory, contains every thing necessary to constitute it *prayer*, in the most proper sense of the word; and therefore Stephen truly prayed to the Lord Jesus. May I, and may the Author of this "Illustration," be found in our last moments, in the exercise of such faith, and such prayer, as this holy martyr, and obtain like him a gracious reception into the realms of bliss and glory!

The reasoning which follows the "Illustration" of this text is very far from being conclusive. Our Author having observed that the word which is here, and in 1 Corinthians i. 2. rendered to *call upon*, is likewise rendered to *appeal to*, and is used to express the *surname* of a person, infers this consequence, "There can be no doubt, therefore, but that it has the same meaning, both in Corinthians i. 2. and also in Acts ix. 21. 'Is not this he that destroyed them who called on this name in Jerusalem?' that is, all who called themselves Christians." By the *same meaning* I suppose our Author intends that expressed in the latter sentence, for he cannot mean the sense of both, or of either indifferently, as they are widely different. But this consequence has no connexion with its premises, as the reader will immediately perceive upon stating the argument. "The word usually translated to 'call upon' signifies in Luke xxii. 3. to be *called by a particular name*, in Acts xxv. 21. to *appeal to*, and in Acts vii. 59. to *address a person;* therefore, in 1 Corinthians i. 2. and Acts ix. 21. it signifies to be called by a particular name." Our Author adds, "The word is so rendered, James ii. 7. 'Do they not blaspheme that worthy name, by which ye are called?' or, as it is more exactly rendered, 'which is called,' or imposed, 'upon you;' that is, by which ye are distinguished. Had it implied *adoration*, it would at least have been *which is called upon by you.*" I grant it, and therefore believe, that in James ii. 7. it does not mean *adoration* any more than it does in Luke xxii. 3. as the construction of the word evinces.

There are very few words in our own, or perhaps any other language, which do not admit of more senses than one; yet this does not hinder, but that the particular sense of a word may be so determined by its connexion with other words in the same sentence, that it cannot in such sentence admit of more than one signification. This remark I could wish the reader to keep in view through the whole of this controversy; and it is very applicable to the subject under consideration. The word commonly rendered *calling upon* signifies, Luke xxii. 3, to be *surnamed*, and can there signify nothing else, as is plain from the connexion; " Then entered Satan into Judas, *surnamed* Iscariot, being one of the twelve." On the other hand, the same word in Romans x. 12, &c. does as certainly signify *divine worship* or *adoration* in the most proper sense, the meaning being likewise absolutely determined by the connexion. " The same Lord over all is rich unto all that *call upon* him. For whosoever shall *call upon* the name of the Lord shall be saved."

20. That Thomas paid such proper *adoration* to our Lord, is plain from the account given of it, John xx. 28. " Thomas answered and said unto him, My Lord, and my God." " This," says the *illustrator*, " is an abrupt exclamation, and no connected sentence at all, and seems to have proceeded from a conviction, suddenly produced in the Apostle's mind, that he who stood before him was, indeed, his Lord and Master raised to life by the power of God;" page 33. What sort of argument our Author intends by saying, the Apostle's words " are no connected sentence

at all," I cannot comprehend: they seem to me to have all the connexion that any exclamation has; they arise from the event, and express the sentiments of the speaker, which were, as we may conclude from the best authority, that he who stood before him was his Lord and his God. In the "Illustration" of this text our Author adds some passages of Scripture, which speak of Christ as raised from the dead by the power of God; as Romans vi. 4. "Raised from the dead by the glory of the Father," Romans x. 9. "If thou shalt confess with thy mouth the Lord Jesus, and shalt believe with thine heart, that God hath raised him from the dead, thou shalt be saved." And then says, "Here we plainly see, that he only who raised Christ from the dead is styled *God*, and not Christ, who was raised by his power;" page 34. This argument is very unfavourable to the cause it is designed to support; for if the being styled God is a proof of divinity, then the divinity of Christ is proved, since he is repeatedly styled God, in the most solemn manner, in Scripture. Or, if the raising Christ from the dead proves the almighty power of him who raised him, then almighty power belongs to Christ, for he raised himself, if he fulfilled his own declaration. "Destroy this temple, and in three days *I will raise it up.*" John ii. 19. See also chapter x. 18.

21. In the "Illustration" of 1 John v. 20. "We know that the Son of God is come, and hath given us an understanding that we may know him that is true: and we are in him that is true, even in his Son Jesus Christ. This is the true God, and eternal life;" our Author says, page 32, "The last clause is manifestly explanatory of the title "him that is true," or *the true one*, in the preceding clauses." This observation, which supposes the title "he that is true" to be the peculiar attribute of the true God, confirms the doctrine which it aims to overturn; for this is the title by which the same Apostle elsewhere speaks of Christ. As Revelations iii. 7. "These things saith he that is holy, *he that is true*; he that hath the key of David, he that openeth, and no man shutteth; and shutteth and no man openeth." These appellations, "the Holy One," and "the True One," are used in many places of Scripture as characteristic of the Almighty, yet we see they belong to Christ; which manifestly proves him to be the true God. Indeed this Book of the Revelation which concludes the sacred code, repeatedly speaks of the Father and of Christ in the same

terms,* represents them as addressed with the same worship,† and declares them to be equally the source of eternal bliss to the happy company of heaven.‡ The *illustrator* remarks, that in this clause of the text, " we are in him that is true, even in his Son Jesus" Christ, the word *even* is not in the original. This the translators have shewn in their usual way, as also in the 4th and 6th verses of the same chapter, but the sense remains the same if this word be omitted. Our Author thinks if the last clause in this text, " This is the true God and eternal life," be allowed to belong to our Lord Jesus Christ, as is evident from the text itself, it will flatly contradict those words of Christ recorded by the same Apostle, John xvii. 3. " This is life eternal, that they might know thee the only true God, and Jesus Christ whom thou hast sent." " For how," says he, " can the Father be ' the only true God,' if the Son be true God also?" He might as well have asked, how the Son can be true God, if the Father be true God; for those terms, " the true God," and " the only true

* Revelations iii. 7. and xix. 11. compared with chapter vi. 10. and xv. 4.

† Chapter v. 8, 13.

‡ Chapter vii. 17. and xxi. 22, 23.

God," are of the same import and extent. If the Son be the "true God," as the Apostle declares, then he is "the only true God," for there is but *one* true God:—and therefore no more can be fairly concluded from the description of the "Father" recorded in the gospel, than may be concluded from the description of the "Son" recorded in the epistle. It is worthy observation, that in both these texts "eternal life" is said to consist in the knowledge of Jesus Christ, as well as in the knowledge of the Father. Eternal life is often spoken of in Scripture as flowing from the knowledge of God, and I think it to be some confirmation of the doctrine I am defending, that such language is likewise used with respect to our Lord, though it is never applied to any mere teacher of God's will, however honoured with credentials of infallibility.

. 22. In the "Illustration" of Philippians ii. 5, &c. a new translation of the words "he thought it no robbery to be equal with God," is still insisted on, page 39; but no notice is taken of the arguments brought, in answer to the "Appeal," to prove, that no good sense can be made of the whole passage without allowing the divinity of Christ. Till this is done,

I may be excused from adding any thing to what I have already said on this portion of Scripture in my "Short Defence."

23. In answer to our Author's comment on that declaration of our Lord mentioned in John x. 30. "I and my Father are one," I shewed in my "Short Defence," that such an union subsisted between the Father and Christ, as no mere man could have with God. All the reply to this which I find in the "Illustration," (except what is included in the exposition of John xvii. 5, page 40,) is, that, "They are one in design and interest. But whatever be the union between the Father and the Son; it is of such a kind, that his disciples are capable of it with respect to them both; for, in his prayer for his disciples, he says, John xvii. 20. 'Neither pray I for these alone, but for them also which shall believe on me through their word: that they all may be one as thou Father art in me, and I in thee; that they also may be one in us;—and the glory which thou gavest me, I have given them; that they may be one even as we are one. I in them, and thou in me, that they may be made perfect in one, and that the world may know that thou hast sent me, and hast loved them as thou hast loved me.'"

page 24. This passage, as many others, speaks of the union which all true christians have with each other, and with Christ: they are one body, of which he is the head; and "out of his fulness they receive grace for grace." It likewise declares the love which the Father hath to all such, who are become his children by adoption and grace. But it does not assert that the disciples are capable of the same union with the Father and Christ, which subsists between them; and many other passages of Scripture evince that they are not, as I have already shewn in my "Short Defence," page 38—40. I would beg leave to ask the *illustrator*, whether he thinks any disciple is capable of such an union with the Father, that the Holy Ghost may be called *his* spirit with as great propriety as he is called the Spirit of God? Yet this is the case with respect to Christ. Romans viii. 9. May it with propriety be said, that the inspiration of the Holy Ghost, by which the prophets foretold the great things which are to come to pass, was the inspiration of the spirit of Paul, or Peter, or any other disciple? Yet this inspiration was from the spirit of Christ. 1 Peter i. 11. Or has the greatest saint that ever entered heaven such an union with the Father, that he can claim the power of commissioning, sending, and directing the Holy Ghost, who is God himself? Yet such union has Christ with the Father, that he may speak of the Holy Ghost as his messenger, who takes of his, and shews it unto his disciples. John xvi. 14. Indeed our Author has invalidated his own argument, as I before observed he must necessarily do,* in his exposition of John v. 23. "That all men shall honour the Son even as they honour the Father." The expression "even as" upon the meaning of which the force of his reasoning in his last argument entirely depends, signifies, he says, *as well as*: and then adds, "The same word is used where it can have no other sense in John xvii. 24. 'And hast loved them as thou hast loved me;' that is, not in the same degree, but *likewise*." So that according to his own interpretation, all that the passage above quoted from John xvii. declares is this, that as there is an union between the Father and Christ, so likewise there is an union of the disciples with each other, and with Christ; and as the Father loveth Christ, he likewise loveth the disciples: but not that the *same* union subsists between the disciples and Christ, as between Christ and the Father;

* "Short Defence," page 39.

or that the Father loveth the disciples with the *same* love, with which he loveth the Son.

24. The *illustrator* endeavours to weaken the arguments drawn from some of the texts in which the peculiar titles of God are applied to Christ, by introducing a new translation of them. How far his translation agrees with the originals, I shall leave to the determination of the learned. The unlearned, for whom he professes to write, can only judge of their propriety by their agreement with the context, and other passages of Scripture: and in this view alone I shall consider them.

The glorious titles given to our Saviour in Isaiah ix. 6. "The mighty God, the everlasting Father," our Author says may be rendered, "the mighty God is my Father for ever." page 30. To read the passage with this translation seems to me sufficient to shew its impropriety. "His name shall be called Wonderful, Counsellor," "the mighty God is my Father for ever," "the Prince of Peace." The text evidently points out the true characters of Christ, and declares what he *was* or *should be*, by saying what he should be *called*, which is a form of expression very common in the Scriptures. The title of "Everlasting Father" applied to Christ does not at all contradict the common doctrine of the Trinity, as this Author supposes; for though he is not *the Father* with respect to the Godhead, yet he may with the greatest propriety be called "the Everlasting Father," with respect to all created beings, since he is the Creator, and in this sense, the Father of all, as, I hope, has been sufficiently proved.

An argument of another kind is likewise used, in which the Author considers the passage as rightly translated; he says, page 29, "These titles may not express what "*Christ is*, but what God will manifest himself to be in him, and by him; so that, in the dispensation of the gospel, God, the wise and benevolent Author of it, will appear to be a wonderful Counsellor, the Everlasting Father, and the Prince of Peace." All the reason he gives for thus expounding the text is, that there are some instances in Scripture, where, "names imposed by divine direction do not express any thing characteristic of the person on whom they are imposed," but which "were intended to be a memorial of some divine promise respecting things of a public and general concern." This remark is very true, but very foreign to the scope of the passage under consideration; for the inspired penman is here giving us the characters of the Messiah, as the preceding and subsequent words plainly shew, and therefore these titles do express what *Christ is*. He who is "the Mighty God, the Everlasting Father," and "the Prince of Peace," is also "a child born," and "a Son given to us; the government is upon *his* shoulders, and of the increase of *his* government and peace there shall be no end." verse 6, 7.

25. The same kind of argument is used with respect to the name *Emmanuel*, mentioned by St. Matthew, chapter i. 23. and, I think, with no great propriety. For the Evangelist having informed us, that the name *Jesus*, which the supposed Father of Christ was commanded to give him, was significant of his character, as the Saviour of sinners, adds, "Now all this was done, that it might be fulfilled which was spoken by the Prophet, saying, Behold a virgin shall be with child, and shall bring forth a son, and shall call his name Emmanuel, which, being interpreted, is *God with us*." So that from the Evangelist's exposition of the Prophet we learn, that the title "God with us," was characteristic of our Lord; being, in effect, applied to him when a name was given him expressive of his mighty power to save, which none but he can claim,

who is "the only Saviour." Isaiah xliii. 11, and "the only wise God." Jude 25.

26. The *illustrator* thinks it has been "fully demonstrated that in the original of 1 Timothy iii. 16. the text was not, '*God* was manifest in the flesh,' but '*who* was manifest in the flesh;'" page 38. Allowing this to have been the case, the sense of the text remains precisely the same; for the relative *who* must refer to *God*, as this is the only antecedent in the passage to which it can refer. The Apostle having concluded, in the thirteenth verse, his directions to Timothy concerning the choice of bishops and deacons, adds the reason why he gave him such particular instructions. "These things write I unto thee, that thou mayest know how thou oughtest to behave thyself in the house of God, which is the church of the living God, the pillar and ground of the truth:" and then concludes the passage with a summary description of the economy of our redemption: "And without controversy great is the mystery of godliness. God was manifest in the flesh, justified in the spirit, seen of angels, preached unto the Gentiles, believed on in the world, received up into glory."

But our Author does not rest his objections entirely upon this full demonstration, for he adds, " Besides, it is even literally true, that God was manifest in the flesh of Christ, the wisdom and power of God being conspicuous in him." If God was no otherwise in Christ than by a communication of wisdom and power to him, these words might have been said of Moses, or Elijah, Paul, or Peter, as well as of Christ; and the manifestation of God in the flesh here spoken of, instead of being a great mystery, as the Apostle affirms, was no mystery at all. Besides, this interpretation of the first clause will by no means suit the subsequent clauses of the sentence; for upon this construction we must suppose the Apostle to say, that wisdom and power were justified in the spirit, seen of angels, believed on in the world, and received up into glory, which are not applicable to a *quality*, but a *person:* on the contrary, if we suppose these things to be spoken of Christ as a mere man, we must imagine the Apostle to tell us, that a man was manifest in the flesh, a piece of information which no one can think an inspired writer capable of giving. In short, whether the passage be translated as our Author says it ought to be, or not, we can never make sense of it without allowing the doctrine of Christ's divinity.

27. In the "Illustration" of Romans ix. 5. "Whose are the fathers, and of whom, as concerning the flesh, Christ came, who is over all, God blessed for ever," it is said, page 32, "This may with equal propriety and truth be rendered, 'God who is over all be blessed for ever,' the former sentence ending with the word *came*." The Author thinks himself justified in making this alteration, as "no ancient manuscripts are pointed," and as "it is usual with the Apostle Paul to break out into a form of thanksgiving to God, after mentioning any remarkable instance of his goodness." The reader will observe, that what is here alleged does not prove it necessary to alter our translation, but, at most, only affords an apology for making such an alteration: the text, as it stands in our Bible, is allowed to be exactly conformable to the original; and the context, instead of affording any reason for the alteration, strongly enforces the contrary. The Apostle, here enumerating the privileges of the Jews, concludes the list with this, that Christ, as concerning the flesh, was descended from them. Now, on the supposition that Christ was but a mere man, the expression "as concerning the flesh" has no meaning at all; and we must believe the Apostle to be here talking nonsense before we can admit

such a supposition to be true. If any man, being asked from what family the King of England was descended, should answer, "that he was, as concerning the flesh, of the House of Hanover;" would not such an one be justly thought to utter words which conveyed no idea to the inquirer? And to alter the last clause of the sentence as our *illustrator* has done, is to make the Apostle's language equally improper; for there remains after such an alteration no antithesis in the passage to give the phrase, "as concerning the flesh," any proper meaning: whereas there is the greatest propriety in the expression, as the text stands in our Bible: Christ, "as concerning the flesh," that is, with respect to his human nature, is of the seed of Abraham; but with respect to his divine nature, he is "God over all blessed for ever."

28. "It is with little appearance of réason," says the *illustrator*, page 23, "that Christ is argued to be very and eternal God, because he is styled the 'Son of God,' for all christians have the same appellation." If no intimation were given us, that this title belongs to Christ in a higher sense than it does to all christians, certainly nothing could be argued from it to prove any superiority of nature in

Christ; but we have abundant intimation in Scripture that this title belongs to him in a sense peculiar to himself. The Jews were well accustomed to the title *sons of God*, for it is a common appellation of the saints in the Old Testament; and therefore when they accused our Lord of blasphemy for saying "that God was his Father," they understood him in such a sense as could belong to no mere man whatever: and it is very plain that our Lord never undeceived them, if they mistook his meaning in such expressions. Our Author says, in his "Triumph of Truth," page 19, "If Christ had not satisfied the Jews that he did not mean to make himself equal with God, would they not have produced it against him at his trial, when he was condemned as a blasphemer, because he confessed he was the Christ only." That the Jews did produce this as an accusation against him is evident from the answer which they gave to Pilate, when he would have released our blessed Saviour, as finding no fault in him. "The Jews answered him, We have a law, and by our law he ought to die, because he made himself the *Son of God.*" John xix. 7. What the Jews here meant by the term "Son of God," may be learnt from their own declarations recorded in the fifth and tenth chapters. In the former, they interpret our Lord's claim to this title, as "making himself equal with God;"* verse 18; and in the latter, they call it still more plainly the "making himself God;" verse 33. We have therefore the greatest reason for believing this to be their meaning in their answer to Pilate. Besides, the Jews had no law to condemn our Lord for claiming this title in its ordinary signification. God had often declared himself the Father of all that trusted in, and obeyed him; and had repeatedly called such his sons. The Jews therefore could not say, "By our law he ought to die, because he made himself the *Son of God*," if they used this appellation in its ordinary signification. But their law did condemn him to death for using such language concerning himself as they understood it, which was, "that he

* Our Author renders this expression, "like unto God," and supposes, that the Jews only meant hereby to charge our Lord with "assuming so much of God's prerogative, as to claim the privilege of working on the Sabbath-day:" whereas the text plainly refers this charge to our Lord's, saying, that God was his Father; and not to his working on the Sabbath. "Therefore the Jews sought the more to kill him, because he not only had broken the Sabbath, but said also, that God was his Father, making himself equal with God."

being a man" *only*, made himself God: and therefore it is plain, that "Christ had not satisfied the Jews that he did not mean to make himself equal with God," because they "produced it against him at his trial, when he was condemned as a blasphemer."

29. I have now taken notice, I think, of every material observation made in the "Illustration" upon those passages of Scripture which I have quoted in my "Short Defence." My plan would not allow me to transcribe all that the *illustrator* says upon each of those passages: what I have transscribed, conveys, in my apprehension, the force of his objections; however, the reader may easily satisfy himself, by comparing these remarks with the "Illustration."

The following texts of Scripture, urged in my "Defence" of the Divinity of Christ, are not taken notice of in the "Illustration." Revelations i. 17, page 11. Hebrews vii. 3, page 13. Revelations xxii. 16, *ib.* Matthew xxii. 45, *ib.* Isaiah xl. 3, page 14. Hebrews ii. 18, page 16. John x. 28, *ib.* Revelations ii. 24, page 17. Luke xvii. 5, page 18. Romans x. 13—15, page 20. 2 Thessalonians ii. 16, page 21. 2 Corinthians xii. 8, 9, *ib.* Revelations v. 8—11, &c. page 22. 2 Corinthians

viii. 9, page 25. 1 Peter i. 10, page 28. John xvi. 7, 14, 15, *ib.* Jude 25, page 29. Revelations vii. 17, chapter xxi. 22, 23, page 31.

30. Before I conclude, I shall take some notice of two other texts which our Author has *illustrated,* though they are not mentioned in my "Defence." The first is Colossians ii. 9. "In him dwelleth all the fulness of the Godhead bodily." To suppose, as the *illustrator* does, page 22, that this text implies no more than that "the wisdom and power of God were manifest in, and acted by Christ," is doing great injustice to it. It expresses, in the strongest manner, that incomprehensible indwelling of the Deity in the human nature of Christ, which no mere man can partake of, and which renders him the proper object of worship to all intelligent creatures. The great privileges of true christians, though spoken of in terms, which at first sight appear similar to this, are found widely different, when attentively considered. God dwelleth in the saints, but it is only by a communication of divine grace, or holy love, as the Apostle declares, 1 John iv. 12. "If we love one another, God dwelleth in us:" and again, verse 16. "He that dwelleth in love, dwelleth in God, and God in him." So the being

"filled with the fulness of God," mentioned in Ephesians iii. 19. is explained in the same passage to be, "Christ's dwelling in their hearts by faith, knowing the love of God," and "being rooted and grounded in love." Besides, it is from Christ we receive these divine benefits, as is intimated in the words immediately following the text under consideration; "Ye are complete in *him*;" and still more plainly in other passages, as John i. 16. "Of *his* fulness have we all received, and grace for grace:" and Ephesians iv. 7. "Unto every one of us is given grace according to the measure of the gift of Christ." But how different is all this from what is here said of Christ: That the Godhead, or Deity itself, yea all the fulness of Deity dwelleth in him bodily. "This expression," says our Author, "that the fulness of the Godhead dwelled or resided in him, seems to imply that it did not naturally belong to him." * page 23. It implies no more, I think, than

* The *illustrator* likewise says, page 46. "To signify that the authority of Christ is not underived, like that of God; and at the same time to inform us from whence it does proceed, the Apostle says, that 'it pleased the Father, that in him should all fulness dwell.'" Colossians i. 19. Our Author might have added, that the word

that the Godhead and manhood of Christ, though united in one person, are not confounded; which is intimated in the phrase "dwelleth in him *bodily*." The word "bodily" fixes the sense of the passage, since it could not have been used with propriety if Christ was but a mere man; for, in this case, it must either convey a false idea, or none at all; it must mean, that wisdom dwelt in his flesh and bones, or mean nothing. We should judge a writer to give a very improper and insignificant description of a wise or learned man by saying, that a great deal of wisdom or learning dwelt in him *bodily*: with still greater impropriety would the Apostle have spoken of the "Godhead" dwelling in Christ "bodily," if he had only meant that Christ was possessed of a great measure of divine wisdom. Whereas, allowing the divine and human nature to be united in our Lord, the Apostle's language has the greatest propriety, being descriptive of such an union.

"Father" is not in the original of this text, as the English reader may observe by the character in which it is printed in our Bibles. It pleased the Father without doubt, that the fulness of the Godhead should dwell in Christ bodily; but how does this prove that Christ has no underived authority?

31. The other text is, Acts xx. 28. " Feed the church of God, which he hath purchased with his own blood." — The *illustrator* after telling us that in the most ancient manuscripts this text is, " Feed the church of the Lord;" and that in some copies it is, " which he purchased with his blood," adds, " As the blood of God is a phrase which occurs no where else in the Scriptures, we ought to be exceedingly cautious how we admit such an expression. If Christ was God, his blood could not be his blood as God, but as man;" page 36. If we ought to be exceedingly cautious of admitting every expression that occurs but once in the Scriptures, there are many besides this which must either be expunged, or regarded as of no consequence. It does not become us to say how often an expression must be repeated in the word of God before we will admit it.— If God speaks, though but once, he requires our diligent attention, and entire credit. There is no danger that any should mistake the meaning of this passage, who accustom themselves to search the Scriptures, or make use of their understanding. Such will readily comprehend, that, by the " blood of God" is meant the *blood of him who is God*, though

manifested to us in the flesh.* The Scriptures abound with similar expressions; not only speaking such things of a person in general, as in truth can only be said of one part of him, which is a very common form of speech; but also applying to one of our component parts what solely appertains to the other. When it was said by Moses, that no *soul* should "eat blood," or "touch a dead body," the Jews were no more at a loss with respect to his meaning, than we are with regard to the Apostle's, when he informs us, that "God purchased the church with his own blood." A similar form of speech we find in John iii. 13; where our Lord calls himself the "Son of man," when speaking of something which could not belong to him as man.

* Some of my readers may perhaps wonder why I have not quoted upon this occasion, 1 John iii. 16. "Hereby perceive we the love of God, because he laid down his life for us." My reason is, that as the word *God* is wanting in the greater part of the best editions of the New Testament which I have seen, I do not chuse to lay any stress upon it; though I think it very agreeable to the context to supply the ellipsis, which is in the original, by that word.

What our Author alleges relating to ancient manuscripts I shall not now inquire into. Thousands, and tens of thousands in this kingdom, have never seen an ancient manuscript of the Bible, nor, if they had, would have been the wiser for it; yet these, being capable of reading, and understanding the Bible in their native language, are called to believe, and obey it, at the peril of their souls. To such I offer these remarks, which a belief of the importance of the subject have given rise to. I shall be extremely glad if they are instrumental, in the hands of Him "who worketh all things after the counsel of his own will," to the establishment of the wavering, or the reclaiming of the erroneous. Or, if this attempt to vindicate the honour of our Redeemer shall excite others, who have greater abilities, and more leisure for such labours, to employ their talents in this important service, my design will be answered.

SHORT DEFENCE

OF THE DOCTRINE OF

ATONEMENT FOR SIN,

BY

THE DEATH OF CHRIST.

WITH

REMARKS UPON SOME LATE PUBLICATIONS ON THAT SUBJECT.

"I will also shew mine opinion." Job xxxii. 10.

"Speaking the truth in love." Ephesians iv. 15.

THE

PREFACE.

The following observations were in part written before the public was informed that the Rev. Dr. Priestley was the Author of the "Appeal," and some other Tracts which are taken notice of in this Essay.* My design being solely to examine sentiments, without any respect to the persons who espouse them, I have chosen to continue the style I had begun to make use of, and to speak of the Author as yet unknown. I could not take the same method of avoiding the appearance of personal reflection, in examining Mr. Graham's Letters, because his name was prefixed to them at their first publication;

* See a Sermon preached on occasion of his resigning the charge of a congregation of Protestant Dissenters in Leeds.

but the freedom used in my remarks upon them is designed to extend no further than to the writings themselves. I think it a shame for any, who profess themselves candid inquirers after truth, to entertain the least malevolence towards those whose opinions they are opposing, and I am sure that such conduct is contrary to the spirit of Christianity.

I have used the term *Socinian*, to distinguish those who deny the doctrine of atonement, both as it prevents the necessity of tedious circumlocution, and as it is adopted by the writers whose works I am examining.*

I have informed the reader in the course of this work, in what sense I use the principal terms belonging to this controversy; and, as far as I know, I have used them according to their most common acceptation. When I speak of repentance or faith, as being the *condition* of pardon, I mean no more by this mode of expression than to assert, that the pardon of sin, considered as the transgression of the moral law, is never obtained without repentance and faith, and that it is always granted to the repenting and believing sinner. When I call the death of Christ the *consi-*

* "Familiar Illustration," page 64. And Mr. Graham's Letters, page 75. *Note.*

deration of our forgiveness, it will be sufficient for my argument if the term *consideration* be construed to imply no more than "something necessary in order to the pardon of sin;" but I would not be understood to mean, that the death of Christ is not the condition of pardon in a higher sense than our faith and repentance are. I have generally preferred the term *consideration* to that of *condition*, in speaking of the relation which the death of Christ bears to our forgiveness, as more readily admitting and suggesting the idea of worth or compensation; but I have not strictly adhered to this distinction.

I have studied to avoid entering upon any question which did not immediately affect the subject in debate, and to express my arguments as concisely as I could without being unintelligible. I do not mean to enter upon a full discussion of all that respects the doctrine of atonement; my design is only to prove that it is a doctrine of divine revelation. Much might be said, and that of considerable importance, upon this subject, which I have wholly omitted; contenting myself with a brief, and yet, I hope, sufficient answer to the principal objections made against the doctrine I have attempted to defend. What I have written is from a full persuasion of the truth and importance of this doctrine; but I shall be ready, I trust, to correct any errors I may have fallen into, when they are pointed out to me.

I wish the reader every spiritual blessing that is offered to sinners through Jesus Christ, "who is made of God" to all that believe "wisdom, and righteousness, and sanctification, and redemption."

SHORT DEFENCE

OF THE

DOCTRINE OF ATONEMENT.

The doctrines which relate to the character and offices of our Lord and Saviour Jesus Christ, are undoubtedly of very great importance in the system of Christianity; and their connexion with our religious conduct is so intimate, that it is impossible we should be right in the latter, if we err considerably with respect to the former. The acknowledgment of the divinity of Christ, for instance, calls for such affections and behaviour towards him, as they who look upon him as a mere man cannot maintain. Our practical regard must likewise be much affected by our belief or disbelief of the doctrine of atonement for sin by his death. If this doctrine is without foundation in Scripture, it must be a high affront to the Divine Majesty, to place any hope of pardon on the cruel treatment which a mere man like ourselves met with in the world. But if our Lord Jesus Christ made a sacrifice for sin by his death, and we are commanded to come unto God through such a mediator, then their condition is dangerous indeed, who despise that sacrifice, and reject that method of approaching God, which is appointed in the gospel for guilty sinners.

The doctrine of atonement has been treated with much contempt by some late writers, who have thought fit to speak (as one of them expresses it) " with great indignation" against it; and to represent it, not only as contrary to the Scriptures, but likewise as so absurd in itself, that it would render the Bible indefensible, if it contained such a doctrine. I have examined, with some attention, the arguments on which this representation is founded; and as they appear to me to be inconclusive, I have ventured to point out wherein I think them faulty, and to give a short defence of what I believe to be a fundamental doctrine of Christianity.

The doctrine of the Socinians respecting

atonement, is this, "That God requires no consideration or condition of pardon, but the repentance of the offender; and that, consequently, the death of Christ was no real sacrifice for sin, but is called so in the Scriptures merely in a *figurative* sense, by way of allusion to the Jewish sin-offerings; as our praises and other good works are called sacrifices, because they are something *offered up* to God." On the contrary, the doctrine which I mean to defend, is, "That God has thought fit to require a consideration of pardon, distinct from the repentance of the sinner; and that this consideration is the death of Christ, which was a real sacrifice for sin, and stood related to the Jewish sacrifices as the antitype to the type."

I. It is evident, that the inspired writers do speak of the death of Christ as a sacrifice for sin. "Christ appeared to put away sin by the sacrifice of himself." Heb. ix. 26. "Christ hath given himself for us, an offering and a sacrifice to God." Ephesians v. 2. "Christ was once offered to bear the sins of many." Hebrews ix. 28. "He is the propitiation for our sins." 1 John ii. 2. "After he had offered one sacrifice for sin, he for ever sat down at the right hand of God." Hebrews x. 12. "By one offering he hath perfected for ever them that are sanctified." Hebrews x. 14, &c. The question then is, Whether this language, which abounds in the New Testament, is proper, and to be understood literally; or merely figurative, and used by way of allusion to the Jewish sacrifices.

It is an allowed rule of interpreting the Scriptures, that every doctrine contained therein must be understood in its most plain and obvious sense, considered in connexion with its context, unless this sense is clearly absurd in itself, or contrary to other parts of Scripture. Now it is self-evidently right, that God should appoint such a way of extending mercy to penitent sinners, as his infinite wisdom saw the fittest to display his hatred of sin, and to maintain the honour of his righteous laws, and just government of the universe. And no good reason can be given, why God, as Governor of the world, might not appoint a sacrifice to be the means of forgiveness for transgressions against his general laws, as he did for offences against those particular laws, which he instituted as Governor of one nation.

Let us then examine whether other parts

of Scripture require us to restrain the sacrifical language, used concerning our Lord, to a merely figurative sense, or whether we are led by them to understand it in its most proper and obvious signification.

The most striking circumstance of the Jewish economy was the appointment of sacrifice as the means of obtaining pardon for offences committed against that constitution, which the Jews were under as a peculiar people. Sacrifice was undoubtedly a consideration distinct from the the moral character of the offender, yet was the standing means of obtaining forgiveness, under the Mosaic dispensation, to those who conformed to the conditions required by the ceremonial law.

Now, if this dispensation was designed to represent that of the gospel, then is pardon granted under the gospel also, to those who comply with the conditions required therein, by virtue of a consideration distinct from the moral character of the offender, in the same manner as it was under the law of Moses.

That the Jewish propitiatory sacrifices were a necessary consideration of forgiveness, and the means of obtaining it, appears both from their institution, and the view which is given of them by the inspired writer of the Epistle to the Hebrews. The words of the institution are plain to this purpose. "And it shall be, when" any one "shall be guilty in one of these things, that he shall confess that he hath sinned in that thing: and he shall bring his trespass-offering unto the Lord for his sin which he hath sinned; and the priest shall make an atonement for him, for his sin which he hath sinned, and it shall be forgiven him." Leviticus v. 5, 6, 10. This passage, compared with Leviticus xvii. 11, which assures us, that "it was the blood which made the atonement," leaves no reason to doubt, that the sacrifice offered by the offender was the appointed means of obtaining forgiveness of his offence.

The same view of propitiatory sacrifices is given in the Epistle to the Hebrews, when it is said, "Almost all things are by the law purged with blood, and without shedding of blood there is no remission:" chapter ix. 22. which proves that the sacrifice was looked upon as the consideration on which the pardon was granted. Now, if it can be shown that these sacrifices were intended to point out the nature of Christ's sacrifice, or the relation which his death bears to the remission of our sins; then it will follow, that the death of Christ is the *consideration* of our forgiveness, with respect to transgressions of the moral law, as the Jewish sacrifices were the consideration of their forgiveness, with respect to transgressions of the ceremonial and political law; and, consequently, that our Lord offered a real sacrifice for sin, *when he offered up himself*.

That the rites of the ceremonial law were intended to represent the manner of our redemption by Christ, is, I think, put beyond all doubt in the Epistle to the Hebrews. For, not to mention here the many instances in which our redemption corresponds with those legal rites, as enumerated in that Epistle, from whence one might reasonably infer a *designed* representation; we are expressly told, that "the law had a shadow of good things to come." chapter x. 1. Not a shadow, *compared with* those things, (which is undoubtedly true, though not the truth here intended,) for that might have been said of any thing unsubstantial, though it had not the least resemblance of them, and is a very different expression from that of the Apostle: his words plainly intimate a resemblance, for he adds, "and not the very image of the things," which words convey no meaning, unless we suppose him to be speaking of a resemblance.* The whole sentence points out the imperfection of that similitude, which the legal rites afforded of good things to come, by a metaphor taken from the art of painting; the former exhibited but the sketch or outlines, and not a finished portrait or complete picture of the latter.† The Apostle uses the term *shadow* in another place, in conjunction with a word which likewise fixes its meaning; "The priests that offer gifts according to the law, serve unto the *example* and *shadow* of heavenly things;" chapter viii. 4, 5. The

* "By a *shadow*, I apprehend, is not meant, that the whole *apparatus* of the Jewish tabernacle and temple was typical of the gospel scheme. Throughout the Epistle to the Hebrews, the two schemes of Moses and Christ are compared, and the preference given, as in justice due, to the latter. But the Apostle never once intimates that the one dispensation was a type of the other. All he says, is, that the religious system of the Jewish legislator, when compared with the nobler one of Christ, is no more than a shadow compared with the substance." Mr. Graham's Sermon, entitled, Repentance the only Condition of Final Acceptance, page 9.

† St. Paul uses the same form of speech in his Epistle to the Colossians; wherein, speaking of the ceremonial ordinance from which Christians are delivered, he says, "which are a shadow of things to come; but the body is of Christ." chapter ii. 17.

me inspired writer says, "Christ is not
tered into the holy places made with hands,
hich are the *figures* of the true," chapter
. 24., which expresses, with sufficient clear-
ss, the typical nature of the ceremonial
w; and that no doubt might remain of the
tention to prefigure by these rites, he informs
, that the first tabernacle was a "figure
r *the time then present*," verse 9., which could
t have been said of it, had it not been
tended to prefigure things then future. But
e evidence of this matter is not yet ex-
usted; for we are further assured, that this
efiguration was designed by God himself;
r the Apostle, speaking of the high-priest
tering into the holy of holies but once a
ar, adds the reason of it in these plain
ords, "*The Holy Ghost this signifying*,
at the way into the holiest of all was not
t made manifest, while as the first taber-
cle was yet standing," chapter ix. 8. And
e are also informed, that Moses was in-
ructed concerning the typical nature of the
remonial law by a divine admonition, "The
iests that offer gifts according to the law,
rve unto the example and shadow of hea-
nly things, *as Moses was admonished of God
hen he was about to make the tabernacle*;"
hapter viii. 5. Thus the doctrine of atone-

ment for sin, by the death of Christ, is demonstrated to be a doctrine of divine revelation; for no terms can be found in language more clear and express, than those which are used to declare the typical nature of the ceremonial law.

II. I might here conclude the positive proof of the doctrine I am defending; but as the *priesthood* and *sacrifice* of Christ are largely treated of in the Epistle to the Hebrews, and we have, therefore, a good opportunity of learning, whether the inspired writer uses these terms in the *proper* or *figurative* sense; I shall take notice of some of the principal passages which serve to fix their meaning.

The Apostle defines, with great perspicuity, the term *priest* in its proper sense. A priest is one who "is ordained for men, in things pertaining to God, that he may offer both gifts and sacrifices for sin." Hebrews v. 1. But the description which is given of our Lord's priesthood, agrees with this; "Wherefore, in all things it behoved him to be made like unto his brethren, that he might be a merciful and faithful high-priest in things pertaining to God, to make reconciliation for the sins of the people," chapter ii. 17. And, therefore, our Lord is a real and proper high-priest, because he has the essential characters of one. To this office he was solemnly instituted by God: for, as "no man taketh this honour unto himself but he that is called of God, as was Aaron: so also, Christ glorified not himself to be made an high-priest; but he that said unto him, Thou art a priest for ever after the order of Melchizedek;" verse 45.

The reality of Christ's priesthood is likewise ascertained by the declaration, that it was "after the order of Melchizedek," who was, in the most proper sense of the words, *priest of the Most High God;* for if our Lord's priesthood was after his order, it was also real, and not figurative.

The Apostle, speaking of the imperfection of the Levitical priesthood, and of its giving way to the priesthood of Christ, says, "The priesthood being changed, there is made, *of necessity*, a change also of the law;" chapter vii. 12. Now this argument requires, that Christ be a true high-priest, otherwise there was no need that the law should be changed; for there were figurative priests under the law, as well as at any other period, that is, persons who offered the *spiritual sacrifices* of prayer and thanksgiving unto God; nay, the whole Jewish nation is called, in this sense, a "kingdom of priests;" Exodus xix. 6. and, therefore, the Apostle could never have argued a change of the law from Christ's priesthood, had it not been a real one.

Our Lord is represented as being a more excellent priest than those of the order of Aaron, in that he was ordained to the office with an oath; "Those priests were made without an oath; but this with an oath, by him that said unto him, The Lord sware and will not repent, Thou art a priest for ever after the order of Melchizedec;" chapter vii. 12. But if Christ is only called a priest because he devoted his life to the service of God, and died in defence of his doctrine; to talk of his superior dignity in being constituted a priest with an oath, is to make a mere jingle of sounds without a meaning.

The superior dignity of our Lord as a priest, is likewise argued from other particulars, which prove his priesthood to be real, and not metaphorical; as that he excelled the high-priests under the law, in having no occasion to offer up a sacrifice for his own sins, but only for those of his people. "Such an high-priest became us,—who needeth not daily, as those high-priests, to offer up sacrifices, first for his own sins, and then for the people's, for this he did once when he offered up himself. For the law maketh men high-priests which have infirmity; but the word of the oath which was since the law, maketh the Son, who is consecrated for evermore; chapter vii. 27, 28.* Now, if Christ did not properly offer any sacrifice for the sins of the people, what can the inspired writer mean by informing us, that he excelled the Jewish high-priests in not offering one for himself? The argument is important and conclusive, if we consider the death of Christ as a *real* sacrifice for sin; on any other supposition, the reasoning is childish.

The *sacrifice*, which this great *high-priest of our profession* offered up for us, was *himself*. This sacrifice, the Apostle informs us, exceeded in its expiatory virtue those which were offered under the law, and therefore we are assured that it was a proper one. If the death of Christ has no influence in procuring the remission of our sins, but as it leads us to repent of them; then it has no expiatory virtue at all, but only a tendency to promote that which properly expiates our guilt. But the Apostle's reasoning does by no means agree with this sentiment: he says, "If the blood of bulls and of goats, and the ashes of

* See also chapter v. 1, 2, 3.

an heifer sprinkling the unclean, sanctifieth to the purifying of the flesh; *how much more* shall the blood of Christ, who, through the eternal Spirit, offered himself without spot to God, purge your conscience from dead works to serve the living God;" chapter ix. 13, 14. It is not good sense to talk of the greater comparative efficacy of a sacrifice, which, as a sacrifice, has no efficacy at all. Nor could it with any propriety be said, that if the blood of bulls was sufficient to purify the flesh, then the blood of Christ was *much more* sufficient to purge the conscience, unless the efficacy of the latter were of the same kind as that of the former.

When the Apostle would point out the dangerous condition of those who reject the Lord Jesus as their Saviour; or, in his own emphatical language, "who tread under foot the Son of God;" he does it by reminding us, that there is no other sacrifice for sin than that which our Lord made by his death. "If we sin wilfully after that we have received the knowledge of the truth, there remaineth no more sacrifice for sin;" chapter x. 26. Now, if Christ made no sacrifice for sin by his death, it is a strange kind of reasoning, to tell us there is no other. And if the term be applied to the death of Christ, only by way of metaphor, then the assertion is false; for there have been many besides our Lord, who have offered their lives in the cause of truth, and for the good of mankind, which is all that the figurative use of the term implies.

When the inspired writers inform us, that some of the circumstances of our Lord's death happened through an *intention* to conform to particular Jewish institutions, they thereby assure us, that they did not compare the death of Christ to those institutions merely by way of allusion, in order to reconcile mankind to the notion of a suffering Saviour. For then the conformity would have been imaginary or accidental, which is inconsistent with an intentional one. But, on the other hand, an intentional conformity was necessary on this supposition, (and on this only,) that those institutions were designed to be typical, and, therefore, an assurance of such a conformity strongly intimates that they were so. "The bodies of those beasts, whose blood is brought into the sanctuary of the high-priest for sin, are burnt without the camp. *Wherefore* Jesus also, that he might sanctify the people with his own blood, suffered without the gate." Hebrews xii. 11, 12. See likewise, John xix. 36.

III. Before I proceed to answer the particular objection made to the doctrine of atonement, I will consider it in another point of view, from whence we may likewise discern that it is founded on divine revelation.

If Christ died only to confirm his doctrine, and to give us an example of patient submission to the will of God; then there is nothing different in the nature or design of his death, from that of any other teacher of Christianity, who suffered in defence of what he taught; Paul and Peter, and all the martyred christian teachers died *for* us, just in the same sense as Christ died for us;* but this is inconsistent with the scriptural account of Christ's death.

St. Paul, reproving the Corinthians for their contentious behaviour in opposing the principal teachers of Christianity to one another, and to Christ, endeavours to rectify their conduct by informing them, that they were to look upon all the ministers of the gospel as

* "The circumstantial account of the sufferings and death of Christ, in the fifty-third chapter of Isaiah, might have been the description of any other good man in the same situation, with this only difference, that the moral effects of it are represented to be more extensive." "Theological Repository," vol. i. page 129.

standing in the same relation to them. "It hath been declared unto me," says he, "that there are contentions among you; that every one of you saith, I am of Paul, and I of Apollos, and I of Cephas, and I of Christ." 1 Corinthians i. 11, 12. "Who then is Paul, and who is Apollos, but ministers by whom ye believed, even as the Lord gave to every man?" chapter iii. 5. Whereas, he rejects with abhorrence the thought of their being considered as standing in the same relation to them as Christ did. "Was Paul crucified for you? Or were ye baptized in the name of Paul?" The Apostle could not mean in this passage to make a question, whether he himself had been put to death, or to assert, that if he died in defence of his doctrine, it would not be for their benefit; for he speaks elsewhere of being "offered up on the sacrifice and service of their faith;" but he evidently means to point out the difference of that relation in which Christ, and that in which their other spiritual teachers stood towards them; and gives this as a proof of such difference, that "Christ died *for* them." Now, if Christ had only died *for* them, in the same sense that Stephen and others had already done, and that he himself shortly was to do, to say that "Christ died *for* them," was giving no proof that he stood in a relation to them distinct from that of other teachers of the gospel.

The Apostle, in other passages, insists upon the particular relation which Christ bears to us different from that of all other teachers of Christianity. As in 2 Corinthians iv. 5. "We preach not ourselves, but Christ Jesus the Lord, and ourselves your servants for Jesus' sake. If Christ was but a mere teacher of God's will, it will be difficult to make such declarations consistent with truth; for in that case, the Apostles preached themselves as much as they preached Christ: and it will not be easy to find a good reason, why one preacher of the gospel should call himself the servant of those to whom he preaches, for the sake of another person, who was simply a teacher like himself.

The Scriptures constantly represent the death of Christ as having a peculiar respect to our forgiveness and reconciliation with God, and this is expressed in a variety of phrases. We are said to be "justified by his blood; reconciled to God by his death;" to have "redemption through his blood, even the forgiveness of sin;" to be "perfected through his offering," &c. Yet not one word is spoken concerning any such relation which the death of the martyrs bears to us, although frequent and honourable mention is made of them. St. Stephen and St. James had suffered death in defence of Christianity, as well as our Lord, before the writings of the New Testament were finished; and a very particular account is given of the behaviour and sufferings of the former, who, according to the Socinian scheme, gave himself a sacrifice for us, precisely in the same sense as Christ did; yet we have not the least intimation that any were "justified by the blood of Stephen," or that he "bore our sins in his own body," and "made reconciliation for us:" nothing like this appears in the whole New Testament; we are only commanded to be followers of their faith and patience. In the Book of the Revelation by St. John, the whole body of christian martyrs is represented as assembled together; many of these, without doubt, had been brought to repentance by the preaching and good example of others; and, therefore, according to the doctrine of Socinus, must have been justified by their blood; but nothing like this sentiment appears; on the contrary, they are all said to have "washed their robes and made them white in the *blood of the Lamb*," and on that account to be before the throne of God. Revelations vii. 14, 15. They, and all the rest who attain eternal felicity, ascribe their salvation to the Lamb, the influence of whose death is declared to be of universal extent. "They sung a new song, saying, Thou wast slain, and hast redeemed us to God by thy blood, out of every kindred, and tongue, and people, and nation;" chapter v. 9.

Again; if the death and resurrection of Christ are only to be considered as motives to our repentance, they could never have been declared in holy writ to be *necessary* for the remission of sins: for if the remission of our sins flows merely from the mercy of God, without respect to any other consideration than our repentance; then nothing else is *necessary* to our forgiveness.* Yet St. Paul says, "If Christ be not raised," (and, consequently, if he has not died,) "ye are yet in your sins." 1 Corinthians xv. 17. Now the

* "It is only necessary," (in order to understand how we are justified 'through the redemption which is in Christ Jesus,') "to suppose that our redemption or deliverance from the power of sin; *i. e.* our repentance and reformation, without which there is no promise of pardon, is *promoted* by the gospel of Jesus Christ." "Triumph of Truth," page 21.

Apostle could not have argued thus, if nothing but repentance was necessary to their forgiveness. He might, indeed, have said, as he does in the preceding verses, "If Christ be not risen, we are found false witnesses of God, because we have testified of God, that he raised up Christ:" but he could not add, that the remission of their sins was affected by the failure of this consideration, if no such consideration was necessary to that remission. On the contrary, if Christ be considered as our high-priest, appointed to offer a sacrifice for sins, and to rise again, that he might enter the holiest with his own blood, there "to appear in the presence of God for us;" then there is some propriety in the assertion, that if Christ be not raised, we are yet in our sins; because the want of his resurrection would prove that he had failed in the execution of his office, and, consequently, that his sacrifice was insufficient to make atonement for transgressions.

Lastly; if forgiveness is granted to penitent sinners without any respect to the death of Christ, we ought to have no respect to it in asking forgiveness at the hands of God. But if we are commanded to come to God through the Lord Jesus Christ, and our views are directed to his mediation while we implore the divine favour, then is pardon granted with a respect to his mediation.*

We are commanded to pray "in the name of Christ," which surely intimates, that we ought to have a regard to him in our addresses to God. "Whatsoever ye shall ask in my name, that will I do, that the Father may be glorified in the Son." John xiv. 13. It is allowed that this is one of the peculiarities of Christianity; but to pray with the temper of Christ, as some interpret the expression, is no *peculiarity* of Christianity, for even natural religion teaches us, that we should worship God with reverence, love, and submission, which is all, I suppose, that is meant by the "mind of Christ." If any one should imagine, it is praying in the name of Christ, to say, "through Jesus Christ our Lord," at the end of our prayers, without meaning any thing by those words, with such an one, I apprehend, it would be needless to argue.

The peculiar regard which is due to Christ in our approaches to God, is clearly intimated in the First Epistle to Timothy. The Apostle, after exhorting that "supplications, prayers,

* "When David and other penitents confess their sins, and intreat for pardon, they refer themselves to the divine mercy *only*, without seeming to have the least idea of any thing farther." "Triumph of Truth," page 21.

intercessions, and giving of thanks be made for all men," adds, "for there is one God and one Mediator between God and men, the man Christ Jesus," chapter ii. 5. Now, if by a *mediator* is only meant one who declares the mind of God to mankind, then there are as many mediators as there are inspired teachers of religion.* But the manner in which the Apostle expresses himself, shows, that Christ is our mediator in a sense peculiar to himself, and the context leads us to understand the term in its most common acceptation, as expressive of one who treats with God on our behalf, as well as with us on the behalf of God.

It may be objected, that Moses is called a "mediator;" Galatians iii. 19.; and, therefore, that it cannot be proved from the application of this title to Christ, that he stands in

* "A mediator, in the sense of Sacred Scripture, is "one between God and the people; who declares to them the mind of God, denounces judgments upon the disobedient, and proclaims pardon to penitent characters; and there being only two authentic revelations from heaven to our world, of course, we read only of "two mediators," employed to communicate the same to the people; and if there was to be a third revelation, there would also be occasion for a third mediator," &c. See Mr. Graham's Sermon before quoted, page 8.

any relation to us different from that in which Moses stood to the people of Israel. In answer to this, I would observe, that Christ is not merely called "a Mediator" in this passage, but the "*one* Mediator between God and men;" a form of speech very different from that made use of with respect to Moses. Moses is likewise called "a god," but surely the Apostle's solemn declaration, that there is but "*one* God" would show, that the title is applied to him in an inferior sense, though the unity of God were taught in no other part of the Bible. And since our Lord is styled the "*one* Mediator" in such a connexion, we may with equal propriety conclude, that he is our Mediator in a sense which can be attributed to no other person.

The author of the Epistle to the Hebrews expressly founds our boldness in addressing the throne of grace, upon the presence of our compassionate high-priest in heaven; which proves that respect is due to him in those addresses. "Seeing then that we have a great high-priest, that is passed into the heavens, Jesus the Son of God; let us, therefore, come boldly unto the throne of grace, that we may obtain mercy;" chapter iv. 14, 16. And again in chapter x. 19—22. "Having therefore, brethren, boldness to enter into the holiest by the blood of Jesus, by a new and living way which he hath consecrated for us through the vail, that is to say, his flesh; and having an high-priest over the house of God: let us draw near with a true heart, in full assurance of faith," &c.

St. John encourages the true christian to hope for pardon from the consideration that he has a powerful advocate with the Father, who is the propitiation for his sins. "My little children, these things write I unto you, that ye sin not: and if any man sin, we have an advocate with the Father, Jesus Christ the righteous; and he is the propitiation for our sins." 1 John, ii. 1, 2. The Apostle, in this passage, is evidently attempting to remove the discouragements with which sincere christians may be afflicted, under a sense of the manifold defects of their obedience; and the argument he proposes for this purpose, is expressed in terms so plain, that no subtlety of criticism, one would think, could ever set aside the obvious sense of it: the different parts of this passage fix the meaning of the principal terms in such a manner, that to alter them from their most obvious signification, is to render the whole sentence obscure or unintelligible. For should it be said, that the word here rendered "advocate," sometimes signifies "a comforter," the expression "with the Father," shows that it cannot mean so in this place. Our Lord promised that he would send the Holy Ghost to reside as a comforter "with all his true disciples," but to tell such, that if they sin, they have "a comforter with the Father," is, in my apprehension, to talk unintelligibly. But the following verse clearly determines the sense of the passage; for this assures us, that Christ is our "advocate with the Father," as being the "propitiation for our sins;" and, therefore, he is here very emphatically styled, "Jesus Christ *the righteous.** Such are the instructions given to

* Mr. Graham says, in his Letters, page 45, that "the Greek word ιλασμος," (propitiation,) "is never used by the sacred writers in the sense of *rendering God propitious.*" The word εξιλασκομαι is perpetually used in the Septuagint for "making atonement," in conformity to which sense of the word, the phrase ιλασμος περι των αμαρτιων ημων, which is twice applied to our Lord, in St. John's First Epistle, cannot be more justly translated, than by *the propitiation*, or *propitiatory sacrifice for our sins.* In the Epistle to the Hebrews also, Christ is said to have become our high-priest, εις το ιλασκεσθαι τας αμαρτιας τȣ λαȣ, "to expiate," or, "make reconciliation for the sins of the people;" chapter ii. 17. So that whatever is meant by "making atonement," thus much is evident, that Christ is *that* with respect to the remission of our transgressions of the moral law, which the Jewish propitiatory sacrifices were with respect to the transgressions of the ceremonial law.

penitent believers in the gospel, and in them we may discern both the truth and importance of the doctrine of atonement for sin by the death of Christ. Were the Socinian hypothesis true, such directions could have no place in the inspired writings, since they are subversive of what that system accounts the true gospel of Christ.

IV. Let us now take a view of the principal objections made to the doctrine of atonement, and consider whether they are sufficient to overturn the arguments proposed in defence of it.

1. The Author of the "Appeal" asserts,* that it is impossible to reconcile this doctrine

* The arguments which our Author has urged against the doctrine of Atonement, in his "Appeal," "Triumph of Truth," and "Familiar Illustration," he has treated rather more diffusely in his "Essay on the proper End of the Death of Christ," contained in the first volume of the "Theological Repository." But as the three former tracts are our Author's latest publications on the subject, if I mistake not, and as in them his sentiments are expressed with more conciseness than in the "Theological Repository;" I have only referred to the latter with respect to those arguments which are not contained in the former. Indeed, I

with those Scriptures, which speak of our being justified *freely* by the grace of God, and that "the declarations of divine mercy to the penitent are all absolute, without the most distant hint of their having any reference to any consideration on which they are made," as Psalm lxxxvi. 5. Daniel ix. 3.*

It is granted, there are in the Scriptures many declarations of mercy, which do not mention an atonement as the consideration on which pardon is granted; there are likewise many, which neither mention an atonement nor repentance itself; but it will not follow from hence, that either the one or the other is unnecessary. If we desire to know the whole counsel of God respecting us, we must take into consideration the whole of divine revelation; and I submit it to the candid reader to determine from the Scriptures already quoted, whether there are not some declarations of divine mercy to the penitent, which contain more than a distant hint of a consideration of pardon distinct from our own

did not know that all the above-mentioned treatises were composed by the same Author, until I had written a considerable part of this "Defence." Page 18.

* "Triumph of Truth," page 20.

penitence. If pardon is granted to all who come unto God through Jesus Christ, in the way he has appointed, that pardon is certainly as *free* with respect to us, as if there were no mediator between God and man; and the Antinomian, who asserts there is no condition of pardon required of us, is as much supported in his opinion by the declarations of *free-grace*, as the Socinian, who asserts there was no condition performed by our Mediator. The inspired writers of the New Testament saw no more contradiction between the freeness of God's grace, and the propitiation made by the death of Christ, than the rest of the Jews did between the goodness of God in remitting their offences against the ceremonial law, and the efficacy of those sacrifices, which were the appointed consideration of that remission; or, than the Socinians do between free-grace, and the necessity of repentance as the condition of pardon. That remarkable passage in Romans iii., is so full to this purpose, that if there were no other in the Bible, it is sufficient to determine this matter. " For all have sinned, and come short of the glory of God; being justified freely by his grace, through the redemption that is in Jesus Christ: whom God hath set forth to be a propitiation, through faith in his blood, to declare his righteousness for the remission of sins that are past, through the forbearance of God: to declare, I say, at this time his righteousness; that he might be just, and the justifier of him that believeth in Jesus;" verse 23—26. The Apostle, in this passage, treats expressly on the method of our justification before God, which he affirms to be "through the redemption that is in Jesus Christ;" and he likewise points out the reason of this method, "that the righteousness of God might be declared," or demonstrated; that he might appear to be just while he justifies the believer in Jesus. Here we have the whole doctrine of atonement concisely delivered to us, and all attempts to take off the force of this Scripture, as a proof of that doctrine, destroy the antithesis which is evident in the passage, and, in my opinion, make the Apostle's arguing to be flat and trifling. The *forbearance* of God in the remission of sins that are past is opposed to his *righteousness*, which is saïd to be *declared* by this method of forgiveness; and this opposition is a principal branch of the Apostle's argument, for he repeats, and lays a particular stress upon it, "to declare, I say, at this time his righteousness, that he might be just, and the justifier of him that believeth in Jesus."* Our Author, and others,

* The Author of the "Illustration" tells us, that the word here rendered *propitiation*, ought to have been translated *mercy-seat*; but he does not extend his criticism on the translation to the whole of the passage. Though I think the translation of this text sufficiently accurate to show, that the scope of the Apostle's arguing is inconsistent with a denial of the doctrine of atonement; yet, in my opinion, the original sets this in a much stronger light than the English translation, which does not clearly express the sense of that very material sentence in the passage, δια την παρεσιν των προγεγονοτων αμαρτηματων, which, I should imagine, might with more propriety be rendered, "because," or, "on account of the passing by of sins committed aforetime." The twenty-fifth and twenty-sixth verses ought, I think, to be translated in some such way as this; "Whom God hath set forth to be a propitiatory, (or, mercy-seat,) through faith in his blood, for a demonstration of his righteousness, because of the passing by of sins committed aforetime, through the forbearance of God: for a demonstration, I say, of his righteousness at this period, that he might be just," &c. The sense of the Apostle will then appear to be, That God, in setting forth Christ as our propitiatory or mercy-seat, by whom we have access to God through faith in his blood, hath given at length the most clear demonstration of his righteousness or justice, which might appear to have been obscured by his having hitherto, in his great long-suffering, passed by the sins of men, without affording a sufficient display of his hatred to sin, or such a display as is now made by the manifestation of our Redeemer. See a further illustration of this passage, in a book, entitled, "Jesus Christ the Mediator," &c. page 85.

who by the *righteousness* or *justice* of God mentioned here, would have us understand his *goodness* or *mercy*, must give some good reason for such an interpretation, before it can be admitted; as the inspired writer himself, in this very Epistle, makes a distinction between the terms *righteous* and *good*. "Scarcely for a *righteous* (or just) man will one die; yet, peradventure, for a *good* man some would even dare to die;" chapter v. 7. When the Apostle, in the context to the passage above quoted, declares, that we are justified by faith, and not by the works of the law; I cannot suppose, as our Author does,* that he only "intended to oppose the doctrine of the Jews, who maintained that the observance of the law of Moses was absolutely necessary to salvation;" because it is added, "Do we then make void the law through faith? God forbid; yea, we establish the law." Which words can only be spoken of the moral law; for the Apostle did not establish the law of Moses by preaching faith in Christ: on the contrary, he made it void, or declared it to be abrogated. Whereas, the moral law is established by this doctrine; its justice being most clearly shown by the pro-

* "Illustration," page 54.

pitiation made for our transgressions of it, and obedience most effectually secured by a true faith in Christ Jesus.

2. "Can we wish for a more distinct and perfect representation of the manner in which God forgives the sins of his offspring of mankind, than our Saviour has exhibited to us in the parable of the *Prodigal Son?*" "Appeal," page 19.

The design of this parable, as the context shows, was to reprove the Jews for their unreasonable conduct, in objecting to our Lord's most gracious attention to notorious sinners, and his kind reception of such upon their repentance; and to teach us with what kindness we ought to behave to all repenting sinners, when they return to the path of duty, however profligate their former conduct may have been. But whether the doctrine of atonement be true or false, cannot be determined from this parable, as the apparent design of it has nothing to do with this question. The parable proves that God is merciful; and I should suppose, that the appointment of a way, whereby sinners may obtain forgiveness from his hands, does not infer that he is unmerciful. Expositors of Scripture should be very cautious of deducing any doctrine from a parabolic representation, but what appears to be designedly enforced by that representation: without this caution the most absurd opinions may be, and, indeed, too often have been, urged from these parts of holy writ.

3. "To say that God the Father provided an atonement for his own offended justice is, in fact, to give up the doctrine. If a person owe me a sum of money, and I choose to have the debt discharged, is it not the same thing, whether I remit the debt at once, or supply him with money wherewith to pay me?" "Triumph of Truth," page 21.

This argument is founded upon these suppositions, that our sins bear no other relation to God than that of debts to a creditor, and that to make atonement for sin is the same kind of transaction as to pay a debt; but till these suppositions are either allowed or proved, no argument can be grounded upon them. As obedience is something that we owe to God, our failures herein are sometimes, with great propriety, called "debts" in the Scriptures. But it is very evident, that the sacred writings do not only represent God as our *creditor*, but likewise as our *moral Governor:* and it must be acknowledged by every reasonable person, that as he alone is acquainted with all the ends aimed at in the punishment of sinners, he is is the sole Judge of the propriety of it in any case, and of the considerations or conditions proper to be required in order to the remission of our sins.

4. " It can never be reconciled to equity, or answer any good purpose whatever, to make the innocent suffer the punishment of the guilty." *Ib.*

Nothing can be plainer, both from Scripture and experience, than that many suffer for the sins of others; and this is undoubtedly by the appointment of God, if he is the Governor and Judge of all the earth: whether the appointment be equitable or not, I leave our Author to judge for himself; the fact he does not deny. " It is allowed," says he, " that we suffer by the sin of Adam, as any child may suffer in consequence of the wickedness of his ancestor."* And if these sufferings are inflicted by God, acting the part of a Judge, they are consequently *penal.* These considerations afford a sufficient answer to any charge of injustice respecting the sufferings of Christ: but, in truth, there is not the

* " Appeal," page 9.

least foundation for such a charge in this case; for the doctrine of atonement supposes, that the undertaking of our Redeemer to suffer for our sins was perfectly voluntary, and that he had full power over himself when he undertook the work of man's redemption.

5. "If it had been inconsistent with the divine justice to pardon sin upon repentance only, without some further satisfaction, we might have expected to have found it *expressly said to be so* in the Scriptures; but no such declaration can be produced either from the Old or New Testament. All that can be pretended is, that it may be *inferred* from it." *Ib.*

Whatever doctrine may be fairly *inferred* from Scripture, demands our assent and practical regard, as much as if it was therein *expressly declared;* nor have we the least right to find fault with the manner in which any truth is made known to us, or to pay the less attention to it on that account.

When our Lord argued with the Sadducees concerning the resurrection, he chose to make use of a passage in the Old Testament which proved this important truth only in a way of inference: and if he thought such a method of reasoning to be conclusive, we have sufficient authority to think so too. The declarations of Scripture respecting the doctrine of atonement are, in my opinion, neither few nor obscure;* but of this the reader must judge when he has considered the passages quoted in defence of this doctrine, and others which I have taken no notice of, that are contained in the Sacred Scriptures.

6. "Though good works are recommended to us in the strongest manner, it is never with any salvo or caution, as if they were not *of themselves* acceptable to God." *Ib.*

If our good works are *of themselves* acceptable to God, in the most strict sense of the word, without any reference to the mediation of Christ, what do the Scriptures mean by telling us that they are "acceptable through Jesus Christ? Ye are an holy priesthood, to offer up spiritual sacrifices *acceptable to God*

* Mr. Graham differs widely from this opinion, for he says, "There is not a single text in all the New Testament, as far as I can remember, that can, by any rules of just and sober criticism, be retained in support of it," (the doctrine of atonement.) "There are only two that seem to look that way, viz. Matthew xx. 28. "He gave his life a ransom for many;" and 1 Timothy ii. 6. "He gave himself a ransom for all." "Letters on the Atonement," page 34.

through Jesus Christ;" 1 Peter ii. 5. "*By Him*, therefore, let us offer the sacrifice of praise to God continually;" Hebrews xiii. 15. The phrases "by Christ," and "acceptable through Christ," cannot mean that our good works, or "spiritual sacrifices," are to be done in the temper or after the conduct of Christ, for that is included in the very notion of their being good. We can offer no "spiritual" sacrifice to God, *i. e.* no true homage or service, but in the temper of Christ: for the "mind of Christ" means nothing more than an humble, thankful, holy, mind; and the "conduct of Christ" is only another expression for a righteous conduct: so that according to the Socinian doctrine, all that can be meant by a command to offer our spiritual sacrifices "through Christ" is, that when we are thankful to God we must be thankful to him, and when we praise him we must give him praise.

To what I have before said on this subject of access to God through Jesus Christ, I would here add, that *holy* persons are represented in Scripture as standing in need of the blood of Christ to cleanse them from sin. "If we say that we have fellowship with him, and walk in darkness, we lie, and do not the truth: but if we walk in the light as he is in the light, we have fellowship one with another, and the blood of Jesus Christ his Son cleanseth us from all sin." 1 John i. 6, 7. By "walking in the light" is undoubtedly meant, living in the true knowledge and fear of God; and to such the assurance is given, that the blood of Christ cleanseth them from all sin. Now if the blood of Christ bears no other relation to the forgiveness of sin, than that of any martyr who dies in defence of the truth,* with what propriety can such a declaration, as this text contains, be made to those who are already in the favour of God? To make this reasoning the more clear, let us suppose, that one

* "Christ being a man, who suffered and died in the best of causes, there is nothing so very different in the occasion or manner of his death, from that of others who suffered and died after him in the cause of Christianity, but that their sufferings and deaths may be considered in the same light with his." "Theological Repository," vol. 1. page 39.

The texts brought to prove this sentiment, are 2 Corinthians i. 5. Colossians i. 24. Philippians iii. 10. 1 Peter iv. 13. Matthew xx. 23. When the sufferings which the persecuted disciples of Christ undergo for righteousness sake, are called the "sufferings of Christ," the expression is undoubtedly figurative, and the reasons for such a figure are very obvious, without supposing, that the sufferings of Christ bear the same relation to the forgiveness of sin as those of any persecuted christian.

who saw the martyr Stephen stoned to death, should have been induced by his conduct to consider the doctrine which he taught, and thereby to have been turned from a wicked course of life to the service of God. With what propriety could it have been said to such an one, that if he walked in the light as God is in the light, the blood of Stephen should cleanse him from all sin? Would such language have conveyed any ideas to the christian convert? Every one, I suppose, will allow, that such an address would have been downright nonsense. And since, upon the Socinian system, the blood of Christ bears the same relation to our forgiveness as the blood of Stephen, we must make the same conclusion with regard to the Apostle's language, or believe that Socinianism and Christianity are, in this respect, opposite systems.

7. " If any of the Jews had had the least notion of the necessity of any atonement for the sins of mankind, they could not but have expected a *suffering Messiah*; and yet it is plain that the very best of them had no such idea." *Ib.* page 22.

It is equally plain that the Jews *ought* to have expected a *suffering Messiah*, their own prophets having clearly foretold his sufferings.

"After threescore and two weeks shall Messiah be cut off, but not for himself." Daniel ix. 26. "He was wounded for our transgressions, he was bruised for our iniquities; the chastisement of our peace was upon him, and with his stripes we are healed," &c. Isaiah liii. Accordingly, the Jews were often reproved for not expecting a suffering Messiah, and on this account charged with ignorance of the Scriptures. Thus our Lord rebuked the two disciples who were travelling to Emmaus; "O fools and slow of heart to believe all that the prophets have spoken: ought not Christ to have suffered these things, and to enter into his glory?" Luke xxiv. 25. And again, he said to the whole body of disciples, "These are the words which I spake unto you, while I was yet with you, that all things must be fulfilled which were written in the law of Moses, and in the Prophets, and in the Psalms, concerning me.—Thus it is written, and thus it behoved Christ to suffer, and to rise again from the dead the third day." *Ib.* verses 44, 46. St. Peter made the same declaration to the Jews in his preaching, after our Saviour's death; "Those things which God before had shewed by the mouth of all his prophets, that Christ should suffer, he hath so fulfilled." Acts iii. 18. And in the same manner St. Paul addresses them; "They that dwell at Jerusalem, and their rulers, because they knew him not, nor yet the voices of the prophets which are read every sabbath-day, they have fulfilled them in condemning him;" chapter xiii. 27. So that the arguments against any part of our Lord's mediatorial character, which are drawn from the ignorance of the Jews respecting it, are evidently invalid, because it appears clearly that they did not know his real character.*

8. "Though our Saviour frequently explains the reason of his coming, and the necessity of his suffering, it is never on any such account," viz. that of making atonement. *Ib.*

Our Lord appears to have paid some attention to the prejudices of the Jews, in the things which he spake concerning himself; and the chief subjects of his preaching seem

* I am quite at a loss how to reconcile this argument against the "Doctrine of Atonement" with our Author's own sentiments; for he frequently speaks of the ancient predictions of our Lord's sufferings and death, without giving the least intimation that he thinks them either unintelligible or obscure. See "Theological Repository," vol. i. page 129, 341, &c.

to have been those, which would lead them to receive him under his proper character, when all things necessary to ascertain that character were accomplished. He taught the truth to his most intimate and faithful disciples in a gradual manner, as they were able to bear it; and professed to them a little before his death, that he still left many things unsaid, which he would afterwards teach them by his Spirit; "I have yet many things to say unto you, but ye cannot bear them now; howbeit, when he the Spirit of truth is come, he will guide you into all truth.—He shall glorify me: for he shall receive of mine, and shall shew it unto you." John xvi. 12, 13. We ought, therefore, to look for these things in the writings of the Apostles; and we may reasonably conclude, that the truths referred to by our Lord were those, which his sufferings and resurrection would make more plain and intelligible. If then we find it declared in the apostolic writings, that one design of our Saviour's death was to make atonement for sin, we have no reason to doubt of the truth of this declaration, though our Lord had not given the least intimation of such a design. But many intimations of this were given during his abode on earth, though it was not taught so explicitly before as after his sufferings. At the first introduction of our Saviour into his ministry, his great herald pointed him out as one who should make atonement for sin; "Behold the Lamb of God, who taketh away the sin of the world." John i. 29.* This was a very uncouth similitude, if Christ took away our sin only by his doctrine and example; for lambs never took away sin in this manner, nor in any other manner but that of expiatory sacrifices; and St. Peter intimates, that the death of Christ bore this relation to our redemption; "Ye were not redeemed with corruptible things as silver and gold, from your vain conversation received by tradition from your fathers; but with the precious blood of Christ, *as of a Lamb* without blemish and without spot." 1 Peter i. 18, 19.†

* The Author of the "Appeal" classes this text among those in which Christ is represented as a "sacrifice." "Theological Repository," vol. i. page 125.

† Should any one object, that the redemption here spoken of is from the *power* of sin, which was not the proper effect of expiatory sacrifices; it should be remembered, that a true faith in Christ, by which we partake of the benefits of his sacrifice, is always attended with holiness of life, and therefore our deliverance from the *guilt* and *power* of sin are always supposed to accompany one another, though one of them is often specified alone, when our salvation is spoken of in Scripture.

Our Lord informed his disciples, that he should "give his flesh for the life of the world." John vi. 51. And added, "Except ye eat the flesh of the Son of Man, and drink his blood, ye have no life in you;" verse 53. This expression is undoubtedly figurative, but the figure is quite unnatural if Christ died merely as a teacher of divine truth; but if his death is to be considered as a sacrifice, then the figure of feeding upon him is easy and familiar. Knowledge is often represented, in metaphorical language, as the food of the mind; but the expression of feeding upon the teacher himself, merely as a teacher, was probably never heard of. St. Paul says, "I have fed you with milk," *i. e.* the most plain doctrines of Christianity, and "not with strong meat," *i. e.* the more obscure; but he never talks of feeding christians with his flesh and blood; nor do we find any declarations of St. Peter's flesh being "meat indeed," and his blood, "drink indeed."

When our Lord, at the institution of that ordinance which was designed to perpetuate the remembrance of his death, informed us, that his "blood was shed for the remission of sins," and that "the new covenant was in or through his blood," he surely gave an intimation, at least, that his death bore the relation of a sacrifice to us, and was the consideration on which our pardon is granted according to the terms of the new covenant.

9. "When our Saviour describes the proceedings of the day of judgment, he doth not represent the righteous as referring themselves to the sufferings or merit of their judge for their justification; and the judge himself expressly grounds it on their good works only." *Ib.*

The conclusion which our Author means to establish by this argument is, that our justification is not grounded on the sufferings or merit of our judge, but on our good works only. If this is his meaning, and I do not see what else he can mean, he has argued as much against his own doctrine, as against that he opposes; for he tells us in his "Appeal," page 18, "That no man who is a sinner (and all men have sinned) can be 'justified by his works.' We all stand in need of, and must have recourse to 'free-grace' and 'mercy.'" But our Saviour does not represent the righteous as referring themselves at the day of judgment to the free grace and mercy of God for their justification, but expressly grounds it on their good works only; therefore, according to our Author's way of arguing, men are not justified by free grace and mercy, but by their works only. The argument, which way soever it is turned, will appear to have no force, when we consider that the justification at the day of judgment is of a different kind from that about which we are now debating: it is neither grounded on the merits of our judge, nor on free grace, but on good works only, and is what some divines, with great propriety, call a *declarative* justification. We are justified *properly*, or "in the sight of God," as St. Paul assures us, whenever with a penitent heart we truly believe on the Lord Jesus Christ; and this justification is through the blood of Christ. We are justified *declaratively*, or "in the sight of men," when we "shew forth our faith by our works," as St. James speaks. Abraham, for instance, was justified in St. Paul's sense of the word, when he "believed God:" he was justified in St. James's sense, when he "offered up Isaac." Compare Romans iv. with James ii. Now as the design of the last public judgment is not that God may *discover* what men are, in order to regulate his distribution of rewards and punishments; but to *shew* what men are to themselves, and an assembled universe, and to *reveal* his righteous judgment; on which account that awful period is called "the day of the *revelation* of the righteous judgment of God." Romans ii. 5; so the justification and condemnation of men which are then to take place, will be solely founded on that which demonstrates what they really were in their state of probation, namely, their works, taking the word in its most extensive sense. "I saw the dead, small and great, stand before God, and they were judged every man according to their works." Revelations xx. 12, 13.

10. "Though St. Peter, in his discourse to the Jews on the day of Pentecost, speaks of their sin in murdering Christ as of a heinous nature, he says not a word of the necessity of any atonement,—but only exhorts to repentance." And "all the discourses of St. Paul upon various occasions, in the Book of Acts, are entirely moral." *Ib.*

If it were true, that the Apostles did not teach the doctrine of atonement in any of those few discourses of their's which are recorded in the Book of Acts, this would not afford a presumption, much less a proof, that they did not teach it at all. It is evident, that they delivered different truths at different times, and we may safely suppose, that in this they adapted their discourses to the state of their hearers. If we are taught this, or any other doctrine in holy writ, it matters not in what part, or upon what occasion. Let the Lord speak, and it is our duty to believe, and obey.

But it is not true, that all the discourses of the Apostles recorded in the Acts are entirely *moral*, if I understand our Author's sense of the word: for St. Paul, after having proved, in his sermon at Antioch, that Jesus was the Christ, and that the Jews had eventually fulfilled all that was written of him, concludes with this application, "Be it known unto you, therefore, men and brethren, that through this man is preached unto you the forgiveness of sins: and *by him* all that believe are justified from all things, from which ye could not be justified by the law of Moses." Acts xiii. 38, 39. The same Apostle gives this solemn admonition to the Elders of the Church of Ephesus, "Take heed therefore unto yourselves, and to all the flock, over which the Holy Ghost hath made you overseers, to feed the Church of God, *which he hath purchased with his own blood*;" chapter xx. 28. And St. Peter, in his discourse before Cornelius, speaking of Christ, says, "To him give all the prophets witness, that *through his name*, whosoever believeth in him shall receive remission of sins;" chapter x. 43.

11. "It is particularly remarkable, that when sacrifices under the law are expressly said not to be sufficient for the pardon of sin, we are never referred to any *more availing sacrifice:* but to good works only." *Ib.*

Let the reader judge of the propriety of this remark, when he has considered the following passage of Scripture. "The law having a shadow of good things to come, and not the very image of the things, can never with those sacrifices, which they offer year by year continually, make the comers thereunto perfect: for then would they not have ceased to be offered; because that the worshippers once purged, should have had no more conscience of sins. But in those sacrifices there is a remembrance again made of sins every year. For it is not possible that the blood of bulls and of goats should take away sin. Wherefore when he cometh into the world, he saith, Sacrifice and offering thou wouldst not, but a body hast thou prepared me. In burnt-offerings and sacrifices for sin thou hast had no pleasure: then said I, Lo, I come (in the volume of the book it is written of me) to do thy will, O God. Above, when he said,

Sacrifice, and offering, and burnt-offerings, and offering for sin thou wouldest not, neither hadst pleasure therein, (which are offered by the law;) then said he, Lo, I come, to do thy will, O God. He taketh away the first that he may establish the second. By the which will we are sanctified, through the offering of the body of Jesus Christ once for all. And every priest standeth daily ministering, and offering oftentimes the same sacrifices, which can never take away sins: but this man, after he had offered one sacrifice for sins, for ever sat down on the right hand of God; from thenceforth expecting till his enemies be made his footstool. For by one offering he hath perfected for ever them that are sanctified." Hebrews x. 1—14. In this passage we are informed, that the sacrifices under the law were insufficient to take away sins, (in the proper sense of the word,) and for this, which the blood of bulls and goats could not do, we are referred to a *more availing sacrifice*, the offering of the body of Jesus Christ, which is sufficient to perfect for ever them that are sanctified. So that the reverse of our Author's objection is asserted in the plainest terms; and if such authority of holy writ cannot decide the matter, we need not wonder, that it is found difficult to put an end to any controversy by Scripture.

In the "Theological Repository," several texts are produced to prove, that, "whenever the legal sacrifices are declared, by the Prophets, to be insufficient to procure the favour of God, the only thing that is opposed to them, as of more value in the sight of God, is personal holiness, good works, or moral virtue. See Psalm li. 16, 17. Isaiah i. 11—20. Hosea vi. 6. Amos v. 22–27. Micah vi. 6, 7, 8."* vol. i. page 129.

In order to understand these, and other texts to the same purpose, it is necessary to consider the design of the legal sacrifices, and the relation they bore to the Jewish

* In this quotation from the Prophet Micah, the fifth verse is omitted, which, in my opinion, directs us to the true meaning of the passage. "O my people, remember now what Balak, king of Moab, consulted, and what Balaam, the son of Beor, answered him from Shittim unto Gilgal, that ye may know the righteousness of the Lord. Wherewith shall I come before the Lord?" &c. Balak was not rejected because his sacrifices were not sufficiently rich or numerous, but because he was defective in justice, mercy, and the love of God: and the Jews were put in mind of this, that they might not vainly hope to compensate for their immoral conduct by the number of their expensive offerings.

people. Besides being *a figure for the time then present* of the great sacrifice, which was to be offered for the sins of the world, they were appointed to remove the effect of those various ceremonial uncleannesses, which prevented those who were defiled by them from all access to God in his public ordinances:* but they could not remove the guilt of any moral offence, considered as such, or free the offender from being obnoxious to the final judgment of God. They "sanctified to the purifying of the flesh," but "could not make him that did the service perfect, as pertaining to the conscience." Hebrews ix. 9, 13. They were instituted likewise as means of freeing the persons who offered them, in the manner prescribed, from the punishment of those civil offences for which the divine lawgiver had not ordained certain

* These uncleannesses, however involuntary and void of moral turpitude were breaches of the ceremonial law, and required an expiatory sacrifice to make atonement, or remove the obligation to punishment from the offender. "If a soul touch any unclean thing, and it be hidden from him; he also shall be unclean, and guilty. And he shall bring his trespass-offering," &c. Leviticus, v. 2, 6. The most ordinary punishment in these cases was exclusion from the public ordinances of God's worship. See Leviticus xii, &c.

death.* They were undoubtedly always sufficient for those purposes for which they were instituted; and, therefore, when their insufficiency is taken notice of, it is in such cases only as their efficacy was not designed to be

* God entered into a particular covenant with the people of Israel at Mount Sinai, and there gave them a body of laws for their government as a nation. This consisted of the moral law, or ten commandments, together with a variety of ceremonial rites, and political injunctions. Temporal blessings and curses were the sanction by which this covenant was guarded. For some offences certain death was appointed; for others pardon was granted upon the offering of the appointed sacrifice, for "without shedding of blood there was no remission." The efficacy of these sacrifices extended no further than to the averting of those temporal evils, which the transgressors of the law of Moses were exposed to. The Jews, therefore, were under the moral law in two respects: 1st. As being God's general law, which extends to all mankind; and 2dly, As being part of that particular law which God instituted for that people, of whom he was, in a peculiar sense, the King and Lawgiver. Hence a transgression of the moral law by a Jew might be considered in a two-fold view. It might be an unpardonable offence against the Sinai-covenant, and consequently expose the offender to capital punishment; yet might be forgiven by God, as his final Judge, upon his true repentance, and faith in the Messiah as then revealed. On the contrary, it might be a pardonable crime, and be actually forgiven through the offering of the appointed sacrifice; and yet expose the sinner, if impenitent, to the final judgment of God.

extended to; either the removal of moral guilt, or deliverance from death in capital offences. When David was lamenting his adultery and murder, he says, " Thou desirest not sacrifice, else would I give it thee; thou delightest not in burnt-offering: the sacrifices of God are a broken spirit," &c. Psalm li. 16, 17. God did desire sacrifice in every case for which he had appointed it, as is plain even from the words immediately following this quotation,* but this was not such a case, and therefore the Psalmist acknowledges its insufficiency. It is true, he only mentions the sacrifice of " a broken spirit, and a contrite heart," as acceptable to God in this instance; but if he understood his own writings as his inspired commentator, the Author of the Epistle to the Hebrews, did, he had some respect to that " Priest after the order of Melchizedek," of whom he elsewhere speaks.

Those passages in the Old Testament which speak with seeming contempt of sacrifices, and other positive institutions, were plainly

* " Do good in thy good pleasure unto Zion; build thou the walls of Jerusalem: then shalt thou be pleased with the sacrifices of righteousness; with burnt-offering, and whole burnt-offering: then shall they offer bullocks upon thine altar;" verse 18, 19.

intended to reprove the Jews for thinking to make up for their neglect of moral righteousness by the abundance of their oblations, &c. For when positive institutions are thus used by way of commutation for moral obedience, they become an abomination in the sight of God:* nay, whenever positive precepts really interfere with those of a moral nature, the preference is always to be given to the latter, as our Lord hath shown in his discourse concerning the Sabbath. Matthew xii. On the other hand, it is equally plain, that legal sacrifices were as much insisted upon in their proper place as any duty of moral obligation, and the people were reproved by the Prophets when they were defective in them. See Isaiah xliii. 22—24. Malachi i. throughout, and chapter iii. 7—10.

12. " Many other things besides the death of Christ are expressly called " sacrifices" by the sacred writers; and if it be universally

* The account of Saul's behaviour in the affair of the Amalekites, 1 Samuel xv. and the reproof given him on that occasion, set this matter in a very clear light. " Hath the Lord as great delight in burnt-offerings and sacrifices, as in obeying the voice of the Lord? Behold, to obey is better than sacrifice; and to hearken, than the fat of rams;" verse 22.

allowed that they are so called by way of allusion only, why may not the same be the case with the death of Christ also?" "Theological Repository," vol. i. page 131. "Christ, being called a 'priest,' can occasion no difficulty, when it is considered that ordinary christians have frequently the same appellation in the New Testament," &c. *Ib.* page 132.

I have already shown, that such things are spoken of the priesthood and sacrifice of Christ, as are inconsistent with the metaphorical use of the terms, and that of consequence they belong to our Lord in the proper sense of the words. Where the terms in question are used figuratively, we are obliged to put this construction upon them, either because the texts themselves intimate their figurative meaning, or because other passages of Scripture require it. When the whole Jewish nation is called a kingdom of priests, Exodus xix. 6, we are obliged to look upon this language as figurative, because other Scriptures assure us, that none could be real priests under the Mosaic dispensation but those who were of the family of Levi. And the services of Christians are plainly distinguished from real sacrifices by being called "*spiritual* sacrifices," "*living* sacrifices," "sacrifices of *praise,"* &c. 1 Peter ii. 5. Romans xiii. 1. Hebrews xiii. 15; but they are never called " sacrifices *for sin;*" by which, and other such like epithets, the sacrifice of Christ is distinguished from those things which have the term applied to them merely by way of allusion.

13. " The death of Christ cannot be considered as a proper sacrifice for sin, because many things essential to such a sacrifice were, in fact, wanting in it.—According to the Jewish ceremonial law, (from which we must borrow all our notions of these things,) it was primarily requisite, in every sin-offering, that it should be provided, and presented by the sinner; Christ, therefore, could not die as a proper sacrifice for a sinful world, except the world had provided and presented him to be sacrificed, and also observed a variety of other forms, of which there is no trace in the history of the death of Christ." *Ib.* page 133.

The sum of this argument is, that nothing is a *sacrifice* in the proper sense of the word, which is not accompanied with all those ceremonies, which were appointed for the Jews by the law of Moses: but if such are not *proper* sacrifices, they must only be *figurative* ones, having that title applied to them in allusion to real sacrifices. Now I would beg leave to ask our Author, of what kind were the sacrifices of the Heathen world? They certainly were not accompanied with all the Jewish ceremonies; and yet I think he will scarcely say they were figurative. He has himself asserted, that "sacrifices" (in the proper sense of the word) "were as familiar to the Gentiles as to the Jews." *Ib.* page 135. and if so, what becomes of this argument against the sacrifice of Christ? The true notion of a "sacrifice for sin," if I rightly understand it, is, that of "something devoted to death as the means of expiating guilt, or removing the obligation to punishment from the offender." The efficacy of this depends entirely upon the appointment of God, and is a distinct consideration.

14. "The death and crucifixion of Christ was the grand objection to the religion which the Apostles preached. It was strongly urged both by Jews and Gentiles. To the former it was a stumbling block, and to the latter foolishness. It cannot, therefore, appear surprising, that the Apostles should make use of all the means in their power to lessen the force of so formidable an objection. And what could tend more to this purpose, than

to take every opportunity of speaking of it in terms borrowed from the Jewish ritual? The same method was equally calculated to strike the Gentiles, to whom sacrifices were as familiar as the Jews." *Ib.* page 135.

When we consider the doctrine of the Socinians, that "Christ taught nothing but the dictates of plain morality, and sober good sense;"* that "there is nothing *new* in the christian system besides the motives to virtue there exhibited;"† that "the New Testament phraseology, of Christ 'dying for our offences, bearing our sins,' and the like, imply nothing more than barely suffering in the cause of virtue and mankind;"‡ that "Christ fell a victim to the licentiousness of the nation he belonged to, and the age he lived in;" and that "cases of this kind are not uncommon in the course of providence:"§ I say, when we consider these things, and suppose that Christianity contains nothing more than these sentences imply; what is there in the death of Christ that should make it a stumbling block to the Jews, or foolishness to the Gen-

* "Theological Repository," vol. i. page 32.

† "Mr. Graham's Letters," page 33.

‡ *Ib.* page 56.

§ *Ib.* page 59.

tiles? Surely there was no need that the Apostles should take every opportunity of referring to the Jewish ritual, to make this doctrine be embraced by the learned Greeks and Romans, to whom the idea of a man's dying in the cause of virtue and mankind was quite familiar. It appears highly improbable, (to say the least,) that such a representation of the death of Christ should have been treated as foolishness and a mysterious affair by the civilized Gentile nations, when cases of this kind were not uncommon in the world, and were greatly applauded by them. And this consideration affords a strong presumption, that the Apostles gave a different representation of the death of Christ, with respect to the relation it bore to mankind. If the gospel be only "the dictates of plain morality and sober sense," with "the assurance that the respective effects of virtue and vice shall take place beyond the grave;" what propriety can there be in the Apostle's representation of it as something "which the world knew not, a mystery hidden from ages and generations, the wisdom of God in a mystery, which none of the princes of this world knew, *nay*, which the angels desire to look into?" But that the "*Word*," who "in the beginning was with God, and was God," should take upon him our nature, and make himself a sacrifice for us, that we might be restored to the divine favour, and partake of eternal felicity; this is such a display of mercy and justice as deserves all those high expressions which the inspired writers bestow upon it.

15. " That the offering of an animal on the altar was considered, in the law of Moses, in the same light as any other gift or offering, and a sacrifice for sin, as any other sacrifice, is evident from several circumstances in their ritual, and several facts in the Jewish history." " Theological Repository," vol. i. page 200. The circumstances and historical facts brought to prove this opinion are these.

(1.) " In many cases, when a person was not able to provide an animal for sacrifice, an offering of flour was accepted." *Ib.*

This shews that God prefers mercy to sacrifice, and, therefore, in cases of necessity, dispenses with the observance of his own positive institutions; but does by no means prove, that sacrifices for sin were only considered as gifts or presents. The necessity of the shedding of blood in the ordinary constitution of the law, is sufficient to warrant the Apostle's declaration, that, " without shedding of blood there is no remission;" especially, as all defects in the particular sacrifices, which were not presumptuous, were remedied by the appointment of a general and annual atonement.

(2.) "The Philistines, convinced of their fault in taking captive the ark of God, return it with a present of golden mice and emrods, to make atonement for them, evidently in the place of sacrifice." *Ib.*

Our Author does not surely lay much stress on this argument. If the priests and diviners of the Philistines thought fit to send their mice and emrods as a trespass-offering, on account of the particular plagues inflicted on them, it will not follow, that the sacrifices for sin instituted by God were considered in no other light than that of presents.

(3.) "In the Jewish ritual the ceremonies attending a sacrifice for sin did not differ in any thing material from those that were used in any other sacrifice," &c. page 201. Hence our Author concludes, that there was nothing vicarious in the sin-offering, and that the use and signification of this and other sacrifices were the same.

It is true, that in making the burnt-offering, and peace-offering, the offerer was commanded to lay his hand upon the head of the victim, as he did in making the sin-offering; and the sprinkling of blood was used in them all: but all this does not shew, that the sacrifices in which blood was shed, "answered exactly to the use of *presents* in civil life," nor invalidate the proofs I have given, that sacrifices for sin were the consideration of forgiveness. The use of the signs mentioned, indicates, I think, that the offerer was considered as a sinner in all these offerings, rather than as one who was merely making a present to the Almighty. Our Author is certainly mistaken when he says, "it was not the *sacrifice*, but the *priest*, that was said in the Old Testament to *make atonement*." *Ib.* For nothing can be more express than the declaration, that the sacrifice made atonement. "The life of the flesh is in the blood, and I have given it to you upon the altar to make an atonement for your souls: for *it is the blood that maketh an atonement* for the soul." Leviticus xvii. 11. Yet this does not contradict what is elsewhere said of the priest making atonement; for since the blood only made atonement as shed by the priest according to the ritual, and the priest only made atonement by shedding the blood as directed, it comes to the same thing, whether the atonement be spoken of as made by the priest, or the sacrifice; for both are included in either expression.

(4.) "Whenever the writers of the Old Testament treat largely concerning sacrifices, it is evident, that the idea they had of them was the very same with that which they had concerning gifts, or presents of any other nature." *Ib.* page 202.

For the proof of this we are referred to the 50th Psalm. "Hear, O my people, and I will speak; O Israel, and I will testify against thee: I am God, even thy God. I will not reprove thee for thy sacrifices, or thy burnt-offerings, to have been continually before me. I will take no bullock out of thy house, nor he-goats out of thy folds. For every beast of the forest is mine, and the cattle upon a thousand hills. I know all the fowls of the mountains; and the wild beasts of the field are mine. If I were hungry I would not tell thee; for the world is mine, and the fulness thereof. Will I eat the flesh of bulls, or drink the blood of goats? Offer unto God thanksgiving, and pay thy vows unto the Most High: and call upon me in the day of trouble, I will deliver thee, and thou shalt glorify me." verse 7—15.

The reader must judge for himself, what sort of proof this passage affords of our Author's premises. I confess I can see no evidence in this Psalm, that God instituted sacrifices to be used as *presents* are in civil life: on the contrary, the people are reproved, in my apprehension, for entertaining such a notion of them, and for thinking to compensate by them for their neglect of moral duties. I agree, therefore, entirely with our Author in his remark subjoined to the quotation above given. "So far did the Heathens give into this idea of sacrifices, as to imagine, that their gods did really feast their nostrils, at least, with the smell of them; and the reproof contained in the passage quoted above, seems to intimate the prevalence of some such gross notion among the Jews."

(5.) "Sacrifice was not universally necessary for the purpose of making atonement; for, upon several occasions, we read of atonement being made when there was no sacrifice. Thus Phinehas is said to have made atonement for the children of Israel by slaying the transgressors. Numbers xxv. 13. Moses made atonement by prayer only. Exodus xxxii. 30. And Aaron made atonement with incense. Numbers xvi. 46, 47." *Ib.*

The passages here quoted shew us clearly what is the scriptural notion of "making atonement," namely, "the removal of the obligation to punishment from an offender," or, which comes to the same thing, the doing of something available for that purpose. What Phinehas did is thus described in the 11th verse; "Phinehas hath turned away my wrath from the children of Israel, while he was zealous for my sake among them:" this is repeated in other words in the 13th verse, after the reward of his zeal had been mentioned, "because he was zealous for his God, and made atonement for the children of Israel." So that "making atonement," and "turning away God's wrath," are plainly synonymous expressions. When Moses said to the people of Israel, "Ye have sinned a great sin, and now I will go up unto the Lord; peradventure I shall make an atonement for your sin:" by "making atonement," he undoubtedly meant, averting the punishment due to their sin. So when Aaron "ran into the midst of the congregation with fire taken from off the altar, and incense thereon," he made atonement for the people, that is, he did something which averted the wrath of God, or stayed the plague begun among them. In these extraordinary cases, extraordinary methods of making atonement were accepted; but this does not at all affect my argument, which is built upon the clear declarations of holy writ, that the standing appointed method of making atonement under the ceremonial law was by sacrifice, and that this was typical of God's method of forgiving offences against the moral law, made known more fully under the gospel dispensation.

It may not be amiss, in this place, to direct the reader's attention to the manner in which this Author opposes the doctrine of atonement. He first proves, as he apprehends, that the death of Christ is no proper or real sacrifice for sin, nor the antitype of the Jewish sacrifices; but that it is called so merely in a figurative sense, by way of allusion to the Jewish sacrifices, because Christ "offered" himself to God for the good of mankind; that we make the same kind of sacrifice as Christ did, when we "yield our bodies living sacrifices" in God's service, or offer him "the sacrifice of praise," or "lay down our lives for the brethren;" and, of consequence, that the sacrifices under the law were transactions of a nature quite different either from our prayers, or Christ's death.

After he has settled this point, he then proves, in like manner, that the legal sacrifices for sin had no relation to the remission of offences, but "that the offering of an animal on the altar was considered in the same light as any other offering or gift." That, "agreeably to the standing and universal custom of the East, with respect to sovereigns and great men, the Jews were never to approach the divine presence without some offering," and that "their sacrifices exactly answered to the use of presents in civil life."

But how are these things consistent with each other? If Christ is said to have made himself a sacrifice because he "offered" himself to God, and real sacrifices are no more than *offerings*, or presents, then the death of Christ had the nature of a real sacrifice. Or if Christ did but make a figurative sacrifice because he merely made an offering of himself to God, then real sacrifices must be more than mere offerings or presents to the Divine Being. These two representations of the matter appear to me to be directly opposite, and, in that case, the arguments deduced from them (and our Author's principal arguments, I think, are deduced from them) must destroy one another.

16. "Some texts of Scripture seem to represent the pardon of sin as dispensed in

consideration of something else than our repentance or personal virtue; and according to their literal sense, the pardon of sin is, in some way or other, procured by Christ. And had the literal representation been all of a piece, &c.—the account would have had more of the air and consistency, at least, of truth: but when the pardon of sin is sometimes represented as dispensed in the consideration of the "sufferings," sometimes of the "merit," sometimes of the "resurrection," and even of the "life" and "obedience" of of Christ;" &c. that the dispensing of pardon is sometimes said to be the proper act of God the Father; and, again, it is Christ who forgives us; we can hardly hesitate in concluding, that these must be, severally, *partial representations*, in the nature of figures and allusions," &c. *Ib.* page 252, 253.

Our Author is as much concerned to answer this objection as they are against whom he brings it. He believes, I suppose, that the dispensing of pardon is the proper act of God the Father, yet if he hesitates to conclude that this is a *partial representation* in the nature of a figure and allusion, he gives up his argument; if he does not hesitate to make this conclusion, I should be glad to know how pardon is really dispensed without figure and allusion. If, by the terms *partial representation*, and *figure*, our Author had only meant that kind of figure, where a part is put for the whole, I should have had no objection to his assertion; but then his argument would have contained nothing against the reality of forgiveness being dispensed on account of the mediatorial undertaking of Christ; his death, resurrection, and intercession, being parts of this, and coinciding with the idea of his making a real sacrifice for sin, as I have already shewn.

17. Many negative arguments, besides those I have taken notice of, are urged against the doctrine of atonement in the "Theological Repository," among which are placed the promises of certain happiness to the righteous, and the threatenings of misery to the wicked; the prayers of holy men recorded in the Old Testament, in which they implore the mercy of God for the pardon of their sins, and make profession of their own sincerity; and the like. I think it quite needless to give a particular answer to every argument of this kind, though our Author thinks them to be of consequence in this debate. "With me, I own," says he, these negative arguments have great weight.

When I find a profound silence concerning this supposed great doctrine of atonement, upon occasions on which I cannot help thinking it would naturally have occurred; when I do not find that frequent mention of it, and that stress laid upon it, which its importance would certainly require; when I find no trace of it in any *direct message* from God, or in any *fact* recorded in the sacred writings; I cannot help thinking that divines must have been mistaken concerning its supposed truth and importance;" page 266.

I readily allow that the Scriptures are silent with respect to this doctrine upon occasions on which this Author thinks it would have occurred, had it been true; and if he will inform me, why divine revelation was not given to mankind at first in its greatest degree of clearness, without the slow succession of dispensations, the last always improving on those which preceded; and why men were left to wait four thousand years before "life and immortality were brought to light," though they had message upon message from God in that long interval; I will then acquaint him why the doctrine of atonement was not clearly revealed on those occasions on which he thinks it ought to have been taught, if it were a doctrine of divine revelation.* I leave the reader to judge, when he has considered what I have urged in defence of this doctrine, whether or not there are " traces of it in *direct messages* from God, and in *facts*, recorded in the sacred writings."

18. Our Author has attempted to shew, in his " Familiar Illustration," that many of those passages of Scripture, which are usually brought to prove the doctrine of atonement, will admit of a natural interpretation upon other principles. In his introduction to these criticisms he says, that the death of Christ " being compared to *so many things*, 'and things of such *different natures*," as a sacrifice, a passover, a ransom," &c. " proves that the

* I might here have answered our Author in his own words, inserting the term *atonement* instead of *a future state*; for thus he argues concerning the latter. " To ask why this important doctrine of a future state was not revealed, or not revealed with the same fulness of evidence before the time of Christ, or why it is not known at present to the whole world, is the same thing as to ask, why, in all the works of nature and providence, and in all the dispensations of God to mankind, a similar gradation is observed, and why nothing under the government of God is brought to perfection at once."—" Theological Repository," vol. i. page 36.

resemblance in all of them is only in *certain respects*, and that they differ considerably in others.—These," says he, "are all bold, but significant figures of speech, the death of Christ really corresponding to them all to a certain degree; but they differ so widely from one another, that no one thing can correspond to any of them throughout; for then it must exclude all, or at least most of the rest." "Illustration," page 47.

There is no necessity to suppose, that each circumstance of every institution which was designed to typify the method of our redemption by Christ, should have something corresponding to it in the antitype; because many, if not all, of those institutions, had other purposes to answer, besides that of being types of our redemption. The propitiatory sacrifices, as I have already observed, were branches of a political law, and had an immediate reference to crimes committed against God as Civil Governor. Various circumstances belonging to them might be needful in this respect, which were not intended to be typical. The same may be said with regard to the passover, and other types of Christ. Besides, so many things were to be prefigured concerning our Redeemer, that no one institution could exhibit them all, and therefore it was necessary that different types should be appointed. The whole ceremonial law did but afford an imperfect resemblance of the things it typified; it was but "the shadow of good things to come, and not the very image of the things."

19. It is asserted, that "sacrifices for sin under the law of Moses are never considered as standing in the place of the sinner." *Ib.* page 49.

The expression "standing in the place of the sinner," is somewhat ambiguous: it may mean either *suffering precisely the same punishment to which the sinner was obnoxious*, or *suffering what is sufficient to free the sinner from punishment*. It is in the latter sense only that Christ is our substitute. He did not suffer precisely the same punishment which we deserve on account of our sins, for that is *eternal death*, or the being given up to a state of perfect sin and misery for ever; but he suffered what is sufficient to free the offender from this deserved punishment, in the way prescribed in the word of God. And in this sense, it is evident, the propitiatory sacrifices under the law stood in the place of the sinner; for the death of the animal, according to the ritual, freed him from that punishment, to which, without it, he would have been exposed. He was not liable to punishment merely on account of neglecting to offer the sacrifice which God had appointed; but he was considered as guilty previously to such an offering. "If a soul sin, and commit any of these things which are forbidden to be done by the commandments of the Lord; though he wist not, yet is he guilty, and shall bear his iniquity. And he shall bring a ram for a trespass-offering," &c. Leviticus v. 17, 18. In these sacrifices the *life* of the animal was given for the offender, and on this account the blood was appointed as the standing means of making atonement. "The life of the flesh is in the blood, and I have given it to you upon the altar, to make an atonement for your souls; for it is the blood that maketh an atonement for the soul,—for it is the life of all flesh, *the blood of it is for the life thereof;*" chapter xvii. 11, 14. It is plain from this text, that it was not the penitent disposition of the offender, but the sacrifice which made atonement.

20. "Many persons are carried away with the sound of the word *redemption*, as if it necessarily implied that mankind, being in a state of bondage, a price must be paid for their freedom, and that the death of Christ

was that price. But the word which we render *redemption*, signifies only deliverance, in general, in whatever manner it be effected." *Ib.*

It is true that nothing can be concluded from the word *redemption*, with respect to the manner in which we are redeemed. This must be inquired after in other parts of Scripture; and from thence we learn, that we are delivered from the punishment of our sins by the interposition of our Redeemer as a sacrifice for sin. "What the law could not do in that it was weak through the flesh, God" hath done, "sending his own son in the likeness of sinful flesh, and for sin, (or, according to the marginal reading, 'by a sacrifice for sin') condemned sin in the flesh." Romans viii. 3. "He made him to be sin (or, 'a sin offering') for us, who knew no sin; that we might be made the righteousness of God in him." 2 Corinthians v. 21.

21. "Stress has been laid upon the word *for*, as if Christ dying *for* all, necessarily implied that he died *in the stead* or *place* of all." *Ib.* page 50.

The mere use of the word *for*, certainly proves nothing in this case; but when it is joined with other expressions which imply substitution, as "propitiatory sacrifice," &c. or when it is intimated to us that Christ died *for* us in such a sense as can be applied to no other, (see 1 Corinthians i. 13.) then we are necessarily led to lay such stress upon the word *for*, as would otherwise be improper.

22. "Much stress has also been laid on Christ being said to 'bear the sins of mankind;' as if they had been ascribed or imputed to him, and he had taken them upon himself, and suffered the wrath of God for them. 'He shall bear their iniquities.' Isaiah liii. &c. But the word does not signify to bear or *take upon another*, but to *bear away*, or *remove*, by whatever means.—The phrase *bearing sin* is never applied in the Old Testament, but to the *scape-goat*, which was not sacrificed, but turned loose into the wilderness, to signify the removal of the sins of the people, which God had forgiven.—The Evangelist Matthew had, most evidently, this idea of the meaning of the passage in Isaiah, when he applied it upon the occasion of Christ's healing the bodily diseases of men, viii. 17. For he says, that he performed these cures, 'that it might be fulfilled which was spoken by the Prophet Isaiah, Himself took our infirmities, and bare our sicknesses.'" *Ib*. page 50, 51.

Supposing the expression *bearing sin* to signify in the New Testament *bearing it away*, the sense of the passages in which it is used will be the same; for how did Christ *bear away* the sins of many, but by being offered up for them as a sacrifice? "Now once in the end of the world, hath he appeared to put away sin by the sacrifice of himself." Hebrews ix. 26. "Christ was once offered to bear the sins of many; and unto them that look for him shall he appear the second time, without sin, unto salvation;" verse 28. The mention of his "appearing a second time *without sin*, will, I think, most naturally lead to the rendering which our translators have chosen; but however that be, the text plainly declares, that Christ "puts away our sins by the sacrifice of himself," and that is all we contend for. The same sentiment is conveyed by St. Peter, when he says, "Who his own-self bare our sins in his own body on the tree, that we, being dead to sin, should live unto righteousness: by whose stripes ye were healed." 1 Peter ii. 24. Here likewise the removal of our sins is attributed to the sacrifice which Christ made on the cross; which was offered up, that we, being healed by his stripes, might serve him in righteousness here, and partake of his eternal felicity hereafter.

I am surprised at the assertion, that "the phrase *bearing sin* is never applied in the Old Testament, but to the scape goat," since that, and *bearing iniquity*, which means precisely the same, are very common phrases in the Old Testament, and generally signify *bearing the punishment of sin*, or *making atonement for iniquity*.* The goat that was slain, and the goat let loose in the wilderness on the great day of atonement, were considered as *one* sacrifice. "And Aaron shall take of the congregation of the children of Israel, two kids of the goats for *a sin-offering*, and one ram for a burnt-offering," &c. Leviticus xvi. 5. Accordingly they are both spoken of as making atonement: they were both likewise made ceremonially accursed, and equally defiled the persons who touched them; for neither the man who led the *scape-goat* into the wilderness, nor he that carried out the flesh of

* As Leviticus x. 17. "God hath given you the sin-offering to *bear the iniquity* of the congregation, to make atonement for them before the Lord;" chapter xxii. 9. "They shall keep mine ordinance, lest they *bear sin* for it, and die therefore, if they profane it." Numbers ix. 13. "The man that is clean, and is not in a journey, and forbeareth to keep the passover; even the same soul shall be cut off from the people,—that man shall *bear his sin*," &c.

the *goat slain*, could return into the camp until he had "washed his clothes, and bathed his flesh in water." From all which it is probable, that the two goats were intended to point out the same thing in different respects, the one by its death, the *means* of pardon, the other by its removal into the wilderness, the *certainty* of it.

Because St. Matthew applies the Prophet's prediction of Christ's "bearing our griefs and carrying our sorrows," to his removing the bodily diseases of men, it will not follow, that this was all the Prophet meant, when he foretold that the Messiah should be "wounded for our transgressions," and "bruised for our iniquities," that "by his stripes we might be healed;" that he should "bear the sin of many," and that the Lord should "lay on him the iniquity of us all." I believe it is impossible for any one to think so while he reads the fifty-third chapter of Isaiah: and it is evident, that our Author himself thinks otherwise, because he speaks of this passage as a prediction of our Lord's own sufferings. "Theological Repository," vol. i. page 129. But the difficulty arising from the application of the Prophet's words by the Evangelist will vanish, when we consider, that sometimes in the New Testament a prophetic declaration is said to be fulfilled in an event, to which it may with great propriety be applied, though it was not originally, or primarily at least, spoken of that event. Such an application proves that the prediction was true in that sense, but not that it is to be restrained to that sense. We have two instances of this kind of application in the gospel written by St. Matthew. See chapter ii. 15, compared with Hosea xi. 1. And verses 17 and 18 of the same chapter, compared with Jeremiah xxxi. 15. Some Socinian writers give a different turn to that clear description of our Saviour's vicarious sufferings in the fifty-third chapter of Isaiah: they look upon this passage as containing only "a beautiful description of suffering innocence," and suppose the Prophet meant no more than to intimate that Christ "was so free from the suspicion of guilt, that his calamity must be charged to the offence of others; and so extraordinary were his sufferings for their number and greatness, that whereas the rest of the nation had been very corrupt, it *seemed as if* God had laid on him the iniquity of them all. The phrase of suffering for the sins of men," say they, "as it necessarily implies innocence in the sufferer, so it does not necessarily imply any thing farther."* This is a very easy method of putting an end to this, or any other controversy. There needs no more than to paraphrase the clearest declarations of holy writ as this Author has paraphrased those of Isaiah, which are almost as clear as any in the Bible, and the matter is settled at once. It *seems*, may any one say, "*as if* the wicked should be turned into hell, and all the people that forget God;" Psalm ix. 17; but this is only a beautiful way of frightening men to their duty. And, indeed, if the phrase of "suffering for the sins of men" necessarily implies no more than "innocence in the sufferer," I cannot see how the inspired writers could by any expressions whatever convey the doctrine of atonement, even supposing it to be their design; for the same liberty of interpretation would set aside any declaration of this kind, and render the most positive evidence of no effect.

23. "Christ is said to die a *curse* for us, because the manner of his death was similar to that by which those who were deemed

* "Mr. Graham's Letters on the Atonement;" page 60, 61.

cursed under the law were put to death. "Christ hath redeemed us from the curse of the law, being made a curse for us; for it is written, Cursed is every one that hangeth on a tree." "Illustration," page 51, 52.

In whatever sense we understand the expression, "being made a curse for us," thus much is plain from the words of the text, that we, *i. e.* all true believers, are delivered from that penalty to which our breach of the law of God exposes us, which is here called the "curse of the law," by the sufferings of our Redeemer: and this proves the truth of the doctrine of atonement. It is not supposed that Christ was "under the displeasure of God," if by *displeasure* is understood *dislike* or *disapprobation*; but that his sufferings, being inflicted by God as a righteous judge, were truly *penal*, and deliver the penitent offender from the curse of the moral law, as the propitiatory sacrifices delivered the Jews from the curse of the ceremonial.

24. "The death of Christ is called a *passover*, because it may be considered as a sign of our deliverance from the power of sin, as the passover among the Jews was a sign of their deliverance from the Egyptian bondage." *Ib.* page 47.

The passover, at its first institution, afforded the Israelites an assurance, and a very significant token, of their preservation from the judgment of God, and of their deliverance from bondage: but what token did the death of Christ afford of our deliverance from the power of sin, according to the account which the Socinians give of it? God permitted an innocent man to be cruelly put to death by a licentious people, therefore we shall be delivered from the power of sin:—I think it requires uncommon penetration to discover here the agreement between the sign, and the thing signified. Whereas, the death of Christ affords a most striking token of our deliverance from sin, if we consider him as giving himself for us, that he might free us from the deserved punishment of our sins, and procure those divine communications of the Holy Spirit, whereby we are delivered from the power of sin, and enabled to serve God in righteousness and true holiness. If to the Apostle's declaration in 1 Corinthians v. 7. "Christ our passover is sacrificed for us," we add the consideration of that special injunction given to the Jews, not to break a bone of the paschal lamb, compared with the reason given for the preservation of our Lord's bones, "These things were done, that the

Scripture should be fulfilled, a bone of him shall not be broken;" John xix. 36. we shall see reason to conclude, that the Jewish institution had a typical respect to the sacrifice of our Redeemer: and it is probable, that this type was designed to exhibit the *benefits* included in our redemption by Christ, as the sacrifices for sin did the *means* of that redemption.

25. " Many divines, finding themselves obliged to give up the notion of Christ's suffering *in our stead*, allege, however, that God forgives the sins of mankind ' on account of the merit of Christ, and his intercession for us;' this opinion, like the former, is favoured by the literal sense of a few passages of Scripture; but is contrary to the general and plain tenor of it, which represents all acts of mercy as proceeding from the essential placability and goodness of God the Father only." *Ib.* page 52.

It is true, that in the Old Testament the mercy of God is generally mentioned alone when our forgiveness is spoken of, though many intimations are there given of the respect which our Lord's sufferings have to this event. It must be acknowledged likewise, that the doctrine of atonement, and some other important truths, were not so clearly taught even by our Lord during his personal ministry, as they were after his ascension by his inspired messengers, agreeably to his own design and declaration; John xvi. 12, 13. But in the epistolary part of the New Testament, the necessity and efficacy of a mediator is constantly inculcated in all the variety of expression. We are said to be "justified by the blood of Christ, accepted through the beloved," to have "redemption through his blood, even the forgiveness of sin," to be "justified in the name of the Lord Jesus, reconciled to God by his death," &c. In short, our acceptance with God through the mediation of Christ is a truth inscribed on almost every page of the Apostle's epistolary addresses to the christian church. And here I would beg leave to remind the reader, that we have the clearest display of Christianity in the Epistles of the New Testament, every thing necessary to complete the system of divine revelation, being finished when the inspired penmen composed these parts of holy writ. All that our Lord thought fit to leave unsaid, had been revealed to the Apostles by his spirit, as he had promised. His death, and resurrection, with the subsequent events, had dispelled all darkness from the minds of the disciples.

They now saw clearly the fulfilment of the Old Testament types and prophecies concerning the Messiah, and were no longer in doubt with regard to his character and offices. In the epistolary part of the New Testament, therefore, we have declared unto us "the whole counsel of God," and herein it is asserted, with the greatest precision, that our justification does not flow solely from the goodness of the Father, without any other medium than our repentance and reformation; but that mercy is extended to repenting and believing sinners through the Son, and that they only are entitled to salvation, who "come unto God through him." *

Our Author has an argument of another kind against that idea of Christ's intercession, which is included in the doctrine of atone-

* The Author of the "Illustration" appears to have a very different notion of this part of holy writ. He talks of the "Jewish disguise," which the Apostles, and especially St. Paul, have put upon the plain truth of God; and, after telling us what he esteems the true gospel, makes this remark, which some of my readers may probably think an extraordinary one. "However, the disguise in which this simple religion appears, as delivered to us through the hands of the Apostles and primitive fathers, is not so close, but that, with proper attention, we are able to look through it, and discern its true lineaments." "Theological Repository," vol. i. page 428.

ment. "Besides," says he, "there are many passages in the Old Testament in which God is represented as forgiving the Israelites, and receiving them into his favour on the account of Abraham, Isaac, and Jacob; and their posterity plead the merit of these their religious ancestors in their prayers.—"Admitting, therefore, that God may grant favours to mankind at the intercession of Christ, this is not a privilege *peculiar* to Christ, but is common to him and other good men who went before him; so that the *general system* of the forgiveness of sin can by no means depend upon the merit and intercession of Christ only." *Ib.* page 53.

The passages of Scripture quoted from the Old Testament on this occasion,* and other texts, plainly show that God has often granted

* Genesis xxvi. 24. "Fear not, I am with thee, and I will bless thee, and multiply thy seed for my servant Abraham's sake." Exodus xxxii. 13. "Remember Abraham, and Isaac, and Israel, thy servants." Deuteronomy ix. 27. "Remember thy servants, Abraham, Isaac, and Jacob. Look not to the stubbornness of this people, nor their sin." In all which texts there is a reference made to that covenant which God graciously established with Abraham, that his seed should be numerous, that they should inherit the land of Canaan, &c. as the reader will find upon consulting the chapters from whence these passages are taken.

favours to men for the sake of their religious ancestors, and at the intercession of others; but they prove nothing further. The doctrine of atonement implies, that no transgression of the moral law, considered as such, is forgiven, without a respect had to the mediation of Christ; and this differs greatly from any efficacy which can be shewn to belong to the prayers of righteous men. Our Saviour in the days of his flesh interceded for others in a manner peculiar to himself. He addressed the Father in his own name, and in language by no means suitable to any other supplicant; "Father, *I will.*" John xvii. 24. Whereas he commands us to approach the throne of grace in *his* name, and promises that he himself will answer our petitions. John xiv. 13, 14, &c. The intercession which Christ is now making in heaven for us, appears from the word of God to be of a different kind from that which holy men are capable of making for others. It is of the nature of that intercession which the High-Priest made on the day of atonement, when he entered the Holy of Holies with the blood of the sacrifice; and, therefore, is mentioned in the Scriptures with a particular reference to his death. "He bore the sin of many, and made intercession for the transgressors." Isaiah liii. 12. "It is Christ that died, yea rather that is risen again, who is even at the right hand of God, who also maketh intercession for us." Romans viii. 34. "He is able to save them to the uttermost who come unto God through him, seeing he ever liveth to make intercession for them;" being "such an High-Priest,—who needeth not daily to offer up sacrifice, for this he did once when he offered up himself." Hebrews vii. 25, &c. "Christ is not entered into the holy places made with hands, but into heaven itself, now to appear in the presence of God for us;" chapter ix. 24. This intercession of our Lord, being the consequence of his giving himself a sacrifice for the sins of the world, and, as it were, the continuance of that transaction, is, therefore, of a peculiar nature, and has a peculiar influence on the remission of sins, which no intercession of any pious man on earth can have.

The intercession of the Spirit of God for us is likewise a distinct thing from the intercession of Christ. The Spirit maketh intercession for us by interceding *in* us, that is, by exciting in the minds of true Christians unfeigned desires after God, and every holy temper implied in the "fervent prayer of a righteous man." "The Spirit also helpeth our infirmities; for we know not what to pray for as we ought:

but the Spirit itself maketh intercession for us, *with groanings which cannot be uttered.*" Romans viii. 26.

V. In the foregoing pages I have taken very little notice of Mr. Graham's "Letters on the doctrine of Atonement," though they are the latest of the publications I have occasion to examine, and are strongly recommended by the Author of the "Appeal."* The principal arguments which they contain are urged, and expressed with more candour, in the tracts I have been considering; and as my intention was to have nothing to do but with arguments, I chose to make my reply to those pieces which were the most candid and argumentative. Indeed, I find myself unwilling to take any notice of an Author, who is perpetually

* "I shall take the opportunity of this preface to recommend that excellent sermon of Mr. Graham's, entitled, 'Repentance the only Condition of Final Acceptance,' and also his 'Letters on the Doctrine of Atonement.' In these pieces the reader will find what I think to be a fair and undisguised account of what is most essential in the religion of the gospel, expressed with a plainness and energy almost peculiar to the Author." "Preface to a Sermon Preached on Occasion of the Author's Resigning his Pastoral Care of a Congregation in Leeds."

misrepresenting the question he debates, and who strives to strengthen his arguments by invective, and abuse of his opponents. However, it may not be amiss to give some specimens of this writer's manner of treating his subject.

1. He observes, that "nothing tends more to introduce confusion into our ideas of religion than equivocal terms, and undefined unscriptural language;" page 5. Yet he seems not to have kept clear of this error, which he justly esteems to be very hurtful to religion. In his first letter he examines into the meaning of the word *satisfaction*. "Sometimes," he says, "it denotes the pleasure which the mind takes in any thing that is the object of our hopes and pursuits; very often it means the redressing of grievances, and repairing damages and injuries done or received; and, lastly, it denotes the obedience due to the command of a superior, properly made known to us;" page 3, 4. This last he calls the Scripture notion of the term *satisfaction* as applied to Christ; page 6. and tells us, that "in the other sense of it, as implying a reparation of injuries, it is not to be found in the New Testament, as applicable to Christ;" page 5. This manner of speaking

of the term *satisfaction*, tends, I should think, to make the reader suppose, that the writers of the New Testament apply it to Christ in the third of those senses which Mr. Graham has here given. Whereas the word is not to be found in the New Testament, nor is it ever applied to the Messiah in the Old Testament, unless Isaiah liii. 11. is to be excepted: "He shall see of the travail of his soul, and shall be satisfied." Our Author might, therefore, have spared himself the trouble of defining a term which the Scripture does not make use of, especially as he himself almost always uses it in a sense different from that which he calls the Scripture notion of the term. I have wholly omitted the word *satisfaction* in my "Defence of the Doctrine of Atonement," for the reason I have just given; and, indeed, I should be far from troubling myself about a doctrine that rested on the meaning of a few equivocal expressions.

Punishment is another of those terms which Mr. Graham has taken pains to clear up; but he often uses the word in a sense that is inconsistent with his own definition of it. "Punishment," he says, "is suffering for immoral behaviour;" page 23. "and, therefore, the *innocent* cannot be *punished* in the room of the guilty, without supposing him capable of those disagreeable sensations which attend the guilty, which is impossible;" page 29. Yet he frequently talks about the punishment of the innocent: as, "Can a manifest act of injustice (for such I consider the punishment of the innocent) ever be the means of conciliating his favour who loveth righteousness?" page 32. "Can the honour of government be vindicated by punishing the innocent in the room of the guilty?" page 24. "Upon this scheme the righteous are not even upon a level with the wicked; for they are punished, while the wicked escape." *Ib.* "Better that many guilty should escape, than that one innocent person should be punished." *Ib.* Here, if I may be allowed the expression, Mr. Graham's common sense gets the better of his critical knowledge, and constrains him to use the word *punishment* in its ordinary signification, that of "suffering inflicted by judicial proceeding."* If the ideas of *innocence* and *punishment* were incompatible, it would be as absurd to talk of the injustice of punishing

* In punishment, the suffering is inflicted by *authority* either real or usurped, and with *design*: the latter distinguishes it from *casualty*, and the former from *violence* or *assault*. This authoritative design constitutes what is here termed judicial proceeding.

the innocent, as of the injustice of murdering the dead.

Atonement being the subject of Mr. Graham's Letters, one might suppose he would be very clear in his definition of this; but he only informs us what it is not, and leaves us to find out its true meaning by ourselves. "Atonement," says he, "I will allow, was made by the death of an animal, but you must not therefore infer that it was slain in the room of the offender. And though I may not be able to assign the precise notion of atonement, what it was, wherein it consisted, and what was the end and design of it, I think I am pretty sure what it was *not*. It did by no means express a *substitution*," &c. page 46. Yet this Author uses the term continually, as if it were a word perfectly understood by the reader.

2. When Mr. Graham represents the sentiments of those who believe the doctrine of atonement, he gives no authorities for his representations, nor does he quote a single Author who has written in defence of this doctrine. I shall not scruple, therefore, to charge him with *misrepresentation*, till he has quoted some Author of credit as an authority for such accounts of this doctrine as the fol-

lowing passages contain.* "The representation given by theologians of the administration of the universe is, that the omnipotent arm at the head of it was actually lifted up, ready to strike the blow, and discharge the thunder-bolt on a sinful world, when Christ seasonably interposed, to wrest it out of his hands;" page 14. "I need not caution you against viewing the best of beings in the light of a tyrant, determined to make sinful men for ever miserable, had not Jesus interposed;" page 15. "Had the advocates for this monstrous scheme been attentive to the amiable light in which nature, not to say revelation, exhibits the Deity, they never would have admitted the idea of *implacability*. By saying he is *placable* only in consideration of a *satisfaction*, it is plain they had no other idea; and yet this is saying nothing, and worse than

* By *authors of credit*, I mean such as Bishop Stillingfleet, among those of the Church of England, and Dr. Watts, among the Dissenters. Both these writers have taken pains to state the doctrine of atonement, that it might be clearly seen what they undertook to vindicate; and from them Mr. Graham might have given a distinct account of what he opposes: but instead of this, he exhibits the reasoning of some anonymous Antinomians, as the language of those who believe this doctrine. See page 31.

nothing; for it is still holding him up in the light of a capricious being, who is pleased with expensive offerings, and moved by foreign considerations to do what he is not naturally and essentially disposed to do;" page 16. "I see a manifest propriety in the sufferings of an innocent and good being to bring about the noblest purposes of providence, but none at all upon the scheme of satisfaction. This is, if I may be allowed the expression, a *luscious doctrine*, which the mobility are exceedingly fond of; and no wonder, indeed, they should, for it permits them to gratify their sensual passions, at the same time that it flatters their heavenly hopes;" page 30. "What else is Calvinism," (and they who hold the doctrine of atonement are generally by this Author denominated Calvinists,*) "but a *commuting system*, where considerations foreign to moral character are made to supply the want of it; where an

* "I know no medium between *Calvinism*, properly so called, and *Socinianism*. The latter is a scheme friendly to virtue, and permits one to go quietly through the world in the exercise of his reasonable faculties. The former is a religious *scare-crow*, that, like the Inquisition, in Popish countries, has long served the purpose of making hypocrites and slaves in Protestant ones;" page 75. *Note*.

external and vicarious righteousness is substituted in the room of a real and personal one;" page 72.

3. Mr. Graham's Letters abound with invective, and abuse of those whose sentiments he opposes. "Whatever charms it" (the doctrine of atonement) "might have for the visionary and licentious, no sober or sensible man would ever become its apologist;" page 52. "I think the doctrine of Christ's atonement, as believed by the bulk of professed Christians, opens a wide gap for the introduction of such evils into society, as would soon sap the foundation of it, were it not checked by better principles of nature's planting." But for this a Calvinist would be a consistent being throughout, and form his practice upon his principles: and in that case, I think, we should have as much occasion for gibbets as we have for churches;" page 64, 65. "The abettors of this doctrine, not much accustomed to argument, and knowing that reason is not in their interest, generally intrench themselves behind the authority of *great numbers* and *great names;*" page 65. Their general character is known to be that of bigotry to their own modes and sentiments, without any grains of charitable allowance for those

that differ from them;" page 69. Some readers may wonder why such abuse is so liberally bestowed on this occasion. Mr. Graham tells us he has received personal affronts from some who hold the doctrine he opposes, and perhaps the remembrance of them might somewhat influence his mind while he was writing. "Where will you find a theologian," says he, "who will defend them" (the sentiments he opposes) "by other arguments than those of *anathemas* and *execrations?* I and others have lately had some specimens of the politeness and humanity by which they are distinguished in this respect;" page 75. Yet we are not to suppose that our Author means to speak contemptuously in all this; for he himself has assured us to the contrary. "I would not," says he, "by what I have said, be understood to insinuate a contempt for popular prejudices, or that they ought to be treated with contempt. I would have them, on the other hand, treated with all imaginable lenity." *Ib.*

4. There is an argument or two in Mr. Graham's Letters, which I have not had occasion to take notice of in examining the tracts before referred to: these I shall now consider.

(1.) Mr. Graham asserts, that the doctrine of atonement is contrary to the principles of natural religion as they are deducible from the conduct of Divine Providence in the world. "The remedies provided in nature for those who hurt themselves by their vices;" "the affection which all animals are observed to have for their offspring," and "the disposition which we find in ourselves to forgive injuries," are, in his opinion, "*proofs* that God will pardon his offending offspring upon their penitence;" page 8, 9, 10. The intelligent reader, I apprehend, will think these proofs not very conclusive; for the conclusion has certainly no necessary connexion with its premises. If our Author would draw a real proof of his doctrine from the constitution of nature, he must make it appear, that repentance does in all cases avert or remove those natural punishments of sin which God has appointed in the world. But it is evidently otherwise. "The miseries which, in the regular course of nature, are the consequences of wickedness, are properly considered as the natural punishments of it. Some of them follow it with a swifter, others with a slower pace; some are transitory, others of longer continuance: but the penitence of a criminal, even before their arrival, affords him no security against the lowest of them; and when either his fears or his feelings have worked a reformation, such as are naturally of longer continuance are not by that reformation presently removed. Whatever then can be alleged, concerning the ends of punishment, or the satisfaction made by a reformed penitent, when applied to this subject, must be trifling. All argumentation is here precluded. We have fact and experience to convince us, that God does not always pardon the repenting sinner."* Whatever notions we may gain by the light of nature concerning the divine mercy and justice, revelation alone can satisfy us how far, and under what circumstances, either the one or the other will be exercised towards sinners. Mr. Graham has sufficiently confuted himself with respect to this argument against the doctrine of atonement: for, although he adopts Dr. Duchal's opinion, that "it must have been an article of natural religion in all ages, and a fundamental article too, that God would forgive sin to the truly penitent," and that all wise men must necessarily have fallen into this sentiment with much assu-

* Dr. Powell's Charge in 1772. See also Butler's Analogy, part 2, chapter 5.

rance;"* he nevertheless asserts, that "mankind, before supernatural light arose upon them, were in a state of great depravity, and alienation from God, sunk in ignorance, vice, and superstition;" and that, "in such a state it is natural to suppose them very much at a loss as to the terms of their acceptance with God;" page 52. But how are these things consistent? If mankind in a state of natural religion were very much at a loss as to the terms of their acceptance with God, how is it that these terms are a fundamental article of natural religion, which every wise man would embrace with much assurance? †

* See Dr. Duchal's Letter to Dr. Taylor, subjoined to Mr. Graham's work, page 81.

† The Author of the "Appeal" seems to have fallen into the same inconsistency in his reasoning upon this subject. For, after having given extracts from several authors, by way of proof that mankind have always entertained just apprehensions of the divine mercy, he makes this inference. "It is almost demonstrable, that mankind have always considered their Maker and universal Parent, in the same light with that, in which reason and the Scriptures, both of the Old and New Testament, uniformly represent him, viz. as of himself gracious and merciful, long suffering, forgiving iniquity, transgression, and sin,

(2.) It is said, page 43, "Had Christ offered himself in the Jewish sense of sacrifice, that is, the literal and original sense of it, he must have incurred the guilt of offering to God a human one, of all others the most offensive in his sight."

Mr. Graham offers nothing by way of proof of his assertion, that human sacrifices are in all cases offensive to God. I suppose, therefore, that he imagines it to be an allowed truth which no one will dispute. For my part, I am so far from thinking a human sacrifice to be in

not willing that any should perish, but desirous that all his offending creatures should repent and live." Yet when he comes to "subjoin, by way of conclusion, a concise view of the scheme of salvation by Jesus Christ," he gives this description of the state of mankind without divine revelation. "Let us, then, suppose the whole race of mankind to be in a state of apostacy from God, lost to all sense of religion and virtue, in the expressive language of Scripture, 'dead in trespasses and sins;' that without a revelation and a Saviour, they were in the most deplorably vicious and wretched circumstances, in a sure way to make themselves miserable both here and hereafter," &c. "Theological Repository," vol. i. page 416 and 422. I cannot conceive how mankind could universally entertain such sentiments of God, as are contained in divine revelation, and yet be lost to all sense of religion, and be in a sure way, without revelation, to make themselves miserable both here and hereafter.

all cases an abomination to God, that I believe such an offering to have been one of the highest acts of obedience that ever was performed by any mere man. "Take now thy son, thine only son Isaac," said the Almighty to faithful Abraham, "and offer him for a burnt-offering." This the holy man executed in intention, which was the same as to the virtuousness or viciousness of the thing, as if he had actually done it;* yet he received the highest applause from his unerring Judge. The doctrine of atonement supposes Christ to have laid down his life for sinners in *obedience* to the will of his Father; the assertion, therefore, that this would have been a crime, or act of *disobedience*, carries absurdity on the face of it. If our Author does not include this in his idea of Christ's sacrifice, he is combating a shadow, and is engaged in a contention in which he has no opponent.

5. Mr. Graham seems to me to have overturned his own arguments against the death

* This seems to be the Apostle's view of the matter, when he says, "By faith Abraham, when he was tried, *offered up* Isaac; and he that had received the promises, *offered up* his only begotten son." Hebrews xi. 17.

of Christ being considered as a sacrifice for sin, in the same manner as the Author of the "Appeal" has done. He asserts that "the death of Christ is styled a sacrifice, not because it was truly and properly such in the Jewish sense of sacrifices; but because it was a distinguished expression of his regard to God. Hence also other moral virtues, such as *praise*, and *thanksgiving*, *doing good*, and *communicating*, are called by that name. In short," says he, "as the New Testament sacrifices are all spiritual and moral ones, that of Christ must be so too." page 42. "Where he is exhibited under Mosaic and Levitical images, such as *propitiation*, and the like, it is plain that the writers use the figurative style;" page 43. "From all which," (speaking of some preceding arguments, he says,) "it is evident, that Christ being called our *propitiation* is only in the allusive way, and that he could in no other sense be an atonement, than that of declaring God's gracious purpose of *passing over* the sins of men, on the condition of their future repentance. Not that what he did and suffered *procured* that mercy, but were only *declarative* of it;" page 48.

When Mr. Graham tells us what was the nature of real propitiatory sacrifices, he gives this description of them. "Propitiatory sacrifices I consider as *public certifications*, that the offerers were either desirous of being restored, or actually were restored to the privileges of citizens; not by virtue of the sacrifice which they offered, but of the penitent disposition accompanying that sacrifice." *Ib.* "So Christ," says he, "is our *propitiation*, declaring us in a state of favour with God; not in virtue of what he suffered, but on condition only of our renewed obedience." *Ib.* Are not these two accounts of the matter manifestly inconsistent? If the proper idea of real propitiatory sacrifices be that of *public certificates*, or *declarations* of God's favour to the penitent; and if Christ is our *propitiation* precisely in the same sense, as is here asserted; then it plainly follows, that he is not called so *figuratively*, but that his death was as *real* a sacrifice as the Jewish propitiatory sacrifices were.

6. The immoral tendency of the doctrine of atonement, and the practical advantages of Socinianism, are favourite topics with Mr. Graham; he enlarges upon them frequently in his Letters. I shall, therefore, make one remark on this head, before I conclude these reflections. Our Author observes, that "the

best and surest criterion of religious principles is their moral influence; this is our Saviour's own rule, "By their fruits shall ye know them;" the fruits which they have a tendency and fitness to produce;" page 63, 64. "Now, Sir," (adds he, addressing himself to his friend,) "I appeal to you, whether principles, that in any degree relax the obligation of the moral law, are principles which a wise man would espouse, or an honest man defend?" *Ib.* Whether our Author's doctrine has not some tendency to relax the obligation of the moral law, I leave the reader to judge, when he has considered the following sentence respecting moral obligation. "To say that every, the least error in moral life deserves eternal torments, is a hard saying, and who can bear it?" page 19. How different is the language of Scripture on this head! "The *wages* of sin is *death*." Romans vi. 23. *Death*, eternal death, as the context plainly intimates, and various other passages declare,* is the *wages*,

* As Galatians iii. 10. "Cursed is every one that continueth not in *all* things which are written in the book of the law to do them." James ii. 10. "Whosoever shall keep the whole law, and yet offend in *one* point, he is guilty of all."

the due desert and reward of sin, of sin indefinitely, of every transgression of the moral law.

May this awful truth be written upon our hearts, that we may apprehend rightly the "exceeding sinfulness of sin," as the Apostle speaks, and be led by this knowledge to embrace the salvation which is by Jesus Christ!

MISCELLANEOUS PAPERS.

Q

ON SUBSCRIPTION

TO

ARTICLES OF RELIGION.

I. It appears from the history of the Christian Church, given us in the Acts of the Apostles, that no adult person was received into her communion, without a declaration of his hearty consent to the leading doctrines, delivered by the Apostles and other first Teachers of Christianity. "If thou believest with all thine heart," said Philip to the Eunuch, "thou mayest be baptized." Acts viii. 37.

Much less was any one admitted to the office of Christian Pastor without such a proof, at least, of his embracing the doctrines which he was to deliver to others. Thus the apostolic injunction runs respecting ordination: "The things that thou hast heard of me among many witnesses, the same commit thou to faithful men, who shall be able to teach others also." 2 Timothy ii. 2. And particular care was taken, that none should be admitted into the ministry, except those who "held fast the faithful word as they had been taught, that they might be able, by sound doctrine, to convince the gainsayers." Titus i. 9.

When the books of the New Testament were all collected, and joined to the Scriptures of the Old Testament, this sacred code contained the Articles to which every candidate for the ministry was to *subscribe*, that is, to testify his assent in the strongest manner, before he could be admitted to teach others.

So far is plain, and, I apprehend, agreeable to the sentiments of all the professors of Christianity. But here it may be asked, Why is not this simple apostolic method still adhered to? Why are candidates for the ministry now required to subscribe to human formularies, instead of the inspired writings;

and that, by those who acknowledge the Bible to contain a perfect rule of faith and practice?

The reason of such conduct is clearly deducible from the very principles upon which the objection is founded.

To make good this deduction, I shall only take for granted the following plain proposition: that words, being only the signs of our ideas, are nothing independent of their meaning. This being allowed, it will follow; that when assent is required to any form of words, it is to the meaning which those words convey, and not to the words considered in themselves. When, therefore, we speak of subscribing to the Holy Scriptures, we mean (if we mean any thing) that such subscription should be made, or assent testified, to the *doctrines* contained in the Scriptures, or to the *meaning* which the *words* of Scripture were designed to convey.

While the sense of Scripture was fixed by the interpretation of those inspired persons, who were employed in writing it, the words of Scripture conveyed the same ideas to all the sincere members of the Christian Church. When any person, under these circumstances, testified his assent to the words of Scripture, it is plain that he assented to their true meaning; and in this case, any other confession of faith than the sacred text, was unnecessary.

But let us suppose, that while the doctrine of the Christian Church was uniform, and the whole body of Ministers held the words of Scripture in their true sense, that one should have offered himself as a candidate for the ministry, to whom the words of Scripture conveyed ideas different from those which they conveyed to the Church. What must have been done in such a case? The Christian Pastors were bound to require subscription to the Scriptures; for this was enjoined as absolutely necessary. But in the case now stated, a subscription to the words of Scripture would not have been a subscription to the Scriptures themselves; because the words did not convey to this candidate their true meaning. Such a person in subscribing, it is evident, must either have testified his assent to something which was not Scripture, or to words without meaning, which is in effect to nothing. The Christian Pastors, in this case, would have been under the necessity of explaining the Scriptures to such an one, that is, of conveying the meaning of Scripture to him in other words, and then of requiring his assent to the Scriptures thus explained, or to the words used as explanatory, which amounted to the same. And whenever the words of Scripture convey different and opposite ideas to the persons whose duty it is to require subscription, and to those who are enjoined to subscribe; one of these methods must be used, if the absurdity of requiring subscription to unmeaning words is to be avoided.

Now that the professors of Christianity are divided in their interpretation of the New Testament, it is the same thing (with respect to the matter of subscription) as if there were more than one New Testament; and each party must require subscription or assent to their formulary, upon the same principle that subscription was required to the words of Scripture, while the interpretation of those words was uniform. To suppose the contrary is to imagine, that words are something independent of their meaning, which is absurd.

If then it is the duty of any Christian Church to require a subscription to the Bible from those who are candidates for the Ministry, it is their duty to require this subscription to the sense in which they understand the Bible; for these are not properly two things with respect to any Church, but are in effect the same.

Thus the necessity of human formularies may be deduced from the plainest principles of Christianity and common sense; and he must not have thoroughly considered this matter, who shall esteem them to be impositions on the consciences of mankind, when they are designed merely to interpret the Christian's only rule of faith, the Bible.

If the preceding observations contain a just account of the nature of Subscription to Articles of Religion, the following consequences will be the result.

1. That a formulary of religion is to be considered as an epitome of the Holy Scriptures, exhibiting, in other words, a summary of the doctrines which they contain.

2. That when a candidate for the ministry declares his assent, by subscription, or otherwise, to Articles of Religion, he does in effect declare, that he understands the Scriptures in that sense in which the formulary represents them.

If, therefore, the Bishops of the Church of England act upon the principles of Christianity and common sense, they must require subscription to the Thirty-nine Articles, as to a form of words expressing the true meaning of Scripture; and giving, in other terms, a summary of the doctrines of the New Testament, by way of ensuring a subscription to the Scriptures themselves.

And if candidates for holy orders act upon the same principles, they must consider their own subscription as tantamount to the following declaration:—"I believe that these Articles do give the true meaning of the words of the New Testament; and I declare my hearty assent to the Scriptures thus explained."

II. The services of divine worship in the Church of England are made conformable to the doctrines contained in her Articles of Religion, and, therefore, it is necessary to a sincere worship of Almighty God, that Ministers do really believe those Articles.

The leading or principal doctrines of the Church of England are these four; the doctrine of the Trinity; the atonement for sin by the death of Christ; (through faith in whom we can alone obtain forgiveness;) the innate moral depravity of mankind; and the necessity of the divine sanctifying influences of the Holy Spirit. These are found in every page of our Liturgy. The service of the Church is founded upon them; and no office can be performed without an acknowledgment of them.

The first of these doctrines describes the object of our worship. The second points out the manner of our addressing the Divine Majesty, through a Mediator. The third teaches us our acknowledgments and confessions. And the fourth leads us to a principal subject of our supplications.

What sort of divine worship must that be, which is neither right in its object, in its mode of address, in its confessions, nor in its supplications! Yet thus monstrous and absurd must the public worship of every Minister of the Church of England be, who disbelieves these Articles of her Faith. He must daily bow down with every act peculiar to divine adoration, to one whom he believes to have been a mere man, and, of consequence, in all his public addresses, he must be guilty of the damnable sin of idolatry: and this not ignorantly, but with a clear understanding of his crime. He must present all his public addresses to God in the name of a Mediator, while he believes the idea of mediation to be a gross affront to the Divine Majesty; and must profess his expectation of divine favour through the death of one, who died by popular tumult, without any peculiarity of nature to distinguish him from other sufferers in a good cause.* He must acknowledge such depravity in himself, as he believes it inconsistent with all just notions of moral agency to allow, and such as he believes to have no existence. And lastly, he must implore certain influences which he believes it absurd to expect; and which, if granted, would destroy the end for which they are implored.

Hence we see how necessary it is, that every Minister of the Church should sincerely believe these fundamental Articles in her formulary of religion.

III. Let us take another view of this subject, and consider the case of a person preparing for the ministry. If such an one act with proper caution, and with sincerity, he will, previously to his entering into the ministry, consider how far the doctrines, of which he is to profess his belief, and which he is to teach, are agreeable to the word of God. Whence can he learn the doctrines of

* This supposes the Minister to be a Socinian, which is generally the case with those who deny the doctrines here mentioned.

the Church of England, but from those authentic documents, the Articles of Religion, the Homilies, and the Liturgy? It is absurd to suppose that he must conform to the opinions of individuals, whether of the clergy or laity in the church. It is not necessary for him to inquire what these opinions are, for he is not to profess any belief of them, nor to take them for the models of his own teaching. Were the opinions of individuals more uniform than they are, he is not at all concerned to know them; much less can this be any part of his duty, when these opinions are discordant with one another.

Were the body of Bishops uniform in their notions of religion, and were he acquainted with their notions, he is by no means bound to conform himself to their opinions. For he is not to declare that he understands the Scriptures in the sense in which they understand them; nor is he to worship God by forms which express their sentiments; nor to teach conformably to their opinions. In the matter of ordination, the Bishop does not propose his own peculiar opinions to the candidate, but the doctrines of the Church: and the candidate's duty is to inquire, whether these doctrines agree with the Christian's rule of faith, the Bible.

The religious opinions of the Bishops may possibly be as opposite to one other, as the opinions of the laity. Supposing this to be the case, how shall a candidate prepare himself for the ministry, if the sentiments of the Bishops are to influence his belief? One Bishop believes the Articles of the Church, and approves of her Liturgy; but it is possible that another may not credit the former, nor approve of the latter. If a candidate for the ministry were bound to conform to the sentiments of the Bishop who should ordain him, he must have no religious sentiments at all, when he knows not who shall ordain him. Upon the idea of conformity to the sentiments of the Bishops, there is no standard of religion left; and, therefore, the duty of preparing for the ministry, by the regulation of the religious sentiments of the candidate, may become absolutely impracticable.

IV. But does every minister act insincerely, who may disapprove of some ceremonies prescribed, or some expressions contained in the Articles or Liturgy of the Church, which affect not the main doctrines of Christianity? By no means; there is an important distinction between essential and non-essential matters in religion. The things contained in the Sacred Scriptures are not all of equal moment: some are fundamental and essential. The rejection of them is inconsistent with the belief and practice of Christianity. Concerning others, true Christians may differ in their belief and practice. The inspired writers delivered certain doctrines as necessary to salvation, denouncing everlasting misery upon all who should reject them. "He that believeth shall be saved, and he that believeth not shall be damned." These truths are never rejected from a mere error in judgment, but from a wrong state of heart. Concerning these our Saviour saith, "If any man will do his will, he shall know of the doctrine whether it be of God." John vii. 17.

On the contrary, the Apostle Paul allows, that there were some true Christians, who differed in less important matters from him, and one another. They were believers, though weak in the faith. "One believeth that he may eat all things; another who is weak, eateth herbs." For such differences Christians were taught not to despise one another, nor to consider those who differed from them as rejecting the Gospel.

Formularies of Religion, which are designed to give the sense of Scripture in other 'ords, may likewise contain essential and on-essential matters. And, as the inspired 'riters did not scruple to acknowledge those › be true believers, who received the fun- amental doctrines of Scripture, though they iffered in some things of small moment; › a person may be said truly to believe a ›rmulary of religion, who believes the fun- amental doctrines contained in it, though he ıay not approve of every expression which ıe compilers have used.

The Scriptures have left several things, elative to christian practice, undetermined, 'hich yet must necessarily be fixed, in order › the very being of christian society. The Iew Testament has not laid down any pre- ise method of public worship; yet, public 'orship cannot be decently conducted with- ut method. The New Testament has not iven a complete code of rules for the go- ernment of the Church; yet the Church annot be governed in an orderly manner 'ithout rules. Whatever is left to the pru- lence and discretion of religious societies, ıay be determined without infringing the livine authority. These human institutions ıust be obeyed if they are not sinful, but re intended to preserve decency and order. A person, in declaring his assent to such

Articles of Religion as relate to these things, does not properly declare that he believes them to be contained* in Scripture; but rather that they are not repugnant to it, and are among those matters allowed to be settled by human prudence.

The Articles of Religion, which relate to these prudential matters, may not improperly be called *Articles of Peace*. A man may conscientiously assent to them, because the Church has appointed them. Should the Church alter her conduct with respect to these matters, a Minister may with truth alter his assent.

But Articles, consisting of fundamental doctrines, stand upon a different footing. They cannot be assented to, consistently with truth, unless they are believed; because (as hath been already observed) they immediately affect our worship of God, and other religious conduct. A Church, fundamentally wrong, must be deserted by the sincere worshipper. No custom can make it right for us to offer to God the sacrifice of fools, nor to worship Him with solemn acknowledgments which we disbelieve. No example can make it innocent for a Minister to declare, that he understands the Scriptures in a sense contrary to that which he judges to be their true meaning. Churches may err fundamentally; but they must then be deserted. Truth requires that we come out from among them, and be separate. Conformity in such a case is only following a multitude to do evil.

THOUGHTS ON THE SABBATH.

PART I.

WHEN we take up the Bible with the view of ascertaining its true meaning, and the extent of our duty; we ought to consider that God speaks to us as intelligent creatures, who are bound to make the best use of our understanding for the discovery of his will. We must not presume to limit the Almighty as to the manner in which he shall make known his will to us: in whatever way this is done, we are called to implicit obedience.

Express command is not the only method by which our great Creator and Governor has pointed out our duty; he has also revealed his will by symbols, by prophetic and somewhat obscure declarations, by significant actions of men divinely inspired, and by parables; and in these the obscurity we sometimes meet with may be designed to excite us to diligent inquiries after the will of God, and to be a test of our humility and sincerity.

Under the impression of these considerations, let us inquire, whether it be not the will of God, that mankind, in all ages, should dedicate one day in seven to the more immediate worship of the Almighty, and other religious exercises; subject to certain limitations which the Bible has pointed out, and which our present condition in this world has rendered necessary.

If, in our researches, we should meet with some passages of Scripture, which, at first sight, appear contradictory; let us apply the following rules of interpretation.

1. Let us endeavour to find out some sense in which the apparently contradictory passages will agree, without doing violence to the expressions on either side.

2. Let us interpret obscure passages by those which are plain; instead of forcing the

plain passages to bend to those which are obscure.

3. Let us, in all doubtful cases, choose that side which is practically the most safe, and agreeable to the general tenor of Scripture.

I shall consider the nature and extent of the command to sanctify the Sabbath, as it stood before the promulgation of the law on Mount Sinai; as it was explained and enforced during the Jewish dispensation; and as it continues obligatory upon the disciples of Christ to the end of the world.

The first intimation respecting the Sabbath is given in the second chapter of the Book of Genesis. This is a very important passage of Scripture, and deserves our most serious attention, both as it respects the meaning of the words, and the period at which they were delivered. The second verse informs us what the Almighty did with regard to his own works: "And on the seventh day God ended his work which he had made; and he rested on the seventh day from all his work which he had made." The third verse proceeds to state; "And God blessed the seventh day and sanctified it;" that is, he set it apart for holy purposes; for such is the meaning of the word *sanctified* in the Old Testament, when applied to inanimate things, or to persons with relation to any office or function. Thus the priests, the tabernacle, and all its furniture, were said to be sanctified, when they were set apart for the service of God. In no other sense can the word *sanctified* be understood with relation to the seventh day, without forsaking the scriptural meaning of the term, and falling into absurdity.

This command, to set apart the seventh day for sacred purposes, was given to man in his primeval purity. Being created upright, he loved the Lord his God with all his heart, and mind, and soul, and strength. The labours of each day, in this happy state of mind, would be dedicated to God's service. There was no need of a day of sacred rest to withdraw the mind from the carnal eagerness of worldly pursuits, or to recruit the body from oppressive labour. Man now enjoyed perpetual communion with God. His labour was light. "The Lord God took the man, and put him into the garden of Eden, to dress it, and to keep it." (*Ib.* v. 15) Thorns and thistles had not yet sprung up to create the necessity of laborious exertions. For "out of the ground made the Lord God to grow every tree that is pleasant to the sight and good for food;" (verse 9.) The earth had not yet received the curse which caused man to "eat bread in the sweat of his face."

If in this state the sacred rest of a seventh day was ordained by infinite wisdom, in what period of time can it become unnecessary to fallen man? Shall the consecration of a seventh day for the cultivation of our minds, blinded by sin, and distracted by corrupt affections, be thought needless; when it was appointed to man in innocence and perfect holiness? Shall the mercies of creation require a frequently-returning day for their celebration; and shall not those of redemption, in addition, call for an equal attention? In short, when we compare the state of fallen man with that of our first parents, during whose original purity this command was given, we shall find a variety of considerations urging upon him the superior necessity of sanctifying a seventh day.

Besides, a general command thus given to the representatives of the whole species, must continue in force for ever; unless it be abrogated by the same authority by which it was enacted.

Whether there be any passages in Scripture

which abrogate the law of a Sabbath, with a clearness equal to that with which it was enacted, will be the subject of our future consideration.

The observance of a Sabbath cannot be opposed with reason, unless it shall appear that there is a clear abrogation of this command. It cannot be said with decency, that the neglect of the Sabbath is a more spiritual service to God than the observance of it.

To attach any ideas of superstition to the observance of a Sabbath would scarcely fall short of blasphemy against the Almighty, whose wisdom made such an appointment before sin had entered into the world.

It is the duty of man, at all times, and in every period of the world, to love God with all his heart, and mind, and soul, and strength; but particular exercises and proofs of this love may be enjoined at different periods. The worship of God, however, is required by a permanent obligation; and the exercise of this worship, especially when it is social, requires a cessation from other employments; and seasons appropriated to itself. Is it not, then, in the highest degree, improbable that man, when employed in the innocent labour of cultivating the garden of Eden, should be required to withdraw, during a seventh portion of his time, from this pleasing employment, to exercise himself in one still more pleasing to a holy soul; yet, that we, who find it so difficult to abstract our minds from the too eager pursuits of worldly things, should be left to follow our own ways on the day originally set apart for the solemn services of religion? Such a supposition I cannot help thinking to be highly improbable, whether I consider the sanctification of the Sabbath in the light of a duty, or a privilege.

In whatever point of view we contemplate it, the Sabbath was instituted when mankind stood the least in need of that institution. Was the Sabbath designed to be a day of rest? It was instituted when the labour of our first parents was merely to keep and dress the garden of Eden. Was it designed to be a season of instruction? The law of God was then written upon the heart of man. He was made after the image of God in righteousness and true holiness. Was it designed to call off the mind from the anxiety of worldly cares? Our first parents had nothing to distract their minds: they saw God in all his works: they walked in innocence, and were not ashamed. Was it a day appointed for more immediate communion with God, in the exercises of holy worship? The pious pair enjoyed a perpetual communion with God: they approached him without fear, and served him with the profoundest reverence.

Can we then imagine, that an institution appointed when there was the least possible need for it, should be set aside when every circumstance in the situation of mankind loudly calls for such an institution? How greatly do the incessant toils of many require a day of rest! What a powerful tendency have the anxious cares of life to shut out the due consideration of the world to come! The ignorance of many, especially of the lower classes of mankind, requires that time for instruction, which no other day, except the Sabbath, will afford; and without stated periods for the public worship of God, the very idea of religion would vanish out of the world.

These considerations forcibly impress my mind with the persuasion, that the sanctification of a seventh day, that is, the setting it apart for holy purposes, was an appointment of God, and is of perpetual obligation.

THOUGHTS ON THE SABBATH,

DURING THE JEWISH DISPENSATION.

PART II.

The sanctification of the seventh day, which was appointed in the time of man's primeval innocence, must have continued to be an institution of constant obligation through the succeeding ages, which intervened between the fall of man and the publication of the moral law at Mount Sinai; since we find no repeal of the original command in the books of Moses.

When a summary of the moral law was promulgated to the Israelites at the Holy Mount, and inscribed by the finger of God on tables of stone, we find this original command of a Sabbath bearing a conspicuous part in the sacred code. The Fourth Commandment explains and enforces this first institution of God to man. " Remember the Sabbath-day to keep it holy:" or, as it is expressed by Moses, when recapitulating the commands in the Book of Deuteronomy, " Keep the Sabbath-day, to *sanctify* it." Deuteronomy v. 12. Let us then inquire what are the duties of the day, and what the limitations of those duties, as they are to be found in Scripture during the Jewish dispensation.

The Fourth Commandment shows that we * are to abstain from our ordinary worldly calling and employments, which it is our duty to pursue, on the other six days, with diligence. " Six days shalt thou labour, and do all thy work; but the seventh day is the Sabbath of the Lord thy God; in it thou shalt not do any work." Exodus xx. 9, 10.

We are commanded also to use our endeavours, that this day be sanctified by all over whom we have any authority or influence: " Thou, nor thy son, nor thy daughter, thy man-servant, nor thy maid-servant, nor thy

* If any reader should think that the use of this pronoun, on this occasion, is begging the question, he may confine it to those who were immediately addressed at that period.

cattle, nor thy stranger that is within thy gates;" *ib.* 10. We are not, therefore, to permit the works of our ordinary worldly occupation to be carried on by others on our behalf; but we ought to put the same restraints upon those who are under our controul, which our duty requires us to put upon ourselves.

The Supreme Legislator has given us, by the Prophet Isaiah, a still more ample account of the duties implied in the sanctification of the Sabbath. "If thou turn away thy foot from the Sabbath, from doing thy pleasure on my holy day, and call the Sabbath a delight, the holy of the Lord, honourable, and shalt honour him, not doing thine own ways, nor finding thine own pleasure, nor speaking thine own words; then shalt thou delight thyself in the Lord," &c. lviii. 13.

This passage of Scripture deserves to be studied with peculiar attention, as it not only describes the duties of the day, but also the temper of mind with which they are to be performed.

The Prophet arranges the command under three heads. The first is, that we are not to do our own ways, which relates chiefly, I apprehend, to our worldly business, as is largely set forth in the Fourth Commandment.

The second, that we are not to find our own

pleasure on the Sabbath. It is not to be a day of merriment, of sports, and pastimes, or of mere amusement. All those ways of spending the Sabbath, which are contrived for the purpose of sensual pleasure, are to be avoided; though the temperate refreshment of the body is not forbidden. It is to be a day of rest from bodily labour; but not a season of mere animal recreation. It is unnecessary, and indeed impossible, to enumerate the various species of pleasure which are forbidden on this day; but as every one knows what is meant by a day of sensual pleasure, so every one may judge what is forbidden under this head.

Thirdly, we are forbidden to speak our own words. The conversation ought to be suited to the sacred offices of the day. For as we are prohibited from pursuing our ordinary labours on the Sabbath, so are we also prohibited from making them the subjects of our discourse. We cease from our own words, when we confine our conversation to subjects of a religious or moral nature; when we employ our time in instructing our dependants, our children, and servants, or in edifying communication with our equals.

Though these three injunctions are expressed in the negative form, yet (according to a well-known rule of interpreting Scripture, a rule derived from the Scriptures themselves) we must understand them as enjoining the opposite conduct.

This beautiful passage of the Prophet teaches us also, what ought to be the temper of our minds in these holy exercises. Far from being weary of the spiritual employments of the Sabbath, we ought to account them our pleasure, " and call the Sabbath a *delight*," as well as " holy of the Lord." This day we are to esteem " honourable" above all others. We are then peculiarly to " honour *Him*," whose bounty created us, whose long-suffering hath preserved us, and whose unsearchable goodness has provided a way for our eternal redemption. Thus is the nature of the duty of sanctifying the Sabbath pointed out with the utmost clearness.

A limitation, however, is sometimes put, by the infirmities of our fallen nature, to some of the exercises which ought, when we are unrestrained, to occupy us on this sacred day. Sickness may confine us to our beds, when we should otherwise be engaged in public worship; and, in such occasional interruptions, we may require the attention and assistance of others. The Lord, by declaring that he prefers mercy to sacrifice, has pointed out our duty on these occasions Whatever the necessities of our nature, as the relief of hunger, or aid in sickness, may require, must be considered as consistent with the sanctification of the Sabbath. Our Saviour, by his precepts and example, has completely illustrated this part of the subject.

Here it is proper to observe, that "God sent forth his Son, *made under the law.*" Christ lived and died under the Jewish dispensation. By his expositions of the moral law, he pointed out its real nature and extent; but made no alterations in it. When he declared that acts of necessity and charity were suitable to the Sabbath, he introduced no new doctrine, but appealed to the Jews themselves respecting the truth of what he taught. "Jesus spake unto the lawyers and pharisees, saying, Is it lawful to heal on the Sabbath-day? And they held their peace." Luke xiv. 3. The question undoubtedly was of this import: Is it agreeable to the law of God, as delivered by Moses? Is it consistent with the Fourth Commandment, and with the illustration of that Commandment by the holy prophets? The silence of the Jewish rulers was a tacit acknowledgment, that such acts of mercy were consistent with the due observance of the Sabbath.

If the ordinary employment of any person

consists in those acts which the proper duties of the Sabbath require, or which are allowed on that day, they certainly cannot be considered as infringements of the Fourth Commandment. The blessed Jesus appealed to the law of Moses on this head. " Have ye not read in the law, how that on the sabbath-day, the priests in the temple profane the sabbath, and are blameless?" Matthew xii. 5.

Our Saviour also taught, that it is consonant to the law of God to take a due care even of the brute creation on the Sabbath, much more of our fellow-creatures; and on this ground he reproved the indignant ruler of the synagogue, who wished to represent our Saviour's healing of the diseased as a work forbidden on the Sabbath-day. " Thou hypocrite, doth not each one of you on the Sabbath loose his ox or his ass from the stall, and lead him to watering?" And again, to the lawyers and pharisees, " Which of you shall have an ass or an ox fallen into a pit, and will not straightway pull him out on the Sabbath-day? And they could not answer him again to these things." Luke xiii. 15. xiv. 3.

These passages of Scripture clearly prove that our Lord was not introducing any relaxation of the Sabbath, suited to the genius of the gospel-dispensation; but that he was speaking the language of the law, as delivered to the Jews; and shewing, that acts of necessity, of mercy, and compassion, were duties suited to the strictest observance of the Sabbath. If this had not been the case, our Saviour could not have charged the ruler with hypocrisy, nor would his appeal to the law of Moses have silenced those who wished to accuse him of breaking that law.

It has been thought by some, that our Saviour exceeded the bounds of the Jewish law, when he directed the man, whom he had healed at the pool of Bethesda, to "take up his bed and walk;" John v. 8; because God had commanded the people, by the Prophet Jeremiah, to "bear no burden on the Sabbath-day;" chapter xvii. 21. Those who entertain such a thought, should consider, that our Lord perfectly understood the law; and if this was a breach of it, he was directing the poor man to commit a heinous offence against the law under which he was living, and also a capital offence against the state; for this, as well as several others of the Ten Commandments, was incorporated into the civil laws of the Jews. "Ye shall keep the Sabbath, for it is holy unto you. Every one that defileth it, shall surely be put to death." Exodus xxxi. 14. But an attentive consideration of the passages, prohibiting the bearing of burthens on the Sabbath, will shew, that they relate to such burdens as were borne in the carrying on of trade or ordinary labour. " If ye diligently hearken unto me, saith the Lord, to bring in no burden through the gates of the city on the Sabbath-day, but hallow the Sabbath-day *to do no work therein*;" Jeremiah xvii. 24. So likewise in the Book of Nehemiah. " In those days I saw in Judah some treading wine-presses on the Sabbath, and bringing in sheaves, and lading asses; as also, wine, grapes, and figs, and *all manner of burdens*, which they brought into Jerusalem on the Sabbath-day." Nehemiah xiii. 15. The cripple, whom our Saviour had healed at the pool of Bethesda, was friendless as well as poor; and probably had nothing but his portable bed, or mattrass, whereon to rest his weary limbs: the Lord Jesus, therefore, directed him to take care of this necessary piece of furniture, when he had strengthened the body of this indigent creature, and enabled him to return to his own house.

Another passage of the Old Testament may be thought to express a degree of strictness in the observance of the Sabbath, which was peculiar to the Jewish dispensation. " Ye shall kindle no fire throughout your habitations on the Sabbath-day." Exodus xxxv. 3. But this, compared with its context, seems to relate only to fires made for the purposes of labour. The whole passage runs thus; "Six days shall work be done, but on the seventh day there shall be to you an holy day, a Sabbath of rest to the Lord: *whosoever doth work therein*, shall be put to death. Ye shall kindle no fire," &c. We may rest assured, that he who prefers mercy to sacrifice would not forbid the use of fire, for the purpose of warmth, in any country where the inhabitants might be compelled to say, "Who is able to abide his frosts?" Nor is it probable, that He who vindicated the conduct of his disciples, when they had plucked the ears of corn, as they walked through the fields, for the purpose of satisfying their hunger, would forbid the use of fire for the necessary preparation of their food. We may conclude, therefore, that the kindling of a fire, for the refreshment of the body, was not contrary to the Jewish law.

Upon the whole, I see nothing in the duties of the Sabbath, as subsisting under the Jewish dispensation, but a most spiritual and rational service; suitable, indeed, to the period of man's innocence, yet accommodated to the necessities which sin has introduced into the world. The sanctions of the Sabbath were undoubtedly increased by the Mosaic law; as the breach of it was, by that law, made a capital offence. But this was not peculiar to the Fourth Commandment; and was a circumstance belonging to the policy, rather than to the religion of the Jews.

I cannot conceive a more delightful exercise to a heavenly-minded person, than that of spending a day in the manner described by the Prophet Isaiah. If the Jews, instead of confining their attention to these spiritual services, preferred a number of unnecessary restraints, we must not form our judgment of the real duties of the Sabbath from their conduct. We know that the further they deviated from the pure word of God in other instances, the more careful they were to make broad their phylacteries, and enlarge the borders of their garments; nor were they ever more strict in tything mint, anise, and cummin, than when they neglected the weightier matters of the law, justice, mercy, and the love of God.

THOUGHTS ON THE SABBATH,

UNDER THE CHRISTIAN DISPENSATION.

PART III.

The approbation of one day in seven to the worship of God, and other religious exercises, having been made a branch of the moral law, as summed up in the Ten Commandments; and that law being confessedly, with respect to nine of the Commandments, of universal and perpetual obligation: nothing more is needful to prove the authority of the Fourth Commandment, under the Gospel Dispensation, than to show that it has not been abrogated in the New Testament.

Our blessed Saviour, in his Sermon on the Mount, hath assured us, in the most explicit terms, that it was not his design to abrogate any part of the moral law.

"Think not that I am come to destroy the law, or the prophets: I am not come to destroy, but to fulfil. For verily I say unto you, Till heaven and earth pass, one jot or one tittle shall in no wise pass from the law till all be fulfilled." Matthew v. 17, 18. He also denounced a curse upon any one, who, by his conduct and doctrine, should set aside the law. "Whosoever, therefore, shall break one of these least commandments, and shall teach men so, he shall be called the least in the kingdom of heaven." Matthew v. 9.

Our Saviour was undoubtedly speaking of the moral law, as contained in the Ten Commandments; for, immediately after these declarations, he proceeded to expound the Sixth, Seventh, and Third Commandments, as parts of that law of which he was discoursing, with a view to remove the false glosses which the Jews had put upon them, and to shew their spiritual nature and their extent.

The perpetual obligation of the whole moral law cannot be expressed in stronger terms than those which our Lord has used. If it had been his design to rescind a tenth part of the law, he surely would not have declared, in this solemn manner, that not one jot or tittle of it should be rescinded.

The same doctrine is taught by the Apostle Paul, in Romans iii. 31. "Do we then make void the law through faith? God forbid: yea, we establish the law." But an important branch of the law is made void through faith, if the gospel annuls the obligation of the Fourth Commandment.

Let us then weigh the import of those passages in the New Testament, which have been thought by some to imply an abrogation of the Fourth Commandment, and consider whether they are not capable of a sound interpretation, which is consistent with these plain declarations of our Redeemer and his Apostles.

An opinion has been adopted, that the appointment of the first day of the week, for the public religious exercises of Christians, is a tacit abrogation of the Fourth Commandment, which appoints the seventh day for the celebration of the Sabbath. But it is obvious that this change is merely circumstantial, and does not interfere with the essence of the command. The last day of the week was undoubtedly appropriated by the Fourth Commandment; but it is remarkable, that the words may be applied to any day in the seven. We are enjoined to pursue our ordinary labours during six days, and on every seventh day to rest. This injunction is fulfilled, whatever day of the seven be the day of rest. The reason given in this Commandment for the observance of the institution is, that it pleased God to occupy six days in the creation of heaven and earth, and to rest from his work on the seventh day. Our regards are not diverted from a due consideration of God's love in creating us, by the alteration of the day appropriated to the Sabbath; though we are thereby directed to the celebration of a blessing superior to that of creation.

It is worthy of observation, that during the Jewish dispensation, another act of love, on the part of our gracious Creator, is mentioned as the reason for observing a sabbatical rest. "Remember that thou wast a servant in the land of Egypt, and that the Lord thy God brought thee out thence, through a mighty hand, and by a stretched out arm: *therefore* the Lord thy God commanded thee to keep the Sabbath-day." Deuteronomy v. 15. Hence we see, that the motive for observing one day in seven, as a Sabbath to the Lord, may be changed, without any change in the Commandment.

Our Saviour seems to have alluded to a future change in the day of the week, to be appropriated to the Christian Sabbath, when he declared that he was "Lord of the Sabbath." Mark ii. 28. A consideration of the context will shew, that this is the most natural interpretation of his words. He had been vindicating the conduct of his disciples, who, to satisfy their hunger, had plucked the ears of corn, and eaten them, as they went through the corn-fields on the Sabbath-day, and had been shewing, that works of necessity and mercy were proper on the Sabbath. On this occasion he declared, that "the Sabbath was made for man, and not man for the Sabbath;" verse 27; and then added, "Therefore the Son of Man is Lord also of the Sabbath;" verse 28. The exercise of Christ's authority over the Sabbath, was a consequence resulting from the former declaration, that "the Sabbath was made for man." Now if he designed to inform us, that the Sabbath would be abolished, the premises and conclusion are by no means coincident. The words of our Lord must then have had this import: "The Sabbath was a gracious institution, designed for the benefit of man, therefore I will take away this benefit from him." Whereas, if we suppose that these words had respect to the celebration of our redemption, a mercy greatly superior to that of creation, or the deliverance from Egyptian bondage, the whole sentence is beautifully connected, and of gracious import. It is as if our Lord had said, "Since the institution of a Sabbath was designed as a favour to man, and has hitherto directed his attention to the celebration of that love and power which created the heavens and the earth; and has also reminded the chosen nation of their deliverance from the most oppressive bondage: I will so regulate the day, as to direct the attention of my disciples to the greatest of all mercies, the completion of my labours for their eternal redemption."

I am aware, that a third sense may be put upon these words of our Saviour. They may be understood as expressive of a design to soften (according to the ideas of some) the rigours of the sabbatical institution. But I hope I have sufficiently shewn, that our Lord introduced no new doctrine respecting the Sabbath, when he declared that works of necessity and mercy were consistent with the sanctification of that day; and that he did not in any other respect alter the law of that institution, as delivered by Moses and the Prophets.* Indeed, the relaxation of the

* See "Thoughts on the Sabbath" during the Jewish dispensation. "Christian Observer," vol. i. page 417.

Fourth, or any other Commandment, would prove a curse instead of a blessing to mankind. "For the law is holy, and the commandment holy, and just, and good." Romans vii. 12.

If it had been the design of our Lord to abolish, under the Christian dispensation, the institution of a Sabbath, I do not see how he could have spoken of it in terms of respect, with relation to an event which he knew would not happen until forty years after the commencement of that dispensation. But when he was privately giving his disciples an account of the dreadful calamities which would take place at the siege of Jerusalem, he directed them to pray, that their "flight might not be on the Sabbath-day." Matthew xxiv. 20. Since in that case, they must either have been inattentive to the peculiar duties of the day, through the multiplicity of worldly concerns which would then press upon them, or have neglected their own safety through fear of breaking the Commandment.

The principal passages in the New Testament, which, at first sight, seem to favour the idea of the abolition of the Sabbath, under the gospel dispensation, occur, 1. in Romans xiv. 5. "One man esteemeth one day above another: another esteemeth every day alike. Let every man be fully persuaded in his own mind." And 2. that in Colossians ii. 16. "Let no man judge you in meat, or in drink, or in respect of an holy-day, or of the new moon, or of the Sabbath-days. But if the sense of these passages be determined by the context, it will appear that they were written with a reference to the ceremonial law, which was designed to be abolished by the gospel dispensation; and that they are not contrary to the idea of a Christian Sabbath.

In order to a right understanding of these passages, it is necessary to remember, that the gospel dispensation did not surpersede the Jewish by a sudden transition, and immediately render the Jewish observances unlawful to all who received Christ as their Saviour. It was the design of God that a gradual change should take place: so that, on the one hand, no violence should be done to the consciences of those, who had been educated in the observance of the ceremonial law; and, on the other, that the Gentile believers should not be brought under the yoke of the Jewish ritual. The Apostles themselves, if we may judge by the conduct of Peter, were not fully informed, at the day of Pentecost, of the intended abolition of the ceremonial law; for he conceived himself bound by the Jewish doctrine of clean and unclean meats, when he was invited to go and preach the gospel to Cornelius, who was a Gentile; though afterwards we find Peter declaring, in the first Christian synod, that the ceremonial law was a "yoke, which neither their fathers, nor they, were able to bear." Acts xv. 10. St. Paul, indeed, seems to have had a full display made to him at once of the whole system of the gospel; yet he continually taught the lawfulness of Jewish observances to those who had been educated as Jews, and himself conformed to them upon all proper occasions.

Many contentions must have arisen, during this state of things, amongst the Christian converts, respecting the authority of the Jewish ritual; and to such contentions the Apostle is evidently referring in the passages above cited. "Him that is weak in the faith receive you, but not to doubtful disputations. For one believeth that he may eat all things; another who is weak, eateth herbs. Let not him that eateth, despise him that eateth not; and let not him which eateth not, judge him that eateth. One man esteemeth one day above another: another esteemeth every day alike." If we understand this last clause as relating to the institutions of the ceremonial law, it will then be agreeable to the scope of the context, and will contradict no other part of the New Testament; but if we conceive of it as intended to cast a slight upon the christian Sabbath, we shall then set it in direct opposition to the declarations of our Saviour, as well as to the doctrines and conduct of the Apostles. They acted, no doubt, by the divine direction, in appointing the first day of the week, instead of the last, to be the day on which Christians should hold their public assemblies for religious worship; on which they should break bread in remembrance of Christ's death: and on which public collections should be made for the benefit of their distressed brethren. To this day they gave the venerable title of THE LORD'S DAY, a title which has been handed down in the Christian Church through every succeeding age, as appropriated to the *Christian Sabbath*.

The same reasoning is applicable to the passage which I have quoted from the Epistle to the Colossians. It is evident from the context, that the Apostle was speaking of the ordinances of the ceremonial law, for the neglect of which no Christian was to be condemned. "Blotting out the hand-writing of ordinances, that was against us, which was contrary to us, and took it out of the way, nailing it to his cross: Let no man, therefore, judge you in meat, or in drink, or in respect of an holy-day, or of the new-moon, or of the Sabbath-days." Colossians ii. 14, 16.

In this passage the Apostle is clearly speaking of *burthensome* ordinances; of something that was *against* them, and *contrary* to the spirituality of the gospel. But can any pious person conceive, that the spending of one day in seven in spiritual services, in the delightful employment of social worship, and other religious exercises, could be ranked by the holy Apostle among the things which were against Christianity, and contrary to it. Was that institution which the people of God had been commanded to call "a delight, holy of the Lord, and honourable," now to be esteemed of so carnal a nature, as to be ranked among the things which Christ "took out of the way, nailing it to his cross?" Were those holy persons, who had been accustomed to adopt the language of the Psalmist, "I was glad when they said unto me, let us go up to the house of the Lord," now taught to esteem a day spent in such services, as a part of that "yoke, which neither the Apostles, nor their fathers were able to bear?" We must destroy all just ideas of the effects which the preaching of the gospel was intended to produce, before we can adopt such an interpretation of the Apostle's words. Whereas, if we suppose him to mean, that no Christian ought to be condemned who had relinquished the Jewish ritual, and joined in transferring the sabbatical institution from the seventh to the first day of the week, in honour of the resurrection of our Redeemer, the passage becomes void of difficulty or contradiction to other passages of the New Testament.

No further arguments, I trust, are necessary to shew the nature and obligation of the Christian Sabbath; but I cannot dismiss this part of my subject without mentioning one reflection, which has often forcibly impressed my own mind.

It is acknowledged on all hands, that Christians are favoured with a clearer knowledge of the divine will than had been vouchsafed to mankind before the coming of Christ; that the motives to love and serve God are increased under the gospel dispensation: and that a more abundant effusion of the Holy Spirit has been granted since the glorification of Christ.

It might, therefore, be reasonably expected,

that the character of pious Christians should be somewhat superior to that of pious Jews; that the clearer views of the love and mercy of God in our redemption, and of our infinite obligations to the Redeemer, should produce greater delight in those holy exercises, which are so well calculated to call forth our gratitude and excite our love. Yet, if a sabbatical institution, as described by the Prophet Isaiah, is not binding upon Christians, as it was upon the Jews, this comparison must be reversed; and the employments of the Sabbath must have been more spiritual under the Jewish than under the Christian dispensation.

I see the pious Jew abstracting himself every seventh day from the cares and concerns of this life; joining in the ordinances of worship with a *delight*, which would render every other employment on that day insipid; and directing his *pleasures* and *conversation* in conformity to the peculiar duties of that holy season. Whereas, the pious Christian (if the observance is not a branch of Christianity) must fall short of the pious Jew in the spiritual frame of his mind on that day; and, as far as the exercises of that day have influence, in the general spirituality of his disposition. The Christian will not, indeed, neglect the public services of religion, which the laws and customs of his country may have appointed for the day; but then "one will go to his farm, and another to his merchandize;" or, at least, his thoughts and conversation will be engaged by these subjects, or his time spent in some unprofitable amusement, unless he performs what he must conceive to be a work of supererogation.

Every one, however, who has made the trial, must be sensible of the advantage which his mind derives from the employment of himself in religious exercises, of one kind or other, during the whole of the Sabbath-day. The influence of such conduct upon the temper of our minds, during the remainder of the week, is not small. On the contrary, a total neglect of the peculiar duties of the day seems, from experience, to be inconsistent with a state of religion.

How forcibly do these considerations point out the value of this institution, and shew, that we ought to regard as a favour, the permission to spend one day in seven as a "Sabbath to the Lord," even if this had not been made the subject of a command!

PART IV.

THOUGHTS ON THE SABBATH.

ANSWERS TO OBJECTIONS.

When I sat down to communicate my "Thoughts on the Sabbath" to the "Christian Observer," my design was to avoid, as much as possible, the appearance of controversy; and merely to state what I conceived to be the doctrine of Scripture. But as this subject has been treated at large by a modern Author, of high reputation in the learned world, who has shewn the great utility of sabbatical institutions, but whose views do not altogether coincide with mine, it might appear supercilious in me to omit taking particular notice of the arguments which he has adduced to prove, that the Sabbath was not instituted till after the departure of the Israelites from Egypt, and remained in force only during the Jewish dispensation. In my preceding papers I have not been inattentive to the arguments of this Author, and have already, in effect, given a reply to some of them. I now proceed to consider those of which I have hitherto taken no notice, or to which my answers have not been sufficiently explicit.

1. This Author candidly acknowledges, that "if the divine command was actually delivered at the creation, it was addressed, no doubt, to the whole human species alike, and continues, unless repealed by some subsequent revelation, binding upon all who come to the knowledge of it."*

It becomes us, then, to weigh with the utmost caution the words of Scripture, respecting the transactions of the "seventh day," as recorded in the Book of Genesis. If this passage declares, that God *then* blessed the seventh day, and sanctified it; all debate about the extent of the obligation of a sabbatical institution is precluded.†

* Paley's Principles of Moral and Political Philosophy, 8vo. edition, vol. ii. page 80.

† Ibid.

But it is objected, that "the words," Genesis ii. 3, "do not assert that God *then* blessed and sanctified the seventh day; but that he blessed and sanctified it *for that reason*," "because that on it he had rested from all his work," &c.; "and if any ask, why the Sabbath, or sanctification of the seventh day, was *then* mentioned, if it was not *then* appointed; the answer is at hand; the order of connexion, and not of time, introduced the mention of the Sabbath, in the history of the subject which it was ordained to commemorate." *

I am here at issue with the Author whom I have quoted, as, in my apprehension, the words in Genesis do clearly assert, that God *then* blessed and sanctified the seventh day, as well as that he sanctified it, *because* that on it he had rested from all his work of creation.

In the first, and beginning of the second chapter of Genesis, we have a distinct chronological account of the transaction of the first seven days, after it had pleased God to begin the stupendous work of creation. The trans-

* Paley's Principles of Moral and Political Philosophy, 8vo. edition, vol. ii. page 70.

actions of the seventh day are as distinctly marked as those of any other day, with this difference only, that with respect to the six preceding days the work is first mentioned, and then the day; whereas, with respect to the seventh, the day is first mentioned, and then its transactions are enumerated.

On the first day, God said, " Let there be light, and there was light." On the sixth, " God created man in his own image;" and, on the seventh day, " God ended his work which he had made; and he rested on the seventh day from all his work which he had made; and God blessed the seventh day and sanctified it, because that on it he had rested from all his work, which God created and made." All the transactions enumerated in this passage belong to the seventh day as clearly, in my apprehension, as the creation of man belongs to the sixth; nor can I discover any thing in the passage, except the division into verses, which could mislead a reader of plain understanding. On the seventh day God ended his work and rested, and blessed the day, and sanctified it. All these things are mentioned as having taken place on that day. It is as expressly declared that he *then* blessed and sanctified the day, as that he rested on it. I do not know how we can prove any thing from the Scripture, if a passage so plain as this is not to be understood in its obvious sense, unless some subsequent revelation, equally clear, had compelled us to adopt another meaning.

The literal sense of the words is confirmed by the reason which is given for the sanctification of the seventh day. God sanctified the day, "*because* that in it he had rested from all his work which God created and made." One design of the original institution was to celebrate the work of creation; and when should we expect the celebration to commence? Surely at the time immediately succeeding the transaction to be celebrated. The Almighty has, since the creation, frequently appointed periodical times and significant actions for the purpose of commemorating signal interpositions of his Providence, or remarkable mercies vouchsafed to mankind. In all these cases the celebration was directed to commence from the period of the mercy to be celebrated. The Passover began with the deliverance of the Israelites, and the Sacrament of the Lord's Supper at the death of Christ. But to suppose that an institution, designed to commemorate the creation of the world, had no existence till two thousand years after the event, is so strange in itself, and so contrary to the conduct of God on similar occasions, that the idea cannot be received without a clear warrant from Scripture.

" 2. If the Sabbath had been instituted at the time of the creation, as the words in Genesis may seem at first sight to import—it appears unaccountable that no mention of it, no occasion of even the obscurest allusion to it, should occur either in the general history of the world before the call of Abraham, which contains, we admit, only a few memoirs of its early ages, and those extremely abridged; or which is more to be wondered at, in that of the lives of the three first Jewish patriarchs, which in many parts of the account is sufficiently circumstantial and domestic."*

If the argument contained in this passage proves any thing, it will prove too much. It will prove, that the observance of the Sabbath ceased during upwards of four hundred years after its institution in the wilderness; for in all that period we have " no mention of it," nor does " the obscurest allusion to it occur." The history of the settlement of the Jews in

* Paley's Principles of Moral and Political Philosophy, 8vo. edition, vol. ii. page 75.

Canaan, as related in the Book of Joshua, is in many parts so circumstantial, that one might have expected to find some mention of this important institution. The Israelites marched round the city of Jericho in military array during seven successive days, (Joshua vi.) one of which must have been the Sabbath; yet no express " permission is recorded to dispense with the institution" during this week. The Book of Judges contains a series of revolts from the worship of the true God, and of deliverances from the miseries which these revolts brought upon the Jews. Yet we find in the history no reproof for the contempt of the sabbatical institution, though this was a crime particularly marked by the Prophets, as a principal cause of the national punishments inflicted on that favoured, yet perverse people.

We argue unfairly, and in a manner injurious to religion, when we oppose the silence of Scripture in one part to its express declarations contained in another. Abraham is particularly commended by the Almighty for his care in " commanding his children and household to keep the way of the Lord :" and we are certain, that " Abraham rejoiced to see the day of Christ, and he saw it, and was glad." John viii. 56. Yet, where do we find, in the Old Testament, the least hint that he communicated this most important branch of knowledge to his family.

The sacrifices under the Mosaic law were typical of the atoning sacrifice made for our salvation by the death of Christ, and Moses was instructed in the typical nature of the ceremonial law, when he received the commands of God respecting that institution. " The law had a shadow of good things to come." Hebrews x. 1. The service of the tabernacle afforded " a figure for the time then present," chapter ix. 9; and the Jewish priests " served unto the example and shadow of heavenly things, *as Moses was admonished of God*, when he was about to make the tabernacle;" chapter viii. 5. Yet where is this chief design of the ceremonial law mentioned in the writings of Moses, though it is explicitly and repeatedly taught in the New Testament?

The silence of some parts of the Scripture respecting the Sabbath, cannot, therefore, with justice be opposed to the declarations which we find concerning it in other parts of the word of God.

3. It is objected, that in the 16th chapter of Exodus, where the Sabbath is first men-

tioned, after the passage in Genesis already quoted, there is not " any intimation that the Sabbath, then appointed to be observed, was only the revival of an ancient institution, which had been neglected, forgotten, or suspended."*

I wish your readers to examine this chapter with attention, and consider, whether the language, upon the first mention of the Sabbath, is more suitable to an old institution, " neglected or suspended," or to one which was totally unknown.

The Israelites having murmured in the wilderness for want of food, God graciously promises them a miraculous supply. " Behold, I will rain bread from heaven for you; and the people shall go out, and gather a certain rate every day, that I may prove them, whether they will walk in my law or no. And it shall come to pass, that on the sixth day they shall prepare that which they bring in; and it shall be twice as much as they gather daily." Exodus xvi. 4, 5. The people obeyed this injunction, and " on the sixth day they gathered twice as much bread; and all the rulers of the congregation came and told

* Paley's Principles of Moraland Political Philosophy, 8vo. edition, vol. ii. page 75.

Moses;" verse 22. "And he said unto them, This is that which the Lord hath said, To-morrow is the rest of the holy Sabbath unto the Lord;" verse 23.

Is this language suitable to a solemnity which had never been instituted? As the Ten Commandments had not, at this time, been delivered to the Israelites, the duty of sanctifying the seventh day must have been totally unknown, if no prior command on this subject had existed. Whereas the preparation for the sabbatical rest, the conduct of the rulers of the congregation, and the reply of Moses, appear much more suitable to the revival of a neglected institution, than to the appointment of a new one. We may be sure that, during the oppressive bondage in Egypt, no such rest could have been observed; but the Israelites having now escaped from their oppressors, the institution is revived, and a preparation for its celebration is commanded, before any mention is made of the institution itself. And when that preparation is completed, the Sabbath is mentioned as a solemnity already commanded: "This is that which the Lord hath said, To-morrow is the rest of the holy Sabbath unto the Lord."

4. "This interpretation," that the Sabbath

was first instituted in the wilderness, "is strongly supported by a passage in the Prophet Ezekiel, where the Sabbath is plainly spoken of as *given*, and what else can that mean, but as *first instituted*, in the wilderness?" —Nehemiah also recounts the promulgation of the sabbatical law amongst the transactions in the wilderness.*

The passage in Ezekiel is as follows: "I caused them to go forth out of the land of Egypt, and brought them into the wilderness. And I gave them my statutes, and shewed them my judgments, which if a man do, he shall even live in them. Moreover also I gave them my Sabbaths;" chapter xx. verse 10, 11.

If this passage proves, that the Sabbath was first instituted in the wilderness, it will prove, that the other commandments of the moral law were then first promulgated: for the language respecting all the commandments is precisely the same. "I *gave* them my statutes, — I also *gave* them my Sabbaths;" Yet we are sure that the moral law was made known to mankind before its promulgation at Mount Sinai. The sixth and seventh commandments, for instance, were ordained from

* Paley's Principles of Moral and Political Philosophy, 8vo. edition, vol. ii. page 76.

the beginning. Genesis ix. 16. Matthew xix. 8. Indeed the whole tenor of the Bible, before the Israelites formed a distinct nation, shews that mankind were not left without the knowledge of God's laws; " for where no law is, there is no transgression." Romans iv. 5.

The passage in Nehemiah is of the same import with that in Ezekiel. " Thou camest down also upon Mount Sinai, and spakest with them from heaven, and gavest them right judgments, and true laws, good statutes and commandments; and madest known unto them thy holy Sabbath." As the *true laws*, and *good statutes* contained in the Ten Commandments were not then first given, though they were then proclaimed in a more awful manner, so neither was the Sabbath then first instituted. As far as we can deduce an argument from the similarity of language, this must be the consequence. The expression, " made known," is used in Scripture, where the first intimation of the thing cannot be intended: as " God *made known* his ways unto Moses, his acts unto the children of Israel;" Psalm ciii. 7; though this was not the first communication of his will, nor manifestation of his acts to mankind.

5. " The Sabbath is described as a sign

between God and the people of Israel, Exodus xx. 12. and xxxi. 16, 17. Now it does not seem easy to understand how the Sabbath could be a *sign* between God and the people of Israel, unless the observance of it was peculiar to that people, and designed to be so."*

By a *sign* I understand something that should distinguish the people of God from all the heathen nations by whom they were surrounded. The Jews, while they continued obedient, were distinguished by their rest from ordinary labours every seventh day, and their dedication of it to the worship of Jehovah. This would mark them out as a peculiar people, devoted to God's service. But this will not prove, that no obligation lay upon any other people to observe a sabbatical institution. The observance of all God's commandments was to be a *sign* or *badge* by which the people of God were to be distinguished from other nations. "Hear, O Israel, the Lord our God is one Lord; and thou shalt love the Lord thy God with all thine heart, and with all thy soul, and with all thy might. And these words which I command thee this day shall

* Paley's Principles of Moral and Political Philosophy, 8vo edition, vol. ii. page 81.

be in thine heart.—And thou shalt bind them for a *sign* upon thine hand." Deuteronomy vi. 4, &c. That is, thou shalt consider them as a *badge*, or mark of distinction, by which the world may know thou art indeed the people of God. But none of the commandments would distinguish them as a people devoted to the service of God, in so peculiar a manner as the fourth. Their disobedience to this command is, therefore, often specified by the prophets as a special cause of the punishments which God inflicted on that nation.

"6. The distinction of the Sabbath is, in its nature, as much a positive ceremonial institution, as that of many other seasons which were appointed by the Levitical law to be kept holy.*

It is not possible to conceive any duty to be more strictly moral, or of more universal obligation, than that of worshipping Almighty God. And if it is our duty to join in acts of public and social worship, some fixed time must be appointed for the exercise of this duty. There is, therefore, nothing more of a positive, or ceremonial nature in a sabbatical

* Paley's Principles of Moral and Political Philosophy, 8vo. edition, vol. ii. page 81.

institution, than what arises from the necessity of the case. He who made us for his own pleasure is surely the best judge what portion of our time ought to be dedicated to his more immediate worship and service. It does not appertain to us to inquire, why the Almighty confined his work of creation to six days; why he rested on the seventh; or why he commanded us to sanctify this portion of our time: but such an institution certainly rests upon different grounds from those festivals which God commanded the Jews to observe in commemoration of mercies peculiar to that nation. It requires no great discernment to see the difference between dwelling in booths at a certain period of the year, to commemorate the protection which the Jewish nation received in the wilderness, and the weekly celebration of the mercies of creation and redemption, which are as extensive as the globe which we inhabit.

Whether the Sabbath should be celebrated on the first or seventh day of the week, is, undoubtedly, a circumstance of a positive nature; but it is a circumstance which does not alter the duties peculiar to the Sabbath. The day on which this institution ought to be observed might have been, and, I doubt not, actually was altered by the authority of our

Saviour, without any alteration in the substance of the commandment.

7. "If the command by which the Sabbath was instituted, be binding upon Christians, it must bind as to the day, the duties, and the penalty; in none of which it is received."*

The *duties* of the Sabbath, are, without doubt, essential to the institution; but the *day* is not essential. By the *penalty*, our Author, I suppose, means that of death, which was directed to be inflicted on the Sabbath-breaker under the Jewish dispensation. But if there be any argument in this assertion, it will prove, that the punishments incurred by a breach of the other Commandments of the moral law, ought to be inflicted upon offending Christians. It will prove, that the idolater, the blasphemer, the adulterer, and the stubborn rebellious son, as well as the Sabbath-breaker, ought to be put to death under the gospel dispensation.

8. "The observance of the Sabbath was not one of the Articles, enjoined by the Apostles

* Paley's Principles of Moral and Political Philosophy, 8vo. edition, vol. ii. page 82.

in the 15th chapter of Acts, upon them, " which from the Gentiles were turned unto God."*

In addition to the ceremonial pollutions, from which the Gentile Christians were commanded to abstain, the Apostle mentions the crime of *fornication*. But we are incompetent to judge, why the breach of one command only of the moral law is interdicted in this place. Little weight ought surely to be attached to such negative arguments, respecting the obligation of the Fourth Commandment of the moral law, since they oppose the positive declaration of our Saviour, that he came not to remove one jot or tittle of this law; which the Apostle Paul also declares was not intended to be made void by faith in Jesus Christ.

Those of your readers, who are unacquainted with the work whence the above quotations are taken, may be ready to conclude, that the Author meant to speak disrespectfully of sabbatical institutions, which is by no means the case. He has shewn their great utility, and has proved that " the *assembling* upon the first day of the week for the purpose of public worship, and religious in

* Paley's Principles of Moral and Political Philosophy, 8vo. edition, vol. ii. page 82.

struction, is a law of Christianity, of divine appointment." He concludes also, that "the resting on that day from our employments," is a duty "binding upon the conscience of every individual in a country, in which a weekly Sabbath is established."*

We who live under the British Government are so happy as to come under the obligation of so excellent a law, which declares, that "every person and persons whatsoever shall, on every Lord's-day apply themselves to the observance of the same, by exercising themselves thereon in the duties of piety and true religion, publicly and privately." 29 Car. II. c. 7.

The most careful consideration which I have been able to give this subject has produced a firm persuasion in my mind, that the obligation to this duty is, however, of universal extent; and this seems to have been the view which the primitive Christians had of the subject, as appears from a quotation which our Author has made from the works of Irenæus. "Unusquisque nostrûm sabbatizat spiritualiter, meditatione legis gaudens, opificium Dei admirans."—"Each of us spends

* Paley's Principles of Moral and Political Philosophy, 8vo. edition, vol. ii. page 91.

the Sabbath in a spiritual manner, meditating on the law of God with delight, and contemplating his workmanship with admiration."

Let it be remembered, that Irenæus had been instructed by Polycarp, who was the disciple of the Apostle John;* that in this passage he is not describing any doctrine or practice peculiar to himself, but the general conduct of Christians; that he appropriates the title of "Sabbath" to that day which was set apart for religious exercises, and which was undoubtedly the first day of the week; that the manner of spending this day by the early Christians, corresponds with the description of the Sabbath given by Isaiah; that what the Jewish prophet commanded, the Christians practised: and can any reasonable doubt remain, that the Christian Church had

* Thus Irenæus speaks. "I can describe the very spot in which Polycarp sat and expounded, and the sermons which he preached to the multitude, and how he related to us his converse with John, and with the rest of those who had seen the Lord; how he mentioned their particular expressions, and what things he had heard from them of the Lord, and of his miracles and of his doctrines. As Polycarp had received from the eye-witnesses of the Word of Life, he told us all things agreeable to the Scriptures."—Milner's Ecclesiastical History, vol. i. page 312. Second Edition, "Life of Irenæus."

been instructed by the Apostles, and their immediate successors, to sanctify the first day of the week as a "Sabbath unto the Lord?" A more direct historical testimony of this important fact need not be required.

OBITUARY.

HIS ELDEST SON.*

Biographical anecdotes of persons deceased, who have exemplified the power of religion, though their lives have not been marked with any uncommon events, are acknowledged to have a beneficial tendency. The utility is increased, when the subjects of these anecdotes have manifested the influence of divine grace during the season of youth. When the service of God is then preferred to the gratifications of sense, and the love of Christ predominates amidst scenes of temptation, we cannot doubt that the heart is truly renewed after the image of him that created us.

* Richard Hey, of whom a short account is given in the Life of Mr. Hey.

The following narratives may not, therefore, be thought unworthy of a place in your useful Miscellany.* It must be remembered, however, that they are the narratives of a father, whom it has pleased the all-wise God to deprive of four children in the bloom of youth. He wishes to divest himself of parental partiality, and to give a faithful account of those whose conduct he describes. He is aware, that true religion is not to be estimated by sudden transports, or rapturous expressions; yet, when it pleases God to afford comfort and holy joy, under trying circumstances, to those who have fled to Christ for refuge under a deep sense of their own sinfulness, and who have dedicated themselves to the service of God, we ought with thankfulness to adore the divine goodness.

My eldest son, of whom I now purpose to give you a short account, had not manifested any remarkable religious impressions in his childhood, though there was often evident in him a strong contest between a sense of duty and the natural corrupt temper of his heart. This he expressed to me at one time in striking terms, when I was reasoning with

* This was first printed in the Christian Observer, October, 1802.

him on the impropriety of his frequent relapses into a fault of which he had often been warned. He replied to my remonstrances by saying, "Indeed, papa, I would be good, but the devil will not let me."

During the time which he passed at a public school, a circumstance occurred, which I shall briefly relate, as it may afford some instruction to parents, and others employed in the education of youth. A theft had been committed at the school, which was laid to his charge by one of his school-fellows. He declared that he was innocent of the crime; but some things relative to the affair casting a suspicion upon him, though no proof of his guilt could be adduced, his declarations were disregarded, and he was considered as guilty. As soon as I heard of this affair, I desired a serious friend of mine to make a strict inquiry into it, and report to me his opinion. He concurred with the master in thinking it proper to urge my son, by the most powerful arguments they could devise, to make a confession of his guilt. He still denied the charge. But at last, being urged with the assurance, that nothing but a confession would ward off my displeasure, the effect of which was represented to him in the strongest manner, he confessed the fault laid to his charge. In his last illness, among other things, in which he opened his mind with great freedom, he solemnly declared, that he was wholly ignorant of the theft which he had confessed, and that he was induced to make this criminal confession, by the terror which the apprehension of my displeasure excited in his mind, and which he was assured could not be avoided but by a confession. He added with great apparent humility, that it was right he should suffer by the false accusation of one, whose sinful example in another instance, he had followed.

If a digression on this subject will not be thought tedious, I would beg leave to remark, that I conceive it to be, in general, an imprudent step, eagerly to solicit a confession of guilt from young persons accused of any crime which they deny, and which cannot be proved. If they are guilty, they are often hereby led to inhance their guilt by strong asseverations of innocence. If they are innocent, their minds are hurt by a disregard to their declarations. It seems to them of less consequence to obey, when obedience cannot insure the good opinion of their friends, nor prevent them from being classed with the guilty. In such cases, it may be the most prudent method, to remind them of the all-seeing eye of God, and of the righteous unerring judgment which will soon take place; and at the same time to manifest a readiness to believe them free from that falsehood, which could only increase their condemnation.

But to return.—Soon after my son had completed his fifteenth year, he returned home, and remained at my house till he arrived at adult age. In this period the happy change took place, which was followed, after a few years, by a triumphant death. I observed, when he was about nineteen, a manifest alteration in his deportment.

A growing attention to the concerns of his salvation was then very apparent; and his whole conduct soon became decidedly religious. In his last illness, he attributed, in a considerable degree, the powerful impressions made upon his mind at this period, to the perusal of "Adams's Evangelical Sermons," of which a pious friend had made him a present.

When he was twenty-one, he made a solemn dedication of himself to God, in the manner, and agreeable to the form proposed by Dr. Doddridge in his "Rise and Progress of Religion," a book which he read with great attention, and which cannot be too strongly recommended. This transaction was, however, unknown to me, and to every one in my family, till after his death, which did not happen till four years afterwards. The form of self-dedication was then found in a small port-folio, which had been observed to be often in his hands during his sickness. It contained the following postscript after the signature.—"At my father's house.—Signed and sealed this——day of——(on which day I am twenty-one years of age,) after full consideration and serious reflection, I do purpose to read over and renew this covenant every return of this day, as also every Christmas-day, and every Good-friday or Easter-day.

From the age of twenty-one to twenty-three he spent his time in London, in a diligent pursuit of those studies to which his profession called him. The great quantity of manuscript observations which he made there, afforded me a clear proof of his industry. At the same time he was diligent in his attendance on the means of grace. I found in his port-folio, after his death, a scrap of paper, on which he had written a set of rules for regulating the manner of spending his time while in London. The following extract of a letter which he wrote to me from thence will manifest the temper of mind, which at that time happily influenced his conduct. It was written on the occasion of a disappointment, which he had just experienced, relative to his future prospects in life:

—"No doubt our merciful God, whose most darling attribute, if I may so speak, is love, has seen perfectly wise reasons for ordering it. We may perhaps come to see how merciful a dispensation it is. But be that as it will, I know I am his creature, and therefore he may with strict propriety do with me whatsoever he pleases. But, dear father, I have solemnly given up myself to serve him, and to be disposed of as he sees fit; and he has graciously promised, that if I seek first the kingdom of God and his righteousness, all other needful things shall be added. Must I not then rest contented? Shall I not rather rejoice that he condescends to order any of the circumstances of my life? Yes, father, and blessed be his love, he does at this moment enable me to admire his goodness."—

After his return home, he continued to enjoy a good state of health, till he caught cold by being exposed in the duties of his profession. The disease which proved fatal to him, came on in the most gentle manner, so that it was probably confirmed before he seemed to have any serious ailment. His physician assured me, that he never before saw such a case; that is, where the distemper proved fatal when accompanied with such mild and favourable symptoms. I first learned that he had a cough, by inquiring why he left off the use of animal food, which I had observed him to do. After the disease was fully confirmed, he was frequently out of bed for seven or eight hours without coughing at all; his pulse, at that time, being frequently as calm as in health: yet under the existence of these mild symptoms, a fatal abscess was formed in his lungs.

During a considerable time in the disease he spake little, as speaking was judged to be an improper exercise; but when it appeared that no rational hope of his recovery could be maintained, I informed him of his situation, and we then talked freely together. He received my information of his danger with perfect composure, as far as I could judge. No expressions dropped from him, but of submission to God's will. He arranged his little affairs and divided his books among his nearest friends. He seemed sensible of the goodness of God to him, in granting him so much ease in his disorder, and, indeed, he had little to complain of but his emaciation. This proceeded to such a degree, that he could sometimes scarcely bear the pressure of his bed. Yet he sat up about eight hours daily in his chair, till within two days of his death.

When confined to his chamber, he spent his time chiefly in reading the word of God, unless when conversing with us. He requested me to pray with him night and morning, as he could not attend our family worship. When reading by himself became too fatiguing to him, he requested his sisters to read to him select passages of the Bible. He addressed his younger brothers, and other young friends who visited him, with great seriousness. He begged that I would contrive, if possible, to sit with him a little every day, that he might open his heart to me; and that I might instruct, and comfort him in his affliction. No communion I had ever before had with him was so pleasing, as were these private conversations. When his departure approached, the tranquillity of mind which he before possessed, (without much sensible joy) rose up to a state of great consolation. On the two last days preceding that on which he died, his mind seemed more strongly comforted, and his hope was full of immortality. I wrote down, as soon as I had left his chamber, some of the things which he then said to me.

Wednesday. He told me he had long since dedicated himself to God's service; and that although his heart had too often grown cold, he trusted he had never relinquished his purpose. He said, "I have sinned greatly against God, but I trust I have sincerely repented of all my transgressions." He lamented the depravity of his heart in strong terms, and said, "O this *foul* heart!" adding, "But it is the grace of God that reigns." He said, "he hoped he did not deceive himself; but he looked forward with joy, trusting that he should shortly see God in his kingdom." He begged of me to read to him that passage in the Epistle to the Philippians,—"To me to live is Christ; and to die is gain. I am in a strait between two, having a desire to depart, and to be with Christ; which is far better." He seemed much delighted with these words. He begged I would tell him, if I thought he deceived himself. He spoke with great feeling of the sufferings of our Redeemer, as described in the fifty-third chapter of Isaiah, and said, "*That* was his joy, that the blood of Christ cleanseth from all sin."

Thursday. Upon my asking him in the morning how he did, he replied, "I grow weaker; perhaps my departure is not far off; and I trust to enjoy a glorious immortality." Looking round upon his relations who were in the room, he said, "God bless you all!" and further expressed his strong hope of approaching bliss.

After a little rest, he broke out in these words; "He was wounded for our transgressions, and I have wounded him by my sins; but now he comforts me." After lying still for some time, he repeated those words in our Saviour's prayer, (John xvii.) "Father, I will that those whom thou hast given me be with me where I am, that they may behold my glory which thou hast given me;" and added, "This prayer, I trust, Christ is now making for me."

Before I left him he said, "Father, I should like once more to receive the cup of salvation, and call on the name of the Lord;" alluding to the Sacrament of the Lord's Supper, which he had before received in his chamber.

In the evening we joined with him in that holy ordinance, and as soon as his friends had left the room, he said to me, "With respect to the state of my mind I cannot now say much, I am so *very* weak; but I trust I am going to sing the song of Moses and the Lamb." Then reposing himself a while, he uttered these words with great emphasis; "Eye hath not seen, nor ear heard, nor hath it entered into heart of man, to conceive the goodness ——" his weakness prevented him from proceeding.

To his cousin J. S. who came up to see him, he said, "Farewell, I shall see you no more. God bless you. May we meet in heaven."

Friday. In the morning he found himself extremely weak. Having usually prayed with him morning and evening, I desired him, as I sat by his bed, to tell me if he found any interval in which he could wish me to pray with him. He answered, "I cannot attend." Upon my saying, "Then we will pray *for* you." He replied eagerly, "Aye, do." He was not forgotten at our family worship, and the Rev. Mr.———, who happened to be with us, recommended him to the protection of our Heavenly Father in that affecting form of worship in our Liturgy, called the "Commendatory Prayer." (Visitation of the sick.)

I sat by his bed the greatest part of the day; but his weakness did not permit him to hold any conversation. At one time, after lying still for about half an hour, he lifted up his eyes as in an act of devotion, and cried out,—"When I wake up after thy likeness, I shall be satisfied." After this he spoke no more, except in asking for a little refreshment, or the like; and in the evening, when he seemed to be asleep, he expired without the least emotion.

OBITUARY.

DAUGHTER ALICE,

(SOMETIMES CALLED LISSY.)

The kind reception which you have given to the short history which I transmitted to you, of my eldest son, encourages me to proceed in sending you some anecdotes of the rest of my children, whom it pleased God to remove from this state of trial, during the vigour of their youth.

Five years after the death of that son, it seemed good to the wise Disposer of all events, to deprive me of one of my daughters, by the same disorder which had proved fatal to her brother.

My daughter Alice was impressed from her infancy with a serious sense of eternal things, so that the work of grace upon her heart was such as our Lord describes in one of his parables. "So is the kingdom of God, as if a man should cast seed into the ground, and should sleep and rise night and day, and the seed should spring up he knoweth not how. For the earth bringeth forth fruit of herself, first the blade, then the ear, after that the full corn in the ear." Mark iv. 26.

Here it may not be improper to remark, that when the Spirit of God makes use of education as the means of producing sound conversion, we are not always to expect such a sudden change of conduct as we see happily to take place in some who have lived in the contempt or neglect of religion. The seed instilled by the care of a parent or guardian, and watered with daily prayers and instructions, groweth up we know not how, but bringeth forth in the end the genuine fruits of righteousness. Those who have been thus gradually led to a right faith in Jesus Christ, and a sincere dedication of themselves to his service, ought not to be disturbed because they cannot fix on any distinct periods of their lives, when their views and tempers were suddenly changed. If such persons, from a consciousness of their guilt and innate depravity, have fled to Christ for refuge from the curse of God's law; if their hopes of justification and salvation are fixed on the merits of their Redeemer; and if the love of God and of all mankind is truly shed abroad in their hearts; they have reason to rejoice in God as their Saviour, and to look forward with a confident hope of future glory.

My daughter Alice was in many respects a pattern to the younger part of the family. She was diligent, frugal, and industrious, while she was at school; and continued to be so when she had arrived at adult age.

The temper of her mind, with respect to spiritual things at this period of life, will be most clearly shewn by a few extracts from the papers found in her bureau after her death. To which I must add, that her conduct was conformable to these private thoughts.

Her watchfulness over her own heart, appears from the following observations which she had made upon herself. "I want to feel a more universal love to God, that all my actions may be governed by that, — my thoughts and my affections. I find dispositions rising daily which are contrary to this I seem to want to *appear religious*, and to be thought well of; and because one in the family behaves towards me as if he thought I was very loose in my notions of religion, I find great risings against him. This is an unchristian temper. If I had that humility which the gospel requires, I should know, that no opinion of me is too mean. My corrupt nature rebels against this; and this will hinder my growth in grace, if not subdued. O God, thy power alone can work a true change in me, and subdue my heart to thee!"

Again she writes thus;—"I fear I do many times dishonour God, by a very hasty temper. If I were truly humble, should I be so soon hurt, or put out of temper, by any little incivility? Oh, I desire it, that whenever I give way to this disposition, I may suffer from it, and feel how hateful it is in God's sight."

Her watchfulness over the state of her mind in company, appears from the following remark. "I have this day had some friends with me who are quite worldly people; and though our conversation has had, I trust, nothing inconsistent with godliness in it, yet my heart has not been with God. O dreadful state of insensibility!"

On this head, I find the following remark, either made by herself, or extracted from some author she had been reading. " Those Christians who are unavoidably obliged to be sometimes in the company of the ungodly, will never have peace in their own minds, if they do not deal faithfully with such."

Her earnest desires after holiness, are shewn in such reflections as these ;—" I want a principle of godliness in the soul at all times guiding me." " I trust I can say with sincerity, that it is, and shall be, my endeavour to strive against sin."

" I find that I have been expecting and desiring to be impelled by the influences of God's Spirit, to do his will, without giving myself the pain of *striving* to overcome by grace.

" Instead of *resolving* to give up my own *ease* and *pleasure*, rather than not do my duty to God and man, I seem to leave that determination till the trial should come. O God, give me power and strength to do *all* thy will, however contrary to flesh and blood !"

Her watchfulness over her mind, in prayer and other religious exercises, appears from the following reflections upon her own conduct.

" Sunday noon. I have attended to the prayers this morning,—my thoughts did not wander much; but it was no worship of the *heart*. My heart did not go along with the words. I thought I never shall overcome this deadness. When I thought this, I was trusting to my own strength; but Christ can be my strength to overcome every thing. O God, by thy Spirit, enable me to see Christ as *my* strength. Let not Satan tempt me to give up all, by leading me to look for deliverance from my own efforts. They are weakness," &c.

I am not certain at what age she wrote down the following rules for spending the day, as the memorandum bears no date; but I apprehend it must have been several years before her death. "Read some portion of Scripture before breakfast. If I have not time before, immediately after. Settle household matters. Then spend half an hour in reading English grammar. After that, work the remainder of the morning, leaving time for walking and dressing. After dinner, work a little,—then read some serious book; after tea, read history,—work if I have time. Retire at half-past seven to my own room, till supper,—after supper, amuse myself as I like best."

In this short account of her daily employments, there is no mention made of visiting, or working for the poor, in both which she was frequently employed. These labours of love, I suppose, were included under the heads of *walking* and *working*.

Some forms of prayer were found written in a small book, which seemed to have been much used.

She had begun a kind of common-place book of the Scriptures, with the view of extracting, and classing under proper heads, such passages as she judged most applicable to her own case, and suitable to advance the Christian life. The heads were such as these,—"The passages of Scripture which excite confidence in God." "The promises of God to those who are desirous to love him, and to those who have chosen him for their God." She had also written out many passages, describing the distinguishing characters of the children of God.

These short extracts will serve to convey some idea how the days of her youth were spent.

When she was twenty-three years of age, she was seized with a spitting of blood, which brought her life into some danger. However, it pleased God at that time to restore her health; but the disease returned in her twenty-sixth year, and brought on a consumption, which proved fatal to her soon after she had completed that year.

Soon after her recovery from the former attack, her mind was much exercised for some time with a trial of too delicate a nature to be minutely related. Suffice it to say, that a considerable struggle took place, in which religion triumphed over a temporary affection.

Whether this struggle had, in any degree, diminished her usual firmness of mind, or whether the trouble which she afterwards experienced was purely of a spiritual nature, I cannot determine: however, a little before the attack of her last illness, she was harrassed with violent temptations to despair. The great enemy of souls was permitted to assault her with ideas of the most distressing kind. She was led to doubt the reality of her former experience. She feared she had been a hypocrite before God, and this terrified her to a very high degree. Her sleep was broken, and the agonies of her mind sometimes made her body tremble. I shall never forget the state of agitation, during which she entered my study one morning early, to communicate to me her fears of eternal perdition, and to beg my prayers.

In this furnace of affliction, her gracious

Saviour meant, I doubt not, to purify her soul; and, indeed, she came out of it as gold purified in the fire. As her disease increased, the tranquillity of her mind was restored; and she was at last enabled to rejoice in God her Saviour.

I shall communicate an account of her behaviour in her last illness, by transcribing part of a letter which I wrote to one of her uncles after her death. She had passed some time at his house between the two attacks of her disease; and having received from him the kindest attention, and most seasonable advice, she entertained a high degree of respect and affection for him.

"Dear Brother;

"During the former part of my dear Alice's illness, she was requested to forbear talking much, lest the spitting of blood should be brought on again by the exertion. When the disease was so far advanced, that there appeared to be no hope of amendment, I left her to follow her own inclinations and feelings, and she conversed as she found herself able to bear the exercise of speaking. Her conversation, when she was restored to a state of comfort, gave me great satisfaction, and evinced a mind deeply impressed with holy affections.

The most prominent feature in her experience was *humility*. She always seemed deeply abased before God. I scarcely ever conversed with her in her last illness, but she reminded me of the parable of the Pharisee and Publican. It seemed as if she thought herself unworthy to lift up her eyes to heaven. The prayer which best suited her feelings was, "God be merciful to me a sinner!" She asked my pardon for any perverseness or impatience that she had shewn to me at any time. This disposition was so clearly genuine in her, that I derived great comfort from our Lord's declaration, "This man went down to his house justified."

"This deep sense of her own sinfulness led her by faith to the Saviour of sinners. Her mind rejected all other ground of dependence, except the merit and intercession of her Redeemer. Her consolation increased gradually, as her death approached; yet it was often assaulted, and sometimes interrupted by fears.

"She manifested a most tender affection to her relations who were about her. One day she expressed to me her fear that she loved us too well; and when I assured her, that love to us was not inconsistent with love to God, she seemed comforted with the idea. She considered it as a great privilege to be permitted to love us.

"Her principal visitor was a poor pious woman, for whom she had contracted a great esteem, on account of the unremitting attention which this woman had shewn to another pauper, who had been bed-ridden a considerable time. My daughter left it as her dying request, that I would never suffer this poor woman to be in want.

"She spoke with great composure of her approaching departure; and looked forwards to heaven with humble confidence. She said several times, that she had never, during any part of her illness, wished to recover. She said one day, with considerable emphasis, 'I feel just now, as if I would not recover if I might.' She often repeated this expression, 'God does not willingly grieve his children; and he has promised, 'I will never leave thee nor forsake thee.' She said to her mother and sisters, at different times, it was a great comfort to her to think, that to be 'absent from the body' was to be 'present with the Lord.' When her desires to depart were the most lively, she expressed great submission to her sufferings, and begged her sisters to pray for her, that her faith might not fail.

"Some weeks before her departure, she was distressed with fears of the agonies of death, and mentioned what her brother had suffered during the last two days of his illness. Her sisters advised her not to distress herself with such apprehensions, as it might please God never to try her in that way, which, through mercy, was the case. She replied, 'Then I will leave it with him, and do you all pray for me, that I may be delivered from the fear of death.' From that time she never expressed any apprehension or dread about the pains of death, except for a short time, upon hearing of the death of a young lady, who had suffered greatly from a cancerous complaint.

"She asked her sisters one evening to talk about heaven, and departed pious persons of her acquaintance. She said it was a comfortable idea to her, that she should meet her pious friends in glory.

"She was aware that many of the distressing thoughts which had harrassed her mind were suggestions of the devil. One day, having mentioned something which she considered as a suggestion of Satan, her sisters said to her, 'But he has no power to hurt you;' she replied strongly, 'No, I do not believe he has.'

"At another time she said to her sister R——, 'Never cavil at the Scriptures; it is a dangerous thing.'

"It pleased God to give her a more easy dismission from this state of trial than we were led to expect.

"The day preceding that of her death, she looked earnestly at her mother upon waking in the morning, who asked her if she wanted any thing? She replied, 'I want to be happy in God. Indeed, I have great need of comfort from him; pray for me, that I may be patient.'

"She requested that she might once more join with us in the holy ordinance of the Lord's Supper, which the Rev. Mr. ——— administered on the following day. She expressed great comfort after joining in this solemn ordinance, and about four hours afterwards quietly fell asleep in Jesus, departing without a sigh, or any other expression of pain."

OBITUARY

OF THE

REV. JOHN HEY.

TWELVE years after the death of my eldest son, and seven years after the death of my daughter, that gracious Being, whose ways are all directed by perfect wisdom and righteousness, saw fit to call hence another of my sons, about a year after he had entered upon the ministerial office.

He had given a preference to the ministry from his early youth; and, when a boy, had often expressed a desire of labouring as a missionary among the heathen. When he was eleven years of age, he wrote a short sermon on those words of the Apostle; "So then they that are in the flesh cannot please God." Romans viii. 8. This text was his own choice, and was explained in the manner which, I believe, is agreeable to its true meaning. He had been accustomed, by the directions of his master, under whose tuition he then was, to write down what he could remember of one of the sermons which he heard at church; and this excellent custom had, no doubt, made him so much acquainted with the composition of a sermon, as to enable him, at the age I have mentioned, to write a discourse, which, if enlarged, would not have been unsuitable to the pulpit.

The subsequent account will be chiefly collected from his private papers, his letters, and conversations with his most intimate friends during his last illness.

When he was seventeen years of age, he wrote the following short history of the preceding part of his life, to which he prefixed, as a motto, these texts of Scripture.

"Because thy loving kindness is better than life, my lips shall praise thee."

"Because thou hast been my help, therefore in the shadow of thy wings will I rejoice."

"I was born March the 8th.—I remember nothing till I was near six years old, except a few trifling circumstances. When I was about six years old, I was sent to Mr. B——'s school, at L——, where I remained till I was nine years old. I was there very guilty of telling lies, and chiefly such as would raise wonder and astonishment. 'Remember not the sins of my youth, nor my transgressions: according to thy mercy remember thou me, for thy goodness sake, O Lord!'"

"When I was nine years of age, I went to the school of the Rev. Mr. ——. There I spent much pleasant time. Mr. —— towards the first was a little severe; but my disposition wanted severity, and I have reason to be thankful that he was so, for he has done me more good than I can express, and more perhaps than I am conscious of.

"I had, at several different times, religious convictions while I was there. Being ill of a fever, when I was about ten years old, I was taken home; and formed there many resolutions of living a good life if I should recover. Nay, I then began, as I thought, to be good, whether I should live or die. But such kind of resolutions have always the same end; I forgot them all when I had recovered my health. Sometimes afterwards, I had again convictions of heart that I was not going on right. The right way, however, I knew not, though I might perhaps have the theory of religion. [Vide sermon written when I was eleven years of age.] But from Mr. R——'s most excellent conversation, and the Rev.

Mr. P——'s preaching, my conscience would not let me go on carelessly. I took up a scheme of self-righteousness. But when I began really to see Christ to be the way, the truth, and the life, then Satan, and my own wicked desires, were permitted to tempt me sorely. This happened when I was fourteen years of age. O how often have I been solicited to act in opposition to the dictates of my conscience! But O my soul, is there not enough, besides that time, enough to make thee sink to the ground in despair, but for my blessed, ever blessed Redeemer? 'Thanks be to God for his unspeakable gift.' Those temptations were to shew me my wickedness, and my weakness, and to engage me to apply to Christ for pardon and strength. But my repentances (so innumerable are they) have need to be repented of.

"By the grace of God in Christ, and by that alone, those temptations have begun to weaken. A sense of my immoderate pride is, I feel, to take place, in order to my humiliation before a holy God. I have not yet done with the former temptations. 'Remember unto thy servant, O Lord, the word on which thou hast caused him to hope.'

"When I was fifteen years old, I left Mr.

R——, and came to H——, O how bountifully has God dealt with me! O how infinitely more than I deserve! Every situation and change in life is better than the former. I hope I shall never be guilty of forgetting Mr. R—— and Mr. P——, they have been of such use to the affairs of my soul. This I know, that I *ought* not to forget them.

"But when I had got some footing in classical learning, as well as in that best of knowledge, how gracious was God in sending me to this place, than which I cannot conceive a better, one more fit for a scholar's proficiency in learning, and for a christian's growth in grace, and in the knowledge of Jesus Christ; I have the best of masters in both things.*

"While I feel the pride of my heart, and find also that my mind is too worldly, may I improve the grace which God hath provided, and make a proper use of all his dispensations.

"By the death of my dear sister Alice, I am to learn, that without God this world is vain and miserable. And other things I have to shew me, that the pleasures of it, and some

* The late Rev. Joseph Milner, Author of the "History of the Church of Christ," &c.

of them that are innocent in themselves, are despicable; for they have a tendency to estrange my mind from God and heavenly things.

"Have I not also just now an instance of of decrease in grace; of opportunities of grace not only lost, but abused? *

"And have I improved aright the privileges I enjoy? Ah no! But through the mercies of God I am what I am. For, thanks be to God, his grace living in me, I trust, has kept me from being dead to God in my soul. But it is his loving-kindness, and not my deserts. For I have deserved to be left long ago to my ownself; and had been so, but that I have to deal with a merciful God.

"Let it be my aim then to live to his glory. Whatever station he may assign me, let me take that as the most proper for me. Whatsoever I do, may I have the honour of God before me. In all my difficulties, let me apply to him, who is my truest friend; for he will direct me right. If I die soon, O may God be with me, and deliver me both in the hour of death, and in the day of judgment. If I am to live longer, may his word be a lamp unto my ways, and a lanthorn to my paths.

* Alluding to the conduct of one of his companions.

"And, O my soul, I charge thee, whether I be in sickness or in health, prosperity or adversity, in whatever way I am to pass through this transitory world, I charge thee forget not God, but be continually receiving Christ, as ever thou wouldest have him receive thee in a dying hour."

The following acknowledgment and address was written in the same year, the day after his birth-day.

"Preserved by thy goodness, O Lord, I would now make an acknowledgment of thy mercies to me. But, indeed, they are more than I can express or conceive. O the infinite goodness of God! I was lost in wickedness and sin; and must have been lost for ever, unless the incomprehensible love of God had snatched the fire-brand from the flame. Fifteen long years spent in open rebellion against a bountiful Creator and Preserver: and not this only, but also against the gospel of Christ, against my Redeemer.

"O blessed Jesus! what love to die for such a wretch as me! Yes, that *was* love. And now these two years that I have in some measure been led to see the value of a Redeemer, how cold and lifeless have I been. But I hope in some measure God has given me his grace, so as to increase in the knowledge and love of God.

"I am now entering upon my eighteenth year. Grant, O Lord, that before the conclusion of it, if I live so long, I may still make greater advances in the knowledge of thee and of myself. May I be preserved from falling away from thee. Thy service is perfect freedom; yea, the greatest pleasantness: and the paths of wisdom are indeed the paths of peace.

"Let me praise thy holy name, O Lord, for those that are departed out of this life in thy faith. May I follow her example,* and take courage, that I may go on in the right way rejoicing, hoping that we shall shortly meet again,—nothing is impossible with thee, and glory be to thee, that thou wilt be intreated by thy people. Thou art, indeed, a prayer-hearing God; more ready to hear than we to pray. When I sought the Lord, he heard me. Yes, Lord, I can see many, many prayers thou hast answered: nor wilt thou forsake me. Thou knowest my inmost thoughts and my desires; but what thou seest better to withhold, thou wilt in goodness there oppose my request.

* Alluding to the death of his sister Alice.

"Gracious God! I would not change; I would not let go my Jesus for all that ten thousand worlds could afford!

"'O that I had an angel's tongue,
And could be heard from pole to pole,
I would to all the listening world
Proclaim thy goodness to my soul.'

"Keep me now, O Lord, by thy mighty power, through the rest of my life. I would be thy ambassador to sinful men: O guide me right, nor let me enter uncalled into that sacred office. Of what importance is it! Let me take care, lest I myself become a castaway! and guide me right with respect to being thy messenger to the beclouded nations of the world. If it be thy will, it is my greatest happiness. Decide thou for me. Into thy hands I commit myself and all my affairs. Do thou with me as will most promote thy glory, and the success of thy glorious gospel. But if I be taken hence sooner, may it be a change to everlasting happiness: may it be a removal from a world of vanity, into Abraham's bosom, there to praise thy glorious name through the countless ages of *eternity*. And now, O Lord, I would commit myself into thy hand. I would be thine, O Lord;

O keep me so! Guide me through this life of darkness; and let thy word be a lamp unto my path. May all my actions tend to the glory of thy name, and the honour of Christianity. Christ is all in all. May I put him on; may he teach me; may he cleanse me; may he daily sanctify me, that I may be at last fitted for the eternal enjoyment of God the Father, Son, and Holy Ghost, the blessed Trinity, one God Almighty for ever! Amen."

The following was written on his birthday, when he entered upon his twentieth year, and while he resided at —— College, in Cambridge.

"When I look back upon the past year, how am I called upon to humble myself before God! I must lay my hand upon my mouth, and my mouth in the dust, if so be there may be hope; for I am vile. I have not walked so faithfully with God as I ought. The sin, which so easily besets me, has had too much encouragement. The table of the Lord has not witnessed that contrition, that fervour in me, which ever it used to do; and my heart has been ever ready to start aside like a broken bow. 'O Lord, examine me, and try me, see what wicked way is in me, and lead me in the way everlasting.'

"But the mercy of God has been renewed to me continually. Before I left H——, when I cast all my cares upon God, he cared for me. Since I have been here, how mercifully has God dealt with me; how has he preserved me from the snares and vanities which surround me! How has he blest me with kind and useful friends! The state of discipline I am now under, is wonderfully calculated for my good, and God blesses my studies. Let me, then, now devote myself afresh to God.

"I have spent nineteen years of my life, and know not how much longer I may be spared.

"I have been warned by the death of my cousin H. H. and the lamentable end of a school-fellow, to prepare to meet my God. O Lord, may I be thine here, that I may enjoy thee for ever hereafter! May I never be ashamed of the gospel of Christ! May I walk closer with thee my God, for this is my greatest happiness!—Preserve me, O Lord, from all evil! 'Thy mercy, O Lord, endureth for ever; forsake not the work of thine own hands.'"

I found a paper written by him at the expiration of that year, in which he entered upon the ministry. He begins his reflections thus:—"I am now come to the end of another year: what an eventful year has this been to me! It has been marked by important events, in all which I hope I have been in the way of duty." Of the last of these events he writes thus:—"In December, I took deacon's orders. May God make me 'a burning and shining light' to his glory! I would endeavour to follow the guidance of Providence, wherever that would lead me. I would have the glory of God to be my chief aim, whatever trials and crosses I may thereby be exposed to; for I know, that even here I shall eventually be the happier, the more uprightly I walk in the path of duty: and hereafter, when time shall appear a mere point, crosses will be nothing, they will be as the light affliction of a moment, but they may 'work out an eternal weight of glory.' May I then devote myself to God and his service!

"'Since God doth thus his wond'rous love
Through all my life extend;
That life to him I will devote,
And in his temple spend.'"

After the disorder, which proved fatal to

him, had rendered him incapable of performing the public duties of the ministry, he left the curacy in which he was placed, and came to my house. He was not aware of the danger of his state, which to the eye of his friends was too strongly pictured in his countenance. The state of his mind, at this period, may be judged of by the following note, which was found among his papers after his death, and, from the date of it, appeared to have been written soon after his return home.

"I think I never had any personal affliction of consequence before this, except a fever when I was young.

"I have been for some time afraid, lest such an uninterrupted series of prosperity and health should draw me from the gracious Author of all my mercies. I prayed that, if it was his will, I might rather suffer affliction, than be permitted to depart from him and cleave to this world. Behold the issue! Am I not warranted to consider my prayer as answered? But it teaches me a lesson of humility; it teaches me that I cannot bear an uninterrupted course of good things. How thankful then should I be, that the Almighty deigns to take me under his paternal care, and to put me into the purifying furnace of affliction!"

A short time before he took holy orders, he made known to me his purpose of entering into the marriage state. From the various conversations which I had with him on this subject, I was satisfied that religion, prudence, and affection, had united in determining his choice. I mention the circumstance in this place, because of the allusion to it in the following reflections, which he wrote in the evening after I had informed him of the danger with which his disease was accompanied. Were I at liberty to give a full account of his conduct respecting this transaction, I should offer one of the strongest proofs of the powerful influence of divine grace upon his mind. I shall only observe, in the language of one who was intimately acquainted with his views and conduct in this affair,—" I think no circumstance can more strikingly exemplify the power of religion, than that of a young man of ardent affections and sanguine hopes, quietly resigning the object of his love; and looking forward to that stroke which should rend asunder the tenderest tie, not only with calmness but with joy."

Reflections written immediately after he had been informed of his danger.

" I have indeed been deceiving myself respecting my complaint. My father has this evening informed me of the dangerous state of health I am in. O Lord, support me, that I may cheerfully accomplish whatsoever thou wouldest have me to do or suffer! This is a severe trial, when I consider my connexion with my dear ——. But *God's will be done.* His will is best. I would glorify God for this consolation, in that I am sure whatever is the issue, I shall have reason to praise and adore him for it. It will be goodness and mercy; only let me put my whole trust in my Heavenly Father. Whilst thousands around me are living the enemies of God, and heirs of eternal wrath, behold God has made me a monument of his mercy. Ah! how unworthy of the very least of his mercies! And yet by his grace, I trust he has made me a child of God, and an heir of eternal glory! 'Behold what manner of love, that we should be called the sons of God!'

'Lord, we adore thy ways,
To bring us near to God;
Thy sovereign power, thy healing grace,
And thine atoning blood!'"

The following day, being Sunday, he attended the worship of God at church, and this was the last time he was able to join the public congregation, which was his delight. Two parts of the service, the collect and the sermon, happened to be peculiarly suitable to his situation. It was the twentieth Sunday after Trinity, when this excellent prayer came in course. "O Almighty and most merciful God, of thy bountiful goodness keep us, we beseech thee, from all things that may hurt us; that we being ready both in body and soul, may cheerfully accomplish those things that thou wouldest have done, through Jesus Christ our Lord." He seemed much struck with its suitableness, and mentioned it in a letter to one of his most intimate friends, as expressing the temper of mind which he laboured to possess.

The Rev. Mr. ——— preached a most instructive sermon from those awful words, "Give an account of thy stewardship, for thou mayest be no longer steward." Luke xvi. 2. He received it as a message from God, reminding him of his speedy departure; and the rest of my family were much struck with the remarkable coincidence of circumstances.

About two months before his death, he received a visit from a young Clergyman, who had been his fellow-student at the University, and who was one of his most intimate friends. They had maintained a correspondence with each other after they were called to labour in different parts of the Lord's vineyard, and at this interview (which continued some days) their conversation appeared to be free and unreserved. At the request of myself and family, my son's friend favoured me with the following account of their conversations.

"He had expressed a readiness to talk with me on the subject of my last letter,—death,—its awfulness,—supports against the fear of it,—and comfort under its approach. I said, I had felt a little misgiving about my letter, whether I had not spoken too unreservedly to him upon the subject. 'No, no,' he replied, 'it grieves me to be written to in any other way; to be considered otherwise than as a dying man.' I said, it gave me great pleasure to find him so supported and comforted in such circumstances, and particularly with such calmness and reflection; and that he had the same sense which I had expressed of the great awfulness of death, and was *yet* so to speak, supported *against* those views. He said, that he did find *great peace;* that God had peculiar consolations to impart at such times; and 'his comforts,' said he, 'refresh my soul!'

"The conversation then turned to *the ground* of his hope. The general ground of all our hopes towards God, there was no need for him to speak of. We knew each other's sentiments upon that subject. They cannot be better set forth, than as they appear in a letter written by him a short time before, where he has these words;—'The enjoyment of that bliss which I hope to receive, *vile* and *unworthy* as *I* am, for the sake of my *blessed* and *adorable Saviour*, in whom alone is my hope and trust, in that he suffered for me, and is now interceding for me at God's right hand.' The point to be shewn at this time was, by what mode of arguing his mind was satisfied and supported in the conclusion, concerning his own personal interest in Christ, and salvation through him. His words upon this subject were few, but very striking, and highly satisfactory. 'I have the Bible,' said he; 'I am perfectly convinced that it is from God: this, therefore, is a sure ground, a firm foundation to rest on. Well,—I read it,—and I cannot but hope and be persuaded, that I do experience what I there read described, as distinguishing the blessed; and *on that ground I cannot but be confident.*' This, he said, was the general ground of his satisfaction and comfort; and then added something again on the assistance of God's Spirit, in enabling him to make use of this hope, and in affording him peculiar consolations.

"He then went on to speak of the necessity of such a hope, and such supports, in the prospect of death; and of the necessity of making religion our care, and most serious concern while in health. On these subjects he spoke with some emotion; and his mind seemed to rise, and become more warm as he proceeded. 'Oh,' he said, '*what should I do, what should I do*, if I were now *unconverted*, and had not this hope!' 'A state of sickness,' he said, 'is not the time first to apply our minds to religion.' He deeply felt this. 'We then need all its sweetest consolations;—to receive them is as much as we are capable of. Then is no time for close self-examination, and the work of repentance. This is too severe, *far too severe* a work for that time.'

"His thoughts then turned to his inexpressible obligations to Almighty God for such hopes; for *his* being 'indulged' with them, (he spoke in the most humiliating language of himself,) who had been such a sinner against God, and who had continued so sinful; who had been so vilely ungrateful to him, and had been brought to love and serve him: that *he* should have such hopes! 'His prospects,' he said, 'might righteously have been quite the reverse. He might justly have been lying in his present situation, with nothing before him but the expectation of *misery for ever*. But instead of this, here,' he said, 'I am enjoying the prospect of everlasting blessedness and glory!'

"'He hath chosen me to this! I can give no reason for it! I am most unworthy!'

"With this subject his mind seemed much affected. He repeated his broken sentences; meditating upon them with himself, as well as addressing them to me, or rather perhaps to God; for his conversation seemed very much turned into devotion at the close: till at length not finding words fully to express his conceptions, he took up the Bible, and giving it to me, desired me to read aloud to him the first chapter of St. Peter's first Epistle, from verse three to verse nine inclusive. 'Blessed be the God and Father of our Lord Jesus Christ, which, according to his abundant mercy, hath begotten us again unto a lively hope,' &c. As I finished this passage, a parcel of his manuscripts arrived from his brother, at ———, and our conversation ended. It was highly edifying, and comforting at the time; and is not less so in the review. 'The righteous hath *hope* in his death.'

"In some part of the conversation I remember he said, I think after mentioning the ground of our hopes towards God, as stated above, — 'This is what I have believed, and what I have been endeavouring to preach; and this is what I now find supports me.'

"On the day I parted with him, I remarked, as I sat near him in the afternoon,— 'It is five years and a fortnight this evening since we first met in the chapel of ——— College.' He seemed a good deal pleased at the recollection, as his kind and affectionate heart always led him to be with any such little circumstance.

"The same afternoon, I think, he told me of some particular fault he had observed in my reading while I was at ———. He said, 'We ought to be assisting one another in every way we can; particularly in whatever may at all tend to the better discharge of our ministerial functions.' He added, 'I have always considered this as a duty, and shall now have little more opportunity.'

"At parting, less passed than I could have wished. It was a night on which we attended service at church; and when I returned to the house, I found him asleep. We had, however, a little time together afterwards. I said to him, it was an afflicting thing now to bring our friendship (which had been of great comfort to me) as it were to a close, and to part probably to meet no more in this world. He said, the separation was not final,—it was only for a short time. His mind seemed fully possessed with such sentiments. He observed, that if we were but where it was our duty to be, and doing what God called us to, the rest was of little importance.

"He desired I would pray with him for a few minutes. I asked if there was any particular thing he would wish me to have in view? At first he said, 'No;' but afterwards calling my attention again, he said, 'Only that I may be *thoroughly prepared to die.*'

"Afterwards he spoke in few words of the peace of his mind. He said, he could not rise to great heights of devotion; his feelings were rather benumbed. His disease in some measure produced that effect, and his medicines still more.* He added, that the state of his mind was not always alike; but that he

* At this time it became necessary to moderate a diarrhœa, which disturbed him much, by the administration of opiates.

had an abiding peace, and an habitual confidence in Christ,—this supported him.

"When I was once speaking of the great calmness and recollection which attended his comfort, (as I have already related,) and was seeming to prefer such a state of mind to that ecstatic joy, which appears in some dying Christians,—he said, 'We are not to make comparisons of that kind, and prefer one state to the other. God is pleased to give his people sometimes triumphant joy in death; and when that is the case, it is a great testimony for religion.'"

The following account was communicated to me by one of his sisters, who waited upon him during the latter part of his illness.

"The conversations which I had with my brother J———, were but short. One day when I was dressing him, he observed how very thin he was become, and added, with a pleasant smile, 'I am glad of it; it is a good sign.'

"At another time he called me to him, and after we had arranged some particulars respecting his food, &c. he said, 'Well, in a little time I shall have done with all these contrivances.' I replied, 'It is a joyful prospect to you.' He said, very feelingly, '*It is indeed.*'

"After speaking to him a little on the firm source of comfort to be derived from that full, perfect, and sufficient sacrifice which our great High Priest has made for us, he said, with great emphasis and animation,—'That is the thing,—without *Christ crucified*, all would be dark and uncomfortable. After a little pause, he added, 'I thank God my mind continues strong,—I think, at least, in some respects, it does.' 'That is, your attention is sooner wearied, but your judgment continues sound, and your mind is not harassed by groundless fears and scruples?' 'No, I thank God, I have none. The Lord is on my side, and he has been my helper.'

"One Sunday, when I staid at home with him, he expressed himself strongly respecting the benefit which he had derived from Mr. ———'s ministry and conversations.* He then desired me to read some passages out of the Revelations, descriptive of the happiness of the blessed; and turning to me with a most sweet look, said, '*That is heaven!*'

"A few days before he died, he asked me to read him the one hundred and twenty-first Psalm. When I had finished it, he said, 'What a sweet Psalm!' and asked me to

* The Clergyman whose Curate he had been.

read the second verse over again,—'My help cometh from the Lord, who made heaven and earth; and then with grateful astonishment he exclaimed, 'What a thing! that the Creator of heaven and earth should be *my* helper,—no less a character than he!' He then spoke of some circumstances which he supposed to be indications of his approaching dissolution, and added, 'I had once hoped to see my brother R———, but I give it up.' I replied, 'If we do but all meet in heaven, the separation will be very short:' he said, 'I trust we shall.'

"After being silent awhile, he said, 'I wish I could bear to say more, but you know the foundation of my hope,—*Jesus Christ and him crucified.*'"

In this state of mind he quietly resigned his spirit into the hands of his gracious Redeemer; and exchanged the society of his friends on earth, I trust, for that of "the spirits of just men made perfect."

OBITUARY.

HIS SON ROBERT HEY.

HAVING intimated ("Christian Observer," Vol. I. page 685) my intention of sending to you some account of my four adult children, whom it has pleased God to remove from me; and having experienced your kind attention to the three accounts which I have already sent, my delay in sending the fourth seems to require an apology.

The truth is, I was afraid of being too obtrusive upon the patience of your readers, by such multiplied anecdotes of my own family. Having now reason to hope, by intimations from different quarters, that the completion of my design will prove agreeable to many who are constant readers of your Miscellany, I proceed to finish the plan which I proposed in my first letter.

The youngest of my departed sons (as he afterwards assured us when in the immediate views of death) had many religious impressions upon his mind during his childhood; but no solid change of heart seemed to take place till about the fourteenth year of his age. When a little boy he was artful and selfish. His capacity was quick; but he wanted the openness and friendliness of his brother, of whom I last sent you an account. They were companions at School and at the University, for they both made choice of the ministry; though that choice was made in a full view of its being a renunciation of all worldly prospects for Christ's sake. This idea I pressed strongly upon their minds. When, by the power of divine grace, their hearts were renewed in righteousness, they became united by the most intimate friendship and tender affection towards each other. The following letter, written by the younger to the elder, when they were school-boys, shews the foundation of their friendship, and manifests the state of the writer's mind.

He was at this time in his fifteenth year, and was about to follow his brother, who had a short time before been removed to H———. It was written after an interview with each other among some friends. The simplicity of the style must be excused.

"Dear J——;

"I was much obliged to you for your wishing to have been able to speak to me on subjects of a religious kind. I often desired it, but one thing or other hindered it. I plainly perceived you would second me in any thing towards the welfare of my soul. I am glad I have an opportunity, by Mr. D——, to thank you for your kind letter which I received at T——. It was more pleasant than one on any other subject. I read it over and over, and I hope it did me much good. Oh! it is a hard thing to be truly humble, so much pride in one thing and another. I try to suppress it as much as I can by passages of Scripture. I pray to God to help me to do it, and I trust I shall in some measure conquer it. I think of these passages: man is only sinful dust and ashes,—a poor worm of the earth. 'Humble thyself under the mighty hand of God, and he shall exalt thee in due time.' So much vanity lies in the heart; prayer seems the best means to conquer it: prayer with diligence and faith. I have looked diligently, and I think I have perceived many things in which God has answered me. I am often troubled with wicked thoughts, yet God in general gives me to conquer them. How delightful is it to meditate on the love of Christ, and to seem to have a view of him with all the holy angels with him in heaven. It makes one wish to depart from this sinful world, and go to him, there to be with him face to face, serving him without ceasing day and night, and to be the sons of God. This is, indeed, such a privilege as no human heart can be aware of. When one's mind seems to grow weary in well doing, then these words are very cheering; ' Be thou faithful unto death, and I will give thee a crown of life," &c.

The greatest part of his life was passed in a state of affliction, as may be seen from the following general account of his trials. When he was about six years old, he had the misfortune to receive a violent blow upon his head, which separated part of the scalp from the bone. During the progress of healing, the glands in his neck, on the injured side, became enlarged, and after the wound was healed the disease extended itself to the opposite side of the neck. Repeated attacks of this disease took place, year after year; on which account it was judged proper that he should spend a considerable part of the summer season either at the sea, or an inland watering place. The latter seemed peculiarly useful to him, and was chiefly the place of his abode. There he promoted the establishment of Sunday Schools, which he superintended with great diligence; and he there contracted a great friendship for two or three poor pious men, who were employed as masters.

Besides the affliction which I have mentioned, he was subject to violent head-aches, especially upon any close mental application. This disorder proved a great impediment to his learning: yet such was his capacity and application at school and at the University, that he obtained two classical prizes in his own college, and was placed on an equality with the first of his year for mathematical knowledge.

Before he left the University a general debility supervened, so that he was at last obliged to forego his disputations in the schools, as he was unable either to prepare for this exercise, or to stand for the purpose of carrying it on. He was carried in a chair to the Senate House, when he took his degree of Bachelor of Arts.

After quitting the University he was unable to attend to any discourse that was long, or that required close application of mind in the hearer. An attempt to exercise his mental powers in this way brought on immediately a head-ache, and an increase of his general debility.

During the winter, after he returned home, he went out frequently in an open carriage, which he preferred to a close one; but the severity of the weather, after some time, affected his breast with a sense of soreness. A spitting of blood came on, which was soon succeeded by a cough and a confirmed consumption, of which he died in May following.

But to return. When he was at school with the Rev. Mr. R——, he was exercised in the excellent customs of writing down the sermon after his return from church, and keeping a journal of his private thoughts and common transactions, with a promise from his master that these secret papers should never be inspected by him. I repeatedly saw these journals lying among his papers when he was at home; but I scrupulously abstained from inspecting them. He continued this custom as long as he was able to write; but during his last illness he destroyed all that he had written previously to his going to the University. The remainder he gave to one of his sisters, with the following note prefixed.

"Some of my journals I have burnt, because there was too much talk and too little sincerity. As far as I know myself, these are more sincere; but they should be called R. H——'s good wishes, and not the account of the state of his soul. Read them so, and if they do you good, I shall be glad of it.

"Your affectionate brother."

In his nineteenth year, while he was yet at school, he made a solemn dedication of himself to God; and in that transaction made use of the shorter form proposed by the pious Dr. Doddridge, adding a sentence relative to his intended future employment in the ministry. This solemn instrument was kept secret from his most intimate friends, but was found among his private papers after his death.

The change wrought in him by divine grace, truly exemplified the description of a real Christian given by the Apostle, "If any man be in Christ, he is a *new creature*." 2 Corinthians v. 17. Instead of the low cunning and selfishness, which prevailed in him when a boy, he became open, generous, and affectionate; and while his attentions to those who were about him partook of an easy politeness, he manifested on all occasions a considerable degree of heavenly-mindedness. His real character will be clearly discerned by the following extracts from his journals, and the minutes of conversations with his most intimate friends and relations. His views of his own spiritual state were not always alike. His disorder often created a depression of spirits, which cast a gloom upon his spiritual comforts, though it did not always destroy his cheerfulness.

Soon after his arrival at the University, in the conclusion of his nineteenth year, he made the following observations in his journal :—" Hither am I come to finish my studies for the ministry. O Lord, impress it upon my mind, that I am now preparing to be thy servant, to speak in thy name to those who are enemies to thee! Since I came hither, I set apart an evening to look over my act of self-dedication, with a design to direct my views aright. I rejoice that I made that act. O that I had kept it with more sincerity, zeal, and love! Lord, by thy grace, I resolve to seek thy face, and be thy servant, and seek the salvation of my soul through my Redeemer, notwithstanding the scoffs and jests of a profane and wicked world! O grant me sincerity, and lead me in the right way; and teach me in all my ways to acknowledge thee, so shalt thou direct my paths!"

After he had been about three months at the University, he took a review of his conduct, his studies, and the temper of his mind. In this part of his journal, I find the following declaration: "I think, as far as I can discover of my heart, I would love my Saviour, and consent more and more to his dominion over me. There is a strong body of sin yet in me. My Saviour, I come to thee without money and without price, hoping for thy merciful aid to enlighten my eyes that I may know thee. As the all-wise Providence of God has placed me here, let me consider the duties more particularly incumbent on me."

These duties he enumerates, and then adds, —"O Lord, teach me this, that laying aside every besetting sin, I may run with patience the race set before me. The more I grow in grace, and the knowledge of my Lord and Saviour Jesus Christ, the more pure and blameless will my conduct be; and the more fitted shall I be for the important office of the ministry. May I here count the cost, and place to the account, labour, and difficulty, contempt, disgrace, and all the trials which those have experienced, who have stood up in their Master's cause, remembering that he suffered too. Yet, on the other side, I must place the abundant recompence of the gospel."

On the following Christmas Day he writes thus;—"O my God, whom I have sworn to serve, and to look up to in all my ways, do thou condescend to direct my path. I hope I can cheerfully submit to thy will, rejoicing that thou art pleased to take any notice of me thy unworthy servant. I have this day looked over my solemn covenant with thee, and confirmed it anew at thy table. Lord, I humbly implore thee, call me not into judgment for my many breaches of it, but strengthen me with divine power and energy, that I may observe it with readiness and constancy, and that an affecting remembrance of it may keep me from sinning against thee, and may hold me in that state of watchfulness in which I should wish to be found at thy awful appearance!"

When he had completed his twenty-second year, he entered the following reflections in his journal:—" I hope God has enabled me to feel a small degree of gratitude for adding another year to my life, and one in which I have received so many mercies at his hand. Perhaps my life is near a close, or perhaps other twenty-two years may be added, if so they will pass to sense much more rapidly than the last; and then, O my soul, thy everlasting doom will be sealed. God grant me his grace to quicken my careless sense to more serious diligence and care for my immortal soul. Surely at the most, to my weak frame, a third of my existence in this world may be completed. Oh, solemn thought! How can my heart be so besotted and tricked by present duties * and enjoyments as to make me forget, that my time of probation must soon for ever end, and I must enter, willing or unwilling, prepared or unprepared, into the world of spirits. It is truly astonishing, that I can pass my moments in so unconcerned a manner. Thy grace alone, O Lord, can incline my thoughtless heart to watchfulness and prayer, that my loins may be girt about, and my lamp burning, that so, when the cry of thy coming shall be heard, I may

* Meaning those secular employments to which he was in duty bound to attend.

be found ready to enter with thee to the marriage."

The accounts which he received in the course of this year, of the indisposition of his brother affected him much. They had been (as I have already observed) companions from their childhood, and had a tender affection for each other. Upon hearing of his brother's danger, he wrote thus in his journal:—"This last week has been a week of affliction to me. On Tuesday I received very unfavourable accounts of my brother J——, so that now it seems scarcely probable I shall ever see him again. Oh, that this news may have an abiding impression! Whether my brother recovers, or whether it should please God that this be his last illness, may I lay to heart the lesson it holds forth to me; that in the present moment I may make the Lord my portion; may I possess an interest in my Redeemer, so that when flesh and heart fail, the Lord Jesus may be the strength of my heart, and my portion for ever."

Having heard of the happy state of his brother's mind, he writes thus in his journal:—"My heart feels knit to him now more than ever; his conduct in this trying hour is so exemplary. He is patient under the hand of God, though it is so severe; and God enables him to place a steadfast trust in his Redeemer. May this lead me to trust in God, who will give strength according to our day, and will certainly with the temptation give an ability to bear it." In this confident expectation he was not disappointed; but experienced the same support and consolation in his last trial as had been vouchsafed to his brother.

His weakness increased about this time, so as to render him unable to walk without crutches. Upon this circumstance he makes the following reflections:—" This day I have been worse, and though it was Sunday I could not attend any place of worship. In the morning, and former part of the afternoon, I felt excessively low, from the idea (perhaps chiefly) that this lameness might long continue, and be a serious impediment to me all my life. I was, however, mercifully much comforted by reading some of our church-prayers, &c. They seemed peculiarly sweet to me. May I learn, O Lord, to " set my affections on things above, where Christ sitteth at the right hand of God." May Christ be *my* comfort, *my* hope, and all *my* trust. On what can my affections be more rationally founded? He is the source of consolation to the poor sinner. May I cordially commit all my concerns to his direction; for " he that spared not his own Son, but freely delivered him up for us all," (for *me* also,) " how shall he not with him freely give us all things ?"

He experienced in his affliction the greatest kindness from his friends in the University, both on account of his own weakness, and the loss which he sustained at this time of a beloved brother. He takes notice of these acts of kindness, in his journal, with strong expressions of gratitude.

In some reflections upon his afflictions, written a short time before he left the University, I find the following remarks :—" If I am not a child of God, I have no reason to complain of my afflictions being too great a punishment for my sins ; and if I am, is there not cause for the greatest thankfulness that God will take thought for my concerns ? Oh, the wonderful condescension of God, that he vouchsafes to order any of the events of our life ! By thy grace, O Lord, this view softens my hard heart, and I would cry out, ' *My* Lord, and *my* God.' In such moments I can say, ' Thy will be done ;' and would not wish to be well. I would not boast. How rarely can I thus exercise myself. It is thy gift, O blessed Spirit !"

Having mentioned in his journal the prizes which had been adjudged to him in the college, he subjoins the following reflections: —"Let not these things puff up my foolish heart, O Lord; but may I learn from them an useful lesson; that although the talents thou hast given me be not great, and my infirmities hinder me from any great exertions, yet from this experience I may hope, that by thy blessing on my future studies, I may so improve myself as to be an useful member in the place thou hast appointed for me, and may, in some measure, glorify thy name. And oh, if it be thy will, strengthen my weak frame in thy due time, that I may come forth in thy name to invite and persuade many poor sinners to turn from the error of their ways, and shew them the knowledge of the adorable Redeemer and Saviour Jesus Christ. Amen."

When reflecting upon his afflictions, and the effect produced upon his mind by them, he makes humiliating confessions too numerous to be inserted here. I shall give the following as a specimen, written about ten months before his death.

"It is God's good pleasure that I should be still afflicted with much weakness. What shall I say of my submission? What of the improvement I have made under these afflictions? I find myself to have been more deficient than I thought I was, when in a state of health. My religion has been too much of a form. When the trial has come to prove the sincerity of my ways, they have been found weak and faithless. I think this is the greatest benefit I have received; a little greater knowledge of my own corruption, and of the deceitfulness and desperate wickedness of my heart before the great and eternal God. O Lord, let me not deceive myself in this, through vanity and ignorance. I would examine my heart now, and call my sins to remembrance, for thou hast visited me. Yet before thee I must confess, that the calls thou hast made to me, and the opportunities now offered to me of weaning my heart from the world and fixing it upon thee, who oughtest alone to be the desire and hope of my soul, have been disregarded and slighted to my shame. Where I might have improved, I have neglected it; and sometimes I have even inwardly murmured at what I should rather have thought a token of thy favour and love: and when thou hast granted me a peaceful acquiescence, I have spoiled it by my pride, and have grieved thee, Holy Spirit, to leave me again to my own natural darkness, and to the wicked suggestions of my own heart. Though I am so hard and perverse, O Lord, still forbear with me! Thou didst not withhold thine only Son from us; O that with Him thou wouldest grant me, through the Holy Spirit, a thorough change of heart!"

His general state of mind was placid and cheerful; and he looked upon his afflictions as mercies sent from God. The following extract points out his reflections upon an increase of his complaints:—"My weakness continues. I was better last week, and my hopes revived. They are now again taken away, in mercy, no doubt. Job saw the end of the Lord, that he is pitiful and of great mercy; therefore, O my soul, be not cast down, for *thou* also shalt see in the end the goodness of the Lord. This weakness and misery of my body shall be health and blessing to my soul. 'Hope thou in God, for *thou* shalt still praise him, who is the help of thy countenance, and thy God.'"

The conclusion of his journal was written about a month before his death, and manifests the state of his mind in the view of a speedy dissolution: "The Lord is righteous in all his ways, and holy in all his works." I would add, therefore, (and I hope heartily,) "Thy will be done." It has pleased God to afflict me with a disorder unto death, which was a great surprise as well as shock to me.* But why should it? Have I not had a long warning? But cease there. — Into what a new and awful situation am I now brought! In a few weeks I shall be in *eternity!* O what a word! and coming upon a great sinner! I thank God for his unspeakable Gift. Through him I have hope; and though the waters often go over my head, my God shows me the hope of the gospel. I will trust in the Lord Jehovah to the end, and not be afraid, for he is my salvation; and here I would acknowledge the mercy shown to my body thus far. I have been confined three months, and have had but little pain: the symptoms of the disease have been mild, and I have received the greatest affection and care from my friends. I would and do pray for them, that they and I may, through the same grace, arrive in the same glory: and now, O Lord, what remains for me during the short remnant of my life? I know not,—thou knowest. I must necessarily suffer more; but be it unto me according to thy word; only grant me thy

* The complaint of which he died was one to which he had had no previous apparent tendency, having never been subject to a cough, or other disorder of the lungs.

gracious presence, and the sense of thy love in Christ, and I ask no more. I now commend my soul and body unto thee, for thou hast redeemed them, O Lord God of truth. Amen."

As a postscript to this he added, with an asterism to the words, "I ask no more." "Should I not have added, that I may glorify that good, and holy, and gracious God and Saviour, whose I am, and whom I would serve? Lord, show me how I may glorify thee now!"

When the cough and spitting of blood had confined him to the house, he thought it his duty to abstain from every thing that might aggravate his disorder, and therefore sat much in silence. When he addressed himself to us it was generally in a whisper, or by writing down his thoughts. He was very desirous of examining carefully into the state of his soul, and lamented to me, that he found himself incapable of pursuing a course of self-examination, as he wished thoroughly to try the foundation of his hopes. He said he was the more desirous of doing this, as he felt much the corruption of his own heart, and saw, with grief, the defects of his obedience to God. As I was convinced of his utter inability to pursue any close train of thinking, and was satisfied of the sincerity of his faith and obedience, I ventured to give him the following advice. After reminding him that he was now called to passive, rather than to active obedience, I requested him, instead of labouring to draw comfort from a close examination of his own heart, of which he was now incapable, to cast himself as a lost sinner at the feet of Christ, trusting only to his precious death, his merits, and intercession. Some time after this conversation he informed me, that he had found great help and comfort from pursuing the method which I had recommended to him.

He did not, however, lose sight of that command so plainly given in the Word of God; " Examine yourselves, whether ye be in the faith; prove your ownselves." 2 Cor. xiii. 5. but took the opportunity, as his enfeebled powers would permit, of doing that by degrees which he could not do at once. He told me one day, at an advanced period of his disease, that he was thankful to God for protracting his affliction, and thereby giving him the opportunity of making that examination " by little and little," (as he expressed himself,) which his debility had rendered him incapable of doing at once.

The mental debility under which he laboured was great beyond any thing that I ever saw or heard of, in a person whose judgment was perfectly clear and correct. I have often been obliged to stop short, when conversing with him on subjects that required pretty close attention, as the application of mind would suddenly bring the head-ache; and what is more remarkable, would evidently increase his general bodily weakness.

Though he delighted to join with us in our family worship, which was never continued to any great length, yet he acknowledged to me that he could seldom keep up his attention to the conclusion, but was obliged to stay the exercise of his thoughts as soon as that exercise began to bring on his head-ache. This cessation of thought he found himself capable of, and was often obliged to have recourse to it.

As soon as the symptoms of a confirmed consumption appeared, I made him acquainted with his danger; and it was very apparent, that from that time he enjoyed more uniform composure of mind, and often a good degree of cheerfulness. Many of his observations, respecting his apparel and food, showed with what serenity he looked forwards to his approaching dissolution.

He often wished us to relate to him any

anecdotes respecting the dying conduct of his two brothers and sister who had gone before; and took great delight in hearing of the patience and pious behaviour of a young man, his cousin, who had died in triumph after a long series of complicated sufferings.

To his youngest brother, who was at some distance from home pursuing his studies for the ministry, he wrote, " How we drop off! four, a little more than a year ago; now, we are three; and, I may add, soon will be two. God give us grace to improve!"

When this brother came home to see him, he addressed himself to him thus: " Don't let your thoughts of me interrupt your studies. I trust, that by the unmerited mercy of God, and through the atonement of Christ, it shall be well with me. Indeed, I have been a great sinner, more than you know of, but Christ died for sinners. Of what consequence is it whether you ever see me again? I hope we are both doing the will of God: in that way we shall have a blessing; and I trust, both you and I, and the remainder of our family, shall join with those who are gone before, and be for ever with the Lord. Oh, S——, that will be happiness worth striving for, and worth dying for."

During the whole course of his illness he

manifested a strong affection to his parents, his brothers, and sisters, and, indeed, to all his friends who were about him. Having one day mentioned his nearest relations to a young person, his cousin, who was sitting by him, he added, " My father and mother, brothers and sisters, I love them better than ever I did before. I love them so as I cannot express; but I love God better,—I MUST LOVE HIM."

At another time, after affectionately kissing his eldest sister, Mrs. D——, who sat by him, he said, " How I love you, and that girl," (looking at his youngest sister, who was in the room;) " I feel the separation. I love you better and better; but I have not loved you as I ought, nor equal to your kindness to me." He said something more about the pain of parting with them, and then added, " Though I feel the mortification of parting, I shall have better company; you will allow that." Some conversation then passed concerning his brothers and sister, whom he hoped shortly to meet in glory, which he concluded by saying, " But I think of that the least;" (meaning the sight of his friends in heaven;) " I shall see God;" (then dwelt awhile on enumerating his attributes;) " and Jesus Christ, the Mediator of the new covenant, I shall see them in all their beauty; I shall be swallowed up in that; I shall want nothing else."

He received the attention and kind offices of his friends about him with great gratitude and humility, and one day expressed his thankfulness in these words;—"What a comfort it is to me to see every body doing things for me with pleasure; if they did them reluctantly, it would be misery to me, *unworthy as I am*."

Throughout the whole of his illness, the grand source of his consolation was the word of God. His great debility, which affected both his mental and bodily powers, rendered him incapable of reading or hearing with attention any considerable portion of Scripture at one time; but he frequently read or heard select portions, on which his mind seemed to feed with delight. The short remarks (too numerous to be recited here) which he made on the passages read to him, shewed that he felt their force, and entered deeply into their spiritual and instructive import. Passages, exciting to a strong faith in God through Christ, and to a deep humiliation of soul, were peculiarly pleasing to him.

When his disease was so far advanced, that

it became necessary to give him food in the night, he frequently requested the person who waited upon him, to read to him some passages of Scripture, when he received his refreshment.

His desire of being present at our morning family exercises was so great, that he requested to be brought down stairs in the arms of two servants, till within a few days of his death. Two days before that awful period, I happened to be near his bed in the morning when he was much oppressed with the cough, and rattling in his breathings, and I overheard him saying to himself, " These light afflictions, which are but for a moment, are not worthy to be compared with the glory that shall be revealed." In the evening he was somewhat relieved, and sent for me to pray with him. Before prayer he spoke to me of the goodness of God to him in many instances, and added, " I have often prayed that God would enable me to glorify him in that way which he saw best. Why should I be surprised that he calls me to glorify him in this way? He will work, and who shall let it?" The same evening he called his mother to him, saying, " Come, mother, give me a kiss and your blessing; I value a father's and a mother's blessing."

The day before his departure, the family met to have prayers in his room, which he seemed to enjoy. He made a sign to one of his sisters to draw back the bed-curtains, that he might see us all. During this day he underwent much bodily pain; and when apparently much distressed, was heard to say, "God's will be done; patience is best." At another time, "The conflict of death will soon be past." His sister, Mrs. D——, hearing him utter this last expression, said to him, "Christ has gone before, and will support you;" to which he replied with great earnestness, "I believe he will."

In the evening he received the sacrament at his own request, as he had twice before since his confinement to the house; and, notwithstanding his extreme weakness, repeated some of the prayers along with the minister. He seemed to bear a remembrance of the solemn dedication which he had made of himself to God when he was a school-boy; and at a very late period of his life was heard to repeat in a low, though very pathetic, voice, that affecting sentence in the form which he had made use of, "O God, look down with pity on thy languishing dying child."

A short time before he expired, his youngest sister, seeing him suffer much, said to him,

"You will soon be released;" to which he replied; "Yes, I trust I shall by the mercy of God." Not long after this it pleased God to grant him his dismission from the burden of the flesh, when, I trust, he entered into the joy of his Lord.

ON THE

LAWFULNESS

OF

DEFENSIVE WAR.

The situation in which our nation is now placed, makes the subject of war a matter of great importance. Leaving, however, to the judgment of politicians the necessity of our present contest with France, and to military men the proper mode of conducting it, I shall confine my observations to the consideration of its lawfulness as a defensive war. I write merely as a christian; and shall endeavour to discuss, in few words, this important question, Is defensive War lawful? Some persons may think this discussion to be a needless employment: but as we cannot be too careful in examining our conduct by the laws of God, and as all who profess to acknowledge the authority of Christ are not agreed upon this subject, I trust your readers will not think their time misemployed in perusing a plain inquiry into this matter, as a question of duty.

Here it must be observed, that no inconvenience, arising from our obedience to the laws of God, must ever be allowed as a plea for disobedience. I shall not, therefore, lay any stress upon the inconveniences or sufferings which the principle of the unlawfulness of war might bring upon us. If war is totally and absolutely unlawful, under every possible circumstance, we ought patiently to submit to all the privations which might ensue from a state of non-resistance. We should give up, not only the comforts and enjoyments of life, but life itself, when it cannot be preserved without committing an act of disobedience to the moral law of God. If this is not our principle of conduct, we have no right to consider ourselves as the disciples of Christ. Let us, therefore, inquire whether we can consistently with that love to our neighbour, which the moral law of God requires, repel with force the invasion, or other aggressions, of our enemies.

The whole of our duty to our fellow-creatures is comprehended in that summary of the second table of the moral law, which was given by our Saviour,—"Thou shalt love thy neighbour as thyself." And this command has been equally binding upon all who have been favoured with the revelation of God's will, under every dispensation.

Our Saviour rescued the moral law from the false glosses which the Jewish teachers had put upon it, but he made no alteration in it. When the Jewish lawyer inquired, "Which is the great commandment in the law?" the inquiry certainly related to the law as delivered to the Jews. "Jesus said unto him, Thou shalt love the Lord thy God, with all thy heart, and with all thy soul, and with all thy mind. This is the first and great commandment: and the second is like unto it, Thou shalt love thy neighbour as thyself. On these two commandments hang all the law and the prophets." Matthew xxii. 36—40. If defensive war, therefore, is contrary to the love of our neighbour under the Christian dispensation, it must have been also contrary to it under the Jewish economy; for Christ here expressly assures us, that to love our neighbours as ourselves was commanded both by the law and the prophets.

The Jewish teachers had, indeed, grossly

perverted the law of God on this head. They had taught, that it was a duty to love our neighbour, in the restrained sense of the word, and to hate our enemy. Matthew v. 43. But the law, as delivered by Moses, spake a language the reverse of this false exposition. It declared, that love to our fellow-creatures was not to be confined to those who were ranked among our friends. "If thou meet thine enemy's ox or ass going astray, thou shalt surely bring it back to him again. If thou see the ass of him that hateth thee lying under his burden, and wouldest forbear to help him: thou shalt surely help with him." Exodus xxiii. 4, 5.

Since then the moral law, respecting our duty to our fellow-creatures, was the same under the Jewish as it is under the Christian dispensation; let us examine in what light *defensive war* was viewed by the great legislator, while superintending, in an especial manner, the affairs of the Jewish nation.

The command which the Israelites received, to exterminate the devoted inhabitants of Canaan, affords no example for the regulation of our conduct. The enormous wickedness of those nations, after long forbearance on the part of the Almighty, was the cause of their destruction. "Speak not in thine heart,—For my righteousness the Lord hath brought me in to possess this land: but for the wickedness of these nations the LORD doth drive them out before thee." Deuteronomy ix. 4.

The authority which was given to the Israelites, to execute the sentence of divine wrath upon the devoted nations, was express and special. "Thou shalt smite them, and utterly destroy them; thou shalt make no covenant with them, nor shew mercy unto them." Deuteronomy vii. 2.

A neglect to execute the authorized and merited vengeance upon these nations subjected the Israelites themselves to severe punishment. "If thou wilt not drive out the inhabitants of the land from before you, then it shall come to pass, that those which ye let remain of them shall be pricks in your eyes, and thorns in your sides, and shall vex you in the land wherein ye dwell. Moreover, it shall come to pass, that I shall do unto you as I thought to do unto them." Numbers xxxiii. 55, 56.

On the contrary, the Israelites were commanded to treat other nations, who were not devoted to destruction, in the most pacific manner, unless they would bring down vengeance on themselves by their own aggression.

" Ye are to pass through the coast of your brethren, the children of Esau ;—take ye good heed unto yourselves. Meddle not with them; for I will not give you of their land, no not so much as a foot-breadth. Ye shall buy meat of them for money, that ye may eat; and water of them for money, that ye may drink." Deuteronomy ii.

Again ;—" Distress not the *Moabites*, neither contend with them in battle." *Ib.* verse 9. So also,—" When thou comest nigh over against the children of *Ammon*, distress them not, nor meddle with them ;" verse 19.

When the Jews were settled in the promised land, they remained surrounded by enemies whom they were forbidden to attack, except in the way of self-defence. And as they remained, for a considerable series of years, under the immediate government of God, or under his special protection, we are enabled to learn his will with respect to defensive war, by the commands and promises which he gave them on this subject, and by the assistance which he afforded them in their contests with an invading enemy.

The Almighty engaged to maintain his people Israel in the quiet possession of the land of Canaan, so long as they should continue obedient to his law. Now this engagement could only be fulfilled in the following ways. 1. He must either restrain, by his secret influence, the surrounding hostile nations from attacking the Jews. Or, 2. He must overthrow, by his own immediate and supernatural exertions, those nations who should at any time commence hostilities against his people. Or, 3. He must aid them in their defensive war, and make their own exertions effectual for their protection, by his assistance given in the ordinary course of warfare.

The Almighty did occasionally make use of the two former means of protection, and thereby shewed, that they were not contrary to the procedures of his infinite wisdom. It can scarcely, therefore, be deemed an act of presumption in us to suppose, that he would not have led his people to, and assisted them in, the last means of defence, if it had necessarily involved in it a breach of his own moral law; for this would have been to reward them for their obedience, by encouraging them in an act of disobedience.

All the adult males among the Jews were commanded to attend the stated worship of God in Jerusalem, three times in every year. He whose almighty power can control "the unruly wills and affections of sinful men," engaged that no attempts to invade the coasts of Judea should ever be made during the three great festivals, while obedience to the divine appointments caused the men to leave their lands and families unprotected. "Thrice in the year shall all your men-children appear before the Lord God, the God of Israel. For I will cast out the nations before thee, and enlarge thy borders: neither shall any man desire thy land when thou shalt go up to appear before the Lord thy God thrice in the year." Exodus xxxiv. 23, 24.

At other seasons it pleased God to permit his people to be invaded by their enemies, even while they exercised a proper trust in his protection, and lived in obedience to his commands. Under such circumstances they entered into a state of warfare, and used the ordinary means of self-defence: nor were they ever reproved for this conduct. On the contrary, they were often incited by their prophets, or inspired leaders, to repel with force the aggressions of their enemies.

Sometimes, indeed, the Almighty appeared so remarkably for their protection, as to render their own exertions unnecessary; as in the case of the pious Jehoshaphat. When he was attacked by the Moabites, the Ammonites, and inhabitants of Mount Seir, whom the Almighty " would not let Israel invade, when they came out of the land of Egypt, (2 Chronicles xx. 10.) he set himself to seek the Lord, and proclaimed a fast throughout all Judah;" verse 3. In this instance God ordained it so, that the confederate army was destroyed by its own weapons. "The children of Ammon and Moab stood up against the inhabitants of Mount Seir, utterly to slay and destroy them; and when they had made an end of the inhabitants of Seir, every one helped to destroy another." verse 23.

Such extraordinary interposition was not always granted, but the people were left to use the ordinary means of defence, which were rendered successful by the gracious, though invisible, assistance of the Almighty, as in the case of Asa. When the land was invaded by Zerah, the Ethiopian, with an army containing a million of men, "Asa cried unto the Lord, and said, Lord, it is nothing with thee to help, whether with many, or with them that have no power? Help us, O Lord our God, for we rest on thee." 2 Chronicles xiv. 9, 11. His prayer was answered, and this enormous army was defeated by the forces of the Jews. This victory was obtained by the blessing of God upon their arms; and so far were the people from receiving a rebuke for engaging in this defensive warfare, that they were afterwards reminded of this victory, as an instance of the divine favour towards them. " Were not the Ethiopians and Lubims a huge host," said Hanani the Seer, " with many chariots and horsemen? Yet, because thou didst rely on the Lord, he delivered them into thy hand." *Ib.* chapter xvi. 8.

An objection to the conclusion drawn from these considerations may arise in the minds of some of your readers. It may be said, that the reasoning hitherto rests upon examples drawn from the Old Testament; whereas the New speaks a different language. I shall proceed, therefore, to examine what is said in the New Testament on this subject.

When John the Baptist " came into the country about Jordan, a multitude *of the people* came forth to be baptized of him." Luke iii. 7. To these he gave reproofs and instructions suited to their several conditions. " When he saw many of the Pharisees and Sadducees come to his baptism, he said unto them, O generation of vipers, who hath warned you to flee from the wrath to come? Bring forth, therefore, fruits meet for repentance." Matthew iii. 7, 8. " Then came also publicans (or tax-gatherers) to be baptized, and said unto him, Master, what shall we do? And he said unto them, Exact no more than that which is appointed you. And the soldiers likewise demanded of him, saying, And what shall we do? And he said unto them, Do violence to no man, neither accuse any falsely, and be content with your wages," or soldier's pay, as the word in the original signifies. Luke iii. 12—14.

Now, can any reasonable person conceive it possible, that this faithful servant of God, this greatest of the prophets, this harbinger of the Prince of Peace, could have given such instructions to the soldiers, if warfare was absolutely, and under all circumstances, unlawful? What! shall a set of murderers be instructed to be content with their wages? For, let it be remembered, that if warfare be absolutely unlawful, a soldier is a murderer by profession. This holy messenger of Christ understood perfectly the nature of the moral law, and faithfully fulfilled his office of calling all men to repentance, and to the forsaking of every evil way. He does not class soldiers, as such, among the "*generation of vipers*," but cautions them against those crimes to which their profession might lead them. He judged that a continuance in the profession of war caused no insuperable obstacle to their repentance; and allowed the lawfulness of that profession, by not calling upon them to forsake it.

When the centurion, or Roman captain, made application to our Saviour on account of his sick servant, and manifested such humility and confidence in the power and grace of Christ, the great searcher of hearts declared that he had not "found so great faith, no not in Israel." So far was our Lord from informing him, that the profession of war was inconsistent with purity of heart, that he strongly intimated the centurion to be of that happy number, "who shall sit down with Abraham, Isaac, and Jacob in the kingdom of heaven." Matthew viii. 10, 11.

Another captain in the Roman army is declared, in the Acts of the Apostles, chapter x. to have been a devout man, and one that feared God with all his house; among whose "household servants" was a "devout soldier." To this military man was the Apostle Peter sent, to bring the glad tidings of salvation. This inspired Apostle did not require from him a renunciation of his profession, but acknowledged him to be of the number whom God had accepted. In consequence of that acceptance, "the gift of the Holy Ghost was poured out" upon him, and he was immediately "baptized in the name of the Lord." *Ib.* verse 44, 48.

It may be supposed, that our Lord forbad the use of the sword, when he said to Peter, after he had smitten the high-priest's servant, "Put up again thy sword into his place; for all they that take the sword shall perish with the sword." Matthew xxvi. 52.

To understand rightly the import of these words, we must take into consideration the circumstances under which Peter used his sword in this violent manner. He was not acting by authority of the government under which he lived; but in resistance to it, a thing which the word of God most clearly condemns. Peter was then in a state of persecution for righteousness' sake; a state in which hostile weapons are forbidden to be used. The weapons of the persecuted church are prayers and tears, not swords and staves. When Christians are persecuted in one city, they are permitted to flee to another; but by no means to resist their persecutors with violence. Besides, submission to our lawful governors is in all cases a duty. If laws are made contrary to the laws of God, "we ought to obey God rather than man;" Acts, verse 29. but we must not act with hostile resistance to that government under which we live. They who use the sword in this way, deserve to perish by the sword. This is the doctrine which our Saviour and his Apostles taught; but they did not represent the authorized warfare (authorized by the supreme magistrate) as in all cases unlawful.

The description of the origin of wars, which is given by St. James, has also been considered as prohibiting every species of warfare. "From whence come wars and fightings among you? Come they not hence, even of your lusts, that war in your members? Ye lust and have not: ye kill and desire to have, and cannot obtain: ye fight and war, yet ye have not, because ye ask not." James iv. 1, 2.

In this passage the Apostle is clearly speaking concerning wars of *aggression*, not concerning those of *defence*. It is the unlawful desire of what belongs to another, and the unlawful means of obtaining it, which he condemns. The corrupt desires which "war in our members" are to be subdued, and not indulged to the injury of our neighbours. Christianity teaches us to be content with the portion which Providence has assigned; and the universal prevalence of this disposition would put an end to all wars between states, and angry contentions between individuals. But this disposition would not prevent an invaded or injured state from standing up in its own defence, and repelling by the sword the unprovoked aggression of an enemy.

The proper expression of love to our neighbour is comprised in that command which Christ hath given us;—"Whatsoever ye would that men should do to you, do ye even so to them, for this is the law and the prophets." Matthew vii. 12. All wars which are undertaken for the purpose of extending the dominions of a state, of acquiring wealth, or subjugating our fellow-creatures, are evident breaches of this command, and highly criminal in the sight of God. But a state of warfare, in which a nation is engaged for the purpose of self-defence, and with the view of inducing perpetual peace, is not contrary to the command of Christ, not inconsistent with the sincere love of our neighbour, that is, of those whose unprovoked attacks we are labouring to repel.

Let all, however, who are engaged in warfare, be watchful against those sins to which a state of hostility exposes them. Let them labour to preserve an unfeigned good-will to their enemies; and let them be ready, on all occasions, to observe such conduct as they might reasonably expect to receive on a change of circumstances. Let all cruelty, or want of compassion, be avoided towards a vanquished foe. Let evil be put away from the camp, lest the Almighty be provoked to withdraw his protection. Let humble trust and confidence in God accompany every measure used for self-defence. And when success attends those measures, let sincere praise be given to Him who ruleth in the armies of heaven and among the inhabitants of the earth.

REMARKS

ON THE

TWENTY-FIFTH VERSE

OF THE

THIRD CHAPTER OF THE EPISTLE TO THE ROMANS.

As "Biblical Criticisms" are among the articles, which it is the design of your miscellany to comprehend; I shall make no apology for sending to you the following observations on an important passage of Scripture, which is somewhat obscured in our authorized translation of the New Testament.

This translation, I apprehend, is, upon the whole, truly excellent: so that no person, who studies the New Testament as we have it in our own language, with humble prayer to the *Father of lights* for the gracious assistance of his Holy Spirit, and with a sincere desire to do the will of God, can be misled, in any point of faith or practice, by the few inaccuracies of interpretation which may be found therein. Yet when any passage can be illustrated or enforced by a recurrence to the original, critical disquisition may be made subservient to practical instruction, the great end ever to be kept in view when we read the Bible.

The important doctrine of justification by faith in Jesus Christ, is, perhaps, in no part of the New Testament more amply displayed than in the third chapter of the Epistle to the Romans. The subject is there treated in the most express and striking manner. Its foundation is laid open, and its necessity confirmed. Yet one sentiment, contained in this most instructive and important passage of Scripture, is somewhat obscured in our translation.

The sentence to which I mean to call the attention of your readers is this;—"To declare his righteousness for the remission of sins that are passed, through the forbearance of God;" verse 25. These words do not clearly convey the meaning of the original; nor, indeed, any other determinate meaning.

The words in the original are;—

Εις ενδειξιν της δικαιοσυνης αυτου, δια την παρεσιν των προγεγονοτων αμαρτηματων, εν τη ανοχη του θεου.

In this sentence the translation seems to fail in three particulars. 1. The word *παρεσις* does not properly signify *remission* or forgiveness, but *passing by*, or *passing over*, as the margin in our Bible properly points out. 2. *δια*, with an accusative case after it, does not mean *for*, or *in order to* a thing; but *because*, or *on account of*.—3. The term *προγεγονοτων*, being evidently opposed to the expression *εν τω νυν καιρω* (at this period of time) in the next verse, must mean not simply *sins that are past*, but *sins committed in former periods of time*. The sentence will then run thus;—"For a demonstration of his righteousness, because of the passing by of sins, committed in former periods of time, through the forbearance of God."

The force of this passage will more clearly appear by a review of the context, which deserves to be studied with the utmost attention.

The Apostle enters upon his subject at the ninth verse; and, by various quotations from the Old Testament, shows the deplorable state of mankind by nature; proving that "both Jews and Gentiles are all under sin. There is none righteous, no not one; there is none that understandeth, there is none that seeketh after God;" verse 10, 11. "So that every mouth must be stopped, and all the world become guilty before God," and stand exposed to his righteous judgment; verse 19. "Therefore by the deeds of the law, there shall no flesh be justified in his sight; for by the law is the knowledge of sin;" verse 10; but no deliverance from its guilt and power. But now the righteousness of God without the law is manifested, being witnessed by the law and the prophets, verse 21. That is, God hath at length clearly made known his method of justifying sinners, who lie under the condemning sentence of the law; which method was revealed, though somewhat obscurely, by the sacrifices and other services of the law, as well as by the more express declarations of the prophets.

All hope of justification by our own righteousness being cut off, we are graciously led to the "fountain opened for sin and uncleanness." Our case is not hopeless. Though we "have sinned, and come short of the glory of God," we may still be justified freely by his grace, through the redemption that is in Jesus Christ; whom God hath set forth to be a propitiation, through faith in his blood;" verse 24, 25.

The Apostle then proceeds to observe that the forbearance of God, in passing by the sins of mankind, committed in former periods of the world, had cast a cloud, as it were, upon his holiness and justice; which were never sufficiently vindicated by the heaviest judgments hitherto inflicted on sinners. But now, at length, by laying our sins upon his own dear Son, that spotless Lamb of God, he hath demonstrated, in the clearest manner, the righteousness of his laws, the justice of his government, and his own immaculate purity, requiring an all-sufficient atonement for sin, while he receives returning sinners to mercy. He hath *declared*, or demonstrated, "at this time his righteousness; that he might be just, and the justifier of him that believeth in Jesus;" verse 26.

O mysterious union of grace and justice!

This passage of Scripture proves, that it would have been inconsistent with the justice of God to receive such guilty wretches as we are to mercy, without giving at the same time a complete vindication of his righteousness. Such a vindication is effected by the sufferings of our Redeemer, who, with infinite condescension, came into the world which he had made, and "bare our sins in his own body on the tree, that by his stripes" we might be "healed."

If then we would form a right conception of the malignity of sin, we must look at our Redeemer, considering at once the dignity of his person, and the greatness of his sufferings.

The punishments inflicted on men, at different periods of the world, for their iniquities are truly awful. Our minds are struck with reverential fear when we contemplate the various judgments of war, of famine, and of pestilence. The overwhelming earthquakes, and the devouring fire from heaven, ought strongly to impress us with a sense of the evil of sin. But neither these, nor the inundation of the whole earth, can convey an adequate idea of the enormity of our transgressions. But when we know that He, "who was in the form of God, and thought it no robbery to be equal with God, humbled himself" to become man for our sakes, that he might magnify the law by bearing the punishment of our transgressions, we may then form some positive notion of the tremendous guilt of sin, and of the wonderful combination of the justice and mercy of God, manifested in our forgiveness and acceptance.

Angels, who behold the face of our Father who is in heaven, obtain more enlarged views of the manifold wisdom of God by the displays which the redemption of sinners has occasioned. Ephesians iii. 10. This subject they willingly contemplate with profound meditation, and no doubt obtain also an increase of happiness from their enlarged views of the divine glory manifested in the mystery of redeeming love. 1 Peter i. 12.

With what astonishment, then, should the believer in Christ reflect on the means required and employed to deliver him from the curse of the law, and to bring him into a state of favour with God. What gratitude should possess his inmost soul for these benefits; and how ardently should he desire to glorify the Saviour of the world by the most steady and active obedience.

MEANS OF PROMOTING

THE

PROSPERITY

OF THE

ESTABLISHED CHURCH.

AMONG the methods which have been devised by those who are friends to the Ecclesiastical Establishment in this kingdom, for increasing the congregations in our churches, there is one which has not received all the attention that it deserves; though it is the most ancient and obvious of all the methods proposed. I mean that of interesting the laity in the erection of churches and chapels.

Those who prefer the dissenting mode of worship, usually find little difficulty in procuring a convenient place of meeting, wherever a congregation can be obtained; while the friends of the Establishment are surrounded with difficulties in their attempts to increase the number of churches, how deficient soever the existing number may be to accommodate the people.

In order to procure a dissenting place of worship, nothing more is necessary than the union of a few opulent persons, who are of ability to purchase a small plot of ground, and erect a convenient building. Even the numerous, though small, contributions of the poor class are often sufficient for this purpose.

If the laity are desirous of retaining in their own hands the presentation to the church which they are proposing to erect, an Act of Parliament becomes necessary, which cannot be obtained without a considerable expense, besides the consent of the diocesan, the patron, and incumbent of the parish church.

Why the consent of any of these parties should be required to the erection of a new church, provided no injury is thereby done to any of them, I have yet to learn.

The plan, which it is the design of this paper to propose, is as follows: that an Act of Parliament should be passed for the purpose of enabling any individual, or body of men, who shall severally or conjointly build and endow a new church, to hold the perpetual presentation thereof, after it has been consecrated by the Bishop. That in such churches the minister shall be restrained to the service of the common prayers, together with sermons, and the administration of the Lord's Supper; or if any advantage should accrue to the public from the permission of funerals, the accustomed fees should be paid to the ancient church or chapel, as if no such new church existed.

To such a plan as this, I can conceive no reasonable objection. Such new church would be under the jurisdiction of the Bishop in the same manner as any other church. The patronage of the parish church would not be injured, because nothing would be taken from the patron. The incumbent of the parish church, or perpetual curacy, would suffer no diminution of his temporalities, since these would remain the same as before.

No clergyman could be minister of the new church without having been twice submitted to the examination of the Bishop, and having twice received his approbation; as the minister must have taken priest's orders.

This method of promoting the interests of the Establishment can afford no injury, nor give any offence, to other societies of Christians. It leaves to them the full enjoyment of all the privileges which they have by law, and therefore obviates all just cause of complaint.

The antiquity of the method which I have proposed, will appear from the following short history of the Christian Church, which I have extracted from a work entitled "Pluralities indefensible."

"Austin, attended with several inferior clergy, came into England, to preach the gospel, in the time of the Saxon Heptarchy." page 9.

"Ethelbert, King of Kent, gave to him ample possessions for the maintenance of himself and his clergy. A church was built for him at Canterbury, in which he might fix his chair; and houses appointed wherein himself and clergy might dwell in common." page 10.

"In this manner cathedral churches were founded and endowed by other Saxon Kings, for the general good of the several dioceses, that is, of their several kingdoms. For in the first foundation of bishopricks among the Saxons, the dioceses had the same limits with the kingdoms, and so they continue at this day, as many of them as have not yet been subdivided.

"The endowment of the church, in the first ages of it, was *general*. Whatever was given by the pious converts within each Bishop's diocese, was the endowment, not of any particular *part* of the diocese, but of the whole diocese. Lands were given in free and irrevocable tenure. Tithes, paid at first as due of divine right, were afterwards confirmed by legislative authority. Oblations were made by the faithful at the times of divine service; and being collected by the itinerant priests, became a part of the common treasure of the diocese." page 12.

"The whole ecclesiastical revenue was vested in the Bishop of the diocese. He therewith maintained himself and his emissaries; repaired the edifices of the church; relieved the poor; and entertained the stranger." page 14.

"The increase of converts occasioned the erection of other churches, as well in the city as in places more remote from the cathedral." *Ibid.* "Itinerant preachers or priests were sent by the Bishop from the cathedral church to celebrate and preach in the rural churches." page 15.

"This was the constant received discipline of the English church about the year 664.

"As the Saxon Kings first founded and

endowed cathedrals for the general good of their respective kingdoms; so great men first founded and endowed parochial churches for the particular good of themselves, their families, and tenants." page 22, 23. "Oratories and chapels were for this end erected by them; which being consecrated by the Bishop, were by the founders or patrons endowed with particular maintenance for the incumbent, who should there reside, and execute the holy function within the limits appointed by the patron." page 23.

"To this endowment by the founder of a parochial church, was added another endowment by the Bishop, of the glebe, tithes, and oblations belonging to the district in which the church was erected.

"This additional endowment was found necessary to excite the laity to erect churches, and make extraordinary contributions for the maintenance of settled ministers, for the Bishops, finding the devotion of the lay-founders restrained, at last condescended, that the whole revenue of the endowment, with all other ecclesiastical profits, which should come to the hands of the priest officiating at such a church, should be taken from the *common treasure* of the diocese, and be perpetually annexed to the church of that clerk who received it. This the Bishops willingly did, as soon as by the erection of many parish churches, the necessity of maintaining so many itinerant priests ceased." page 42.

These extracts shew us the origin of parish churches, and of lay-patronage. Churches of an inferior order were afterwards erected upon the same plan. And if this method had been closely pursued, the number of dissenting places of worship would not have been so numerous as they now are.

Soon after the first-fruits and tenths had been set apart for the augmentation of small benefices, the legislature of this kingdom evidently entertained a favourable idea of the measure which I have recommended. For, in the first year of George I. a statute was made, entitled, " An Act for making more effectual her late Majesty's gracious intentions for augmenting the maintenance of the poor clergy," 1 Geo. chapter 10, in which, after premising that " inasmuch as the right of presentation or nomination to small livings is of inconsiderable value, and yet it may be a great inducement to such benefactions, if the benefactors may have some right of presentation to the cure which himself contributes to augment," it is enacted, that the King, or any bodies politic or corporate shall have power to alienate their right of presentation in favour of any benefactor who shall augment the living. Section 8. Now, if the legislature thought right to hold out the prospect of the advowson, for the purpose of encouraging the *augmentation* of small livings, surely he who both builds and endows a church ought not to have less than the perpetual presentation as the recompence of his bounty.

Here an inquiry may arise respecting the value of the endowment proposed to be annexed to a new church. To this inquiry the legislature have already given an answer. For, as they have judged that seventy-five pounds per annum is a sufficient stipend for any curate, they have in effect determined, that an endowment of this value would be sufficient from the founder of any new church.

As the Bishops of the English Church had recourse to this plan in the original formation of parish churches; and as it has received the sanction of the legislature, when providing for the augmentation of small livings; it certainly deserves the consideration of our ecclesiastical superiors, and of the legislature in general.

The support of our Ecclesiastical Establishment, by peaceable measures, and such as can give no just cause of offence to any religious sect in the kingdom, has no weak tendency to preserve the tranquillity of the State.

I have tried to find objections to the plan here proposed; but have hitherto discovered none which a reasonable person could support. Permit me to add, that a careful attention to the state of religion in this kingdom, during the course of half a century, has convinced me, that the adoption of this plan would have proved highly favourable to the interests of true religion, as well as to those of our Ecclesiastical Establishment.

ON THE

RELIGIOUS EDUCATION

OF

CHILDREN.

A CORRESPONDENT, who signs himself a "Christian Parent," having requested, in your number for January last, the communication of "a few hints, respecting the means that have been found most successful, in impressing the minds of children with the important truths of our holy religion, and bringing them to an early acquaintance with its sanctifying influence;" I take the liberty of suggesting a few considerations on this important subject.

Though a pious education is not universally successful, in bringing children into a truly religious state; yet it is undoubtedly appointed by God for this end, and is perhaps more frequently attended with success than any other means of grace.

Education may be comprised under these three heads, *discipline*, *instruction*, and *example*. These must all concur, and be agreeable to the word of God, in order to form what is comprehended under the idea of *christian education*.

Children are the proper subjects of DISCIPLINE, before they are capable of receiving much instruction; and a system of discipline ought to commence as soon as ever they are able to discern between good and evil. This branch of education is of more consequence than parents in general are aware of. We shall see its importance if we consider the nature of true religion, and the ideas which a child forms in infancy of the authority of his parents.

True religion consists in choosing the will of God in preference to our own. His authority is absolute. It should silence all our perverse reasonings; and obtain from us an implicit obedience. And as a parent is to his child in God's stead, he ought to require from the child an entire submission to his authority.

A child naturally conceives the authority of his parent to be absolute; and if a proper discipline is maintained, this branch of education will be a handmaid to religion. Let the object be changed, and filial obedience becomes piety.

All the commands of a parent should be *reasonable;* and as the understanding of the child advances, their reasonabless should be unfolded: but implicit submission must be enforced long before the reason of the command can be understood.

We may easily discover, that children are perpetually endeavouring to break through the absolute authority of their parents. This is attempted with amazing sagacity even in early infancy. Children will sometimes disobey in the most trifling circumstances, in hope that the parent will not think it worth the trouble to persevere in requiring obedience. They will endeavour by some humorous trick to disarm the displeasure of a parent, when they see him serious in requiring obedience. They will seize the opportunity when the parent is engaged with company, or with some close employment, to evade obedience to a command, which they know would be enforced if the parent was more at leisure to pay attention to their conduct. In these, and similar instances, parents should be upon their guard, and never suffer their children to break a known command by any device or artifice whatever.

That discipline may be effectual, it must be *steady*. A child will soon discover, whether the commands of the parent depend upon his humour, or his principle. Commands urged merely because the parent is angry, will harden the heart of a child, instead of producing a spirit of obedience. We too often see the authority of a parent directed by caprice. Alternate fits of indulgence and severity occupy, in too many instances, the greatest share of family government. Such conduct is completely destructive of christian discipline.

Discipline must not only be steady, but *gentle*. Commands that appear to flow from love naturally dispose the child to obey. A child sees no hope of escaping from a system of discipline, that seems to arise from the tenderness of a parent. The harshness of a command is generally more grievous to a child than the thing commanded. Displeasure in the parent should only be excited by wilful disobedience; and should rise in proportion to the contempt of authority.

When the understanding of a child is sufficiently matured, the christian parent should shew, that, in the commands which he gives, he himself is subject to a higher authority. If the conduct of a parent is formed upon this principle, he will be ready to grant indulgence where that is not inconsistent with the commands of God. And when a child is convinced, by the uniform conduct of the parent, that restraints are not the effect of caprice, or want of affection; discipline loses all its galling effects, and becomes truly subservient to holiness and happiness.

As soon as a child is capable of understanding the nature of God's law, religious INSTRUCTION should keep pace with discipline. It must not, however, be confined to stated times, as in the ordinary branches of learning, but it must also occupy a considerable share in the common conversation of the parent. This is the method which divine wisdom has appointed for parental instruction. "Thou shalt teach them diligently unto thy children, and shalt talk of them when thou sittest in thine house, and when thou walkest by the way, and when thou liest down, and when thou risest up." Deuteronomy vi. 7.

It is scarcely necessary to observe, that children should first be taught the plainest truths of religion; which, indeed, they are capable of understanding at a very early period. They can comprehend, as well as the most acute philospher, that God created all things; that he is in every place, though we cannot see him; that he sees all our actions, and knows all our thoughts; and that he will bring every work into judgment.

But the scheme of religious instruction must not rest here. The whole system of evangelical truth is not above the comprehension of children, if it be laid before them in plain language, and in a familiar manner. The vehicle which conveys instruction to their minds in the most pleasing and impressive form, is the History of the Bible. The facts recorded in the Books of the Old and New Testament are so striking, that we often see children extremely desirous of hearing them repeated, when a repetition of mere moral precepts would prove wearisome.

From this history the principal doctrines of Christianity may be collected, as they are therein exemplified. We see, in the conduct of the Almighty towards his creatures, the most affecting instances of his power, his justice, and his mercy. In this history appears the original purity of man, and his apostacy from God. The degenerate state of the human heart is marked throughout the

Bible in the strongest characters: and the necessity of holiness, in order to the enjoyment of God, is clearly displayed. The method whereby alone we can obtain pardon of sin, and be restored to the divine favour, is illustrated by the whole series of the Jewish economy, and the repeated details of our Saviour's sufferings. A parent, who is able to make a plain and judicious comment on these recorded facts, enjoys the surest means (through divine grace) of impressing evangelical truths upon the minds of his children.

A spiritual exposition of the moral law should always accompany the history of redemption, as an enlightened conscience must lead us to sincere self-condemnation, before the offers of mercy made in the gospel can be truly valued and accepted.

The doctrines of Christianity, being all of a practical nature, requiring of us corresponding affections and conduct, the *practical application* should always attend the *system* of religion.

It is a prudent measure in parents to keep out of sight the various controversies which have unhappily taken place among the sincere disciples of Christ. The conduct of the great Creator and Governor of the world towards his creatures, though founded on *per-*

fect righteousness, is in many respects to us inscrutable. Yet through this cloud the goodness and grace of the Almighty shine forth with such bright beams, as are sufficient to enlighten the understanding, and warm the heart, of every true believer.

Children should be taught to hear and read the word of God with the most profound reverence; and to be content with such knowledge as removes all doubt with respect to their own duty.

As God has been pleased to manifest himself to us in the person of Jesus Christ, the history of the Redeemer should be inculcated upon the minds of children in the most forcible manner. The discourses, the actions, and sufferings of Christ, should be impressed by a frequent and minute detail; nor should his present intercession for us ever be forgotten.

I have already observed, that religious instruction ought to make a part of the familiar conversation of a christian parent; yet the appropriation of certain seasons for this important work remains indispensably necessary. Among other invaluable benefits which the institution of the Sabbath offers, that of affording the most suitable opportunity for private instruction is not the least. When we are detached in this sacred season, from worldly considerations and employments, the minds of parents and children are then in the best state of preparation for giving and receiving the knowledge of those things that appertain to our salvation.

But at whatever time, and in whatever manner, religious instruction is given, the greatest care should be taken to impress such sentiments on the minds of children as are in exact conformity to the word of God. We are more apt to form such ideas of the Supreme Being as are dictated by self-love, than implicitly to receive the declarations of the Bible respecting the character of God. In this sacred book we have a history of the conduct of the Almighty towards his creatures, under a variety of circumstances, and from these historical facts, as well as from express declarations, our notions of the divine character should originate. It is of the utmost consequence that children should be taught to draw their ideas of God from the declarations and historical facts of the Bible; for, without this foundation laid in the mind, their whole system of religion must be erroneous.

With the scriptural character of God are intimately connected the purity of the divine law, the method of salvation by a Mediator, and the necessity of personal holiness. The instructions which are given to children should always keep those fundamental truths in view: for without a deep sense of these things, our knowledge must be superficial, and our service formal.

Children should be taught, as soon as they become capable of reflection, to attend to the workings of their own minds: that they may discover the deceitfulness of their hearts, and become thoroughly acquainted with their inbred corruption. Christ is precious to those only who know their own vileness; and the influences of the Holy Spirit will be earnestly sought by those alone, who are deeply conscious of their own depravity, and moral inability.

Christian education will still be imperfect, unless to pious instruction there be added the pious EXAMPLE of the parent. Children are acute in discovering any deviation from those precepts which are enforced upon them. They keep a watchful eye upon the conduct of their parents; and are glad to discover any thing that can prove an argument in favour of relaxation in their own obedience. On the contrary, a constant visible regard in the parent to the commands of God, which he is daily enforcing, tends to make the most powerful impression on the minds of his children, and to remove all doubt of the rectitude of the instructions which they receive.

I have already observed that one great benefit which we derive from the institution of the Sabbath, is that of affording time for more ample instruction than can, in many situations, be obtained on the days of labour. I would here remark, that a conscientious regard in the parent to the sacredness of this holy season, is of great importance in a system of religious education. Let all worldly and trifling conversation be avoided on this day, that the impressions made by the public or family exercises of religion may not be obliterated, by a carelessness to improve the intervals of religious service.

Children are not ignorant of the truth of that divine aphorism, " Out of the abundance of the heart the mouth speaketh:" nor will they be easily persuaded that religious truths make deep impressions on the minds of their parents, when nothing is heard that can direct the mind to eternal objects, except at the stated hours of instruction. And as God has expressly forbidden us to " speak our own words" on the Sabbath, an example of conformity to this gracious command should be shewn by every master of a family, whose peculiar office it is to direct the subjects of discourse to those who are in his presence, and under his care.

The influence of example should make parents extremely cautious in the choice of companions for their children. With this view those schools should be chosen where pious example may be added to religious instruction and useful learning. It gives me pleasure, while on this subject, to be able to congratulate the friends of religion, that instructors may be found in this kingdom, in whom are combined the excellent qualities required in a christian teacher.

The company to which children are introduced in other places should be such as shall have no tendency to make them slight the religious instructions of their parents and masters.

This great object should also be kept in view in the choice of situation for the trade or profession to which they are educated; as the highest interest of a child ought to have the first place in our regard. But my design is not to write a system of education, a subject too copious for an article in your Miscellany, and too complex for my abilities. I wish merely to throw out a few hints in compliance with the request of your correspondent, and such as have been suggested by the experience of a parent.

I must not, however, conclude these hints without reminding the christian parent, that, to all his endeavours (be they ever so judicious) must be added constant prayer for the influences of the Holy Spirit, without which true religion will never be implanted in the minds of his children. Though Paul should plant, and Apollos water, without the influence of divine grace no fruits of righteousness will appear; for it is God that giveth the increase. But we have the strongest reason to hope for this blessing, while diligently, and with an humble dependence on his grace, we use the means which God hath appointed.

ON THE

ETERNITY

OF

FUTURE PUNISHMENT.

Being fatigued with the labours of the preceding day, I awoke this morning somewhat later than is usual with me at this season of the year; when the first sound that reached my ear was that of a passing-bell,—the signal that one of my fellow-creatures had just entered upon a state of eternal duration. The thought of eternity and its immense importance, pressed forcibly upon my mind; and a variety of reflections on this awful subject held me for some time in serious contemplation. Among other things, the danger and absurdity of the doctrine of universal salvation occurred; and I thought with regret on the profession of this pernicious doctrine, which was said to have been made on his death-bed, by a late eminent philosopher, who died not long ago in America.

A passage of Scripture occurred to my mind, as it has often done before, which affords a full demonstration of the falsehood of this doctrine. The terms of this passage are so clear, that they will admit of no sense but one, which proves the certainty of an eternal duration of the misery of the damned, unless we allow the doctrine of annihilation.

The idea of applying mathematical demonstration in support of any doctrine of divine revelation, may, at first sight, appear strange and absurd; but in this peculiar instance such demonstration will not be found inapplicable; and may be urged with propriety in confutation of such persons as boast of the rationality of their religious principles.

The doctrine which I mean to oppose, and which is held by too many who call themselves Christians, is this,—That those who are not truly righteous shall suffer a certain degree of punishment in a future state, proportioned to their criminality; but shall at last, after this *time* of discipline, (to use the expression of the philosopher, to whom I allude,) be admitted to a state of eternal happiness.

This doctrine is in direct contradiction to the declaration which our blessed Saviour, the great Judge of all, made with respect to the traitor Judas.—" Woe to that man by whom the Son of Man is betrayed: it had been good for that man, if he had not been born." Matthew xxvi. 24.

This woe could not, consistently with truth, have been pronounced against any man for whom an eternal state of happiness was prepared, let his preceding punishment be ever so great, or of ever so long duration.

To demonstrate the truth of this proposition, it is only necessary to appeal to the judgment of any one, whether this woe could with truth be applied to the life of a person (a future state being now out of the question) who was appointed to live a hundred years in uninterrupted felicity, excepting the short space of a single hour, during which he should suffer any conceiveable punishment. No doubt can be entertained of the answer to this inquiry.

Let us further suppose this perfectly happy life to extend as far as the age of Methusaleh, and that the intervening period of misery had but the duration of one second of time. Could it be said of such a one, " It had been good for this man that he had not been born?" We must suppose the person to have lost his understanding who should hesitate to conclude that such a life was truly desirable.

Yet even these proportions of happiness and misery, dissimilar as they are, do not exhaust the force of my argument; for the least imaginable portion of time, call it the ten thousandth part of a second, bears a greater proportion to the longest limited duration which the imagination can reach, than that duration does to eternity.

The conclusion, therefore, is clearly demonstrated, that eternal happiness will not succeed to any period of misery to the damned; because on this supposition it could not be said of any one, "It had been good for that man, if he had not been born."

If this awful truth had its proper influence on our minds, we should account every worldly enjoyment but as "dung and dross," in comparison with the favour of God, and the attainment of that holiness, without which no man shall see the Lord.

ON

FORMS OF PRAYER.

Objections have been frequently made to pre-conceived forms of prayer. They have been represented as impediments to true devotion in public worship; as improper restraints upon those who are endued with the gift of prayer; and as proofs of a low state of religion in those who use them as helps to devotion in their seasons of retirement.

An inquiry into the validity of these objections will involve in it several important practical considerations. It will lead us to consider,

1. What is the nature of prayer.

2. What association subsists in the human mind between the affections of the heart, and the words in which those affections are expressed.

3. What assistance we are taught by the word of God to expect in the discharge of this duty.

4. What examples the Scriptures afford us of forms of prayer.

5. What may be collected on this subject from the experience of devout persons.

1. Prayer is the expression of our desires and affections towards God; whether in *confession* of our sins, in *supplication* for the blessings which we need in *thanksgiving* for mercies received, or in *intercession* for others.

He who searches the heart is perfectly acquainted with all our desires and affections. The manner in which they are expressed is of no consequence in his sight; but in acts of social worship our expressions are of great consequence, and in our most retired devotions they are not totally without effect upon our own minds.

Whether forms of prayer are helps or hindrances to private devotion, is so much a question of experience, that the solution of it, as far as it regards our own conduct, might with propriety be submitted to the determination of every sedate and devout Christian. Our conduct in this respect ought to be such, as upon experience we find to be most conducive to the suppression of our wanderings, and the maintenance of a true spirit of prayer.

The Scriptures represent that prayer which is acceptable to God in a variety of figurative terms, expressive of earnest desire, and strong affection. It is called, "pouring out the complaint, pouring out the heart," and "pouring out the soul" to God, &c. And as our blessed Redeemer, who was a pattern of righteousness, "in the days of his flesh, offered up prayers and supplications with strong crying and tears," we should aspire after such a holy temper in the practice of this important duty, and estimate every external circumstance in proportion to the assistance which our minds receive from it in this holy and delightful exercise. We should never forget, that the most excellent form of prayer, or the most pathetic *extemporaneous* address, is nothing in the sight of God, where the heart does not pour forth its devout affections. The more we are impressed with a sense of these important truths, the less shall we be inclined to despise any mode of addressing our Maker, which a pious mind may find helpful to devotion.

2. As all acceptable prayer must be the language of the heart, it may seem unnecessary to clothe our thoughts with words in our private devotions. But a due consideration of the nature of man will convince us, that words form an important, though not an essential, part of prayer. There is such an association between our thoughts, and the language in which they are usually expressed, that we may be said to think in words. Every considerate person must be sensible, that our affections are often excited, or rendered more vehement, by the force of well adapted expressions The most experimental writers on the subject of prayer have recommended the use of verbal addresses. It is natural, therefore, to suppose, that a judicious and pathetic form of prayer may often be an auxiliary to the devout Christian in his retired exercises. Expressions which have once powerfully affected our minds, are perhaps better calculated to re-kindle the same feelings, than other expressions which in sense may be equivalent. Every serious and attentive reader of the Scriptures may have experienced the

truth of this observation. He feels an energy in many passages, which a different mode of expressing the same sentiments would not, perhaps, have produced. Upon this principle, an excellent form of prayer may prove a help to devotion. If we find this to be the case, let us not despise, but improve, that mental constitution with which God has created us. Let us avail ourselves of such associations as may prove handmaids to devotion.

3. To encourage our addresses to the throne of mercy, God hath promised to pour out upon them that fear him the spirit of grace and supplication. This promise is fraught with great consolation to those who are conscious that they know not what they should pray for as they ought. They rejoice at the declaration, that " the Spirit helpeth our infirmities." But in what manner is this help vouchsafed to us? The Spirit helpeth our infirmities in various ways; by enabling us to discover our wants, and by showing us our weakness, sinfulness, and danger from temptation. A deep sense of these things must excite, in every serious mind, an earnest application to him whose grace is sufficient for us. The Spirit also helpeth our infirmities, by producing those holy desires and affections towards God and

our Redeemer, which naturally lead the mind to the throne of grace. But the promise of a spirit of prayer does not imply, that the words in which we express our desires shall be the subject of inspiration. These desires are sometimes too vehement to be fully expressed by any words: "The Spirit maketh intercession for us with groanings which cannot be uttered;" that is, which language is unable to express. But supposing the very words of prayer to be inspired, it is not necessary that those words should be uttered as soon as they are conceived. A pious person may be as much inspired in writing, as in uttering a prayer; and, therefore, forms of prayer argue no less inspiration than extemporaneous addresses.

They who find their minds elevated by psalms and hymns, and yet condemn forms of prayer, as beneath the spirituality of christian worship, are inconsistent with themselves. For, what are psalms and hymns, but forms of prayer in verse? Surely none will argue, that forms of prayer are unsuitable to true devotion when in prose, but perfectly suitable when in verse. Yet such must be the reasoning of all who condemn forms of prayer, while they find hymns to be no impediment to their devotion. Is the ear of the Almighty captivated by the jingle of our rhymes? But I forbear,—hoping that this consideration may, in some degree, silence the clamour of an ill-directed censure; and show the ingenuous reader how far want of caution may lead some well-meaning persons to urge or receive the weakest and most absurd arguments.

4. If we look into the Holy Scriptures, we shall find them abounding in the most pathetic forms of prayer on every head of devotion. We shall see the most affecting confessions of sin, in which that enemy of human happiness is represented in its native deformity. We shall be struck with the most earnest supplications for mercy, flowing from a heart impressed with the deepest penitence. We shall hear the glad voice of thanksgiving, loudly proclaiming the mercies of a gracious God; and be affected with the intercessions of the most exalted saints recorded in holy writ.

The Book of Psalms contains a series of devout forms, suited to every occasion in the christian life. We cannot surely suppose, that the pious Christian would lose the end of his devotion, by adopting these, as occasion might require.

Our Saviour and his Apostles constantly attended the Jewish Synagogues, where the public worship, as the learned inform us, was conducted by a prescribed liturgy. John the Baptist seems to have given his disciples a form of prayer, which served not only the purposes of devotion, but constituted also a badge of their adherence to that eminent prophet. All this is implied in these words addressed to our Saviour by his disciples, "Lord, teach us to pray, as John also taught his disciples," when the import of this request is explained by the answer which our Saviour returned. In answer to this request, the blessed Jesus gave us that most excellent form, commonly called the LORD'S PRAYER. This was designed, not only as a pattern for our prayers, "After this manner pray ye;" but also as a form to be used in our devotional exercises, "When ye pray, say,—Our Father," &c. It must, therefore, be highly unbecoming the disciple of our heavenly Master to treat such forms of prayer, as are composed on a scriptural model, in a light or contemptuous manner. Rather let us endeavour to frame our devotions aright, by studying the import of that form, while we use, or imitate it, in our addresses to the throne of grace.

It may be objected to the use of pre-conceived forms of prayer in public worship, that we have no intimation, that the Apostles, and those ministers who were ordained by them, made use of such forms in their public ministration. To this it may be answered, that the disciples of Christ would undoubtedly be mindful of our Lord's injunction, so far as to use that form which he had taught them in compliance with their own request. Also the command which the Apostle gives, respecting psalms and hymns, and spiritual songs, implies that these were used in the social worship of the first Christians: and these, as I have already observed, are in reality forms of prayer.

Hence we may conclude, that forms of prayer are not contrary to the nature of a truly spiritual worship of God in public. But the truth is, that we have no exact model of public worship prescribed, or related, in the New Testament. We know that the word of God was preached in the public assemblies; that prayers were offered up to God; and we have reason to believe that psalms and hymns were sung, as they certainly were by our Saviour and his disciples at the celebration of the passover. But in what order the public service was conducted, we know not. The account given of the public worship of the Corinthian Christians, 1 Corinthians xiv. is the most particular of any that I recollect; yet this seems to be mentioned chiefly with the view of correcting it; and it consisted so much in the exercise of supernatural gifts, that it cannot in our days be imitated.

Of the office of baptism, we have no more than that it was to be performed "in the name of the Father, and of the Son, and of the Holy Ghost." The Lord's Supper we are forbidden to use as a common meal; and are commanded to take the bread and wine as the memorials of Christ's sufferings for us, thereby "showing forth the Lord's death till he come." Further regulations were undoubtedly made by the Apostle Paul;—"The rest will I set in order when I come;—but we are not informed in what those regulations consisted. In short, it is impossible for us to regulate, with certainty, our public worship after the model of the first Christians, since we know not the order observed in their religious assemblies. The substantial parts of public worship are clear; the rest is left to our prudence and discretion.

Whether the use of a liturgy, when all extraordinary gifts are withdrawn from the Church, be eligible, deserves a serious and temperate discussion. Among other considerations, it will be of importance to inquire, whether a liturgy, framed during the pure state of a Christian Church, where the worshippers are of the same nation, may not be the means of preserving a belief of the essential doctrines of Christianity; and whether, in fact, the Liturgy of the Church of England has not produced in some measure this benefit. My present design is only to show, that they mistake who represent forms of prayer as inconsistent with the spirituality of divine worship, and as manifesting a low state of religion in those who make use of them.

5. It would tend to throw further light on this subject, if we could obtain a fair representation of the experience of pious Christians in their devout exercises, when using, and when rejecting, the assistance of forms of prayer. This information, however, it is difficult to obtain. Education, habit, and opinion, create a leaning to one side or the other; so that it implies no want of sincerity in men to suppose their experience to be different. Were I to propose the example of the excellent Mr. Bonnell on one side, others might be found whose antipathy to forms had led them to a conduct different from his. It

happens, however, that there is one instance upon record of a pious man, well acquainted with the nature of spiritual worship, who, having forsaken the use of a public liturgy, had the honesty to confess, that it proved no hindrance to his devotion while he used it without prejudice. This evidence will be esteemed unexceptionable by all who reverence the character of Mr. Richard Baxter. In the account of his life, written by himself, he makes this remarkable confession. "Till this time I was satisfied in the matter of conformity. While I was young, I had never been acquainted with any that were against it, or that questioned it. I had joined with the common-prayer with as hearty fervency, as afterwards I did with other prayers; as long as I had no prejudice against it, I had no stop in my devotion from any of its imperfections." Baxter's Life, folio edition, page 13.

This declaration deserves to be attentively considered. Mr. Baxter declares, that the fervour of his devotion was in no wise lessened by the forms prescribed in the liturgy; but that it was as hearty as when afterwards he made use of extemporaneous addresses. He acknowledges, that the imperfections of the liturgy (and what human composition is without imperfections) created no stop in his devotion. What then could make him afterwards prefer extemporaneous prayer in public worship? He contracted prejudices against the liturgy, and then its devotional excellencies vanished. It is hinted, that these prejudices were contracted by his acquaintance with some persons who were against it. Let those who now slight this form of public worship ask themselves, whether prejudice, contracted by an acquaintance with its enemies, may not have warped their minds as it seems to have done that of Mr. Baxter.

Upon the whole, let us endeavour to cultivate a devotional spirit, in every thing by prayer, with thanksgiving, making our requests known unto God. Let us draw near to Him through our great Mediator and High Priest, trusting only in the merit of his atoning sacrifice and intercession. Let us "pray always with all prayer, and watch thereunto with all perseverance." Let fervent and frequent ejaculations be mixed with the ordinary business of life. Let regular retirement at the appointed seasons of private devotion be observed and improved; neglecting no prudential help to check our wanderings, and excite our drowsy affections. And let us go to the house of God with delight, endeavouring to hold communion with the Father.

and with his Son Jesus Christ. So shall our days pass on sweetly, and our souls be prepared for the fellowship of the blessed saints and angels in the kingdom of glory.

ON THE

CUSTOM OF SAYING,

"NOT AT HOME."

CONFIDENT that I shall not, at least from you, incur the charge of expending zeal on trifles, I take the liberty of offering a few observations on a common practice,—trifling and harmless, no doubt, in the estimation of many who conform to it; but not so, I conceive, in the view of those who measure things by a juster standard. The practice to which I allude, is that of freeing ourselves from the intrusion of unwelcome visitors by informing them (contrary to truth) that we are "not at home."

There are, doubtless, many persons, by no means generally lax in point of principle, who defend this custom. " It has," say they, " become, by universal usage, a mode of speech, a phrase, ascertained and understood as such by both masters and servants,—by any person, in short, who knows the world. It is the same, in fact, as subscribing yourself the ' humble servant' of the man whom you feel inclined neither to obey nor serve." —This argument, I apprehend, will not bear examination. Let a servant, who has once given the customary *denial*, be asked whether his master is really gone out or no; and will he feel himself at liberty to answer in the negative? I appeal to common experience, whether such cross-examination is unfrequent; and I ask, whether servants have, in such cases, appeared to consider their prior assertion as a phrase, or as a falsehood; a falsehood which they feel called upon to support, for their master's credit, and for their own? And I ask, whether, when some peculiar claim for admission has been urged, an embarrassment, and even a blush, have not sometimes seemed to shew that the servant had not wholly lost the better feelings of a man; and that, though bad example might have taught, or the authority of his master might have compelled him to utter a falsehood, he was not yet entirely unmindful that he had a Master also in heaven?

Such instances, in my opinion, clearly prove, that "Not at home" is by no means understood as a phrase, or as any peculiar mode of speech, by at least the generality of servants. — Will, then, our grammatical refinements justify a custom which habituates them to falsehood?

Others have urged, in defence of this practice, that it implies no intention to deceive. I grant, that persons who abhor deception have conformed to it, and have really done so without being conscious of such intention: but whether they have themselves been deceived or not, in this particular, I will rest on one simple point:—Would such persons feel no reluctance to being seen at home, (suppose through a window or an open door,) when they were "not at home?" Would no involuntary emotion, no rising blush, no secret shame, betray that there was something of detection in the case?—I suggest this to the conscientious only: let them, if they can, reconcile this feeling with the absence of all intention to deceive.

The generality, however, justify this custom on a broader principle: "Not at home" is, in a word, with them a *white lie*. If, however, we admit this plea, we renounce the cause of truth altogether. A white lie is, in fact, another term for pure falsehood; it is falsehood unmixed with any other principle. But, however paradoxical it may appear to some, I will venture to assert, that it is only by strictness in this very instance; it is only by an undeviating adherence to truth in indifferent matters—and, consequently, in what are termed trifles—that the lover of truth can evince the sincerity of his attachment. I may abhor a slanderous lie, a boasting lie, a dishonest lie; but if I practise lies which bear no other character than that of simple deception, I shew, in the above instances, only that I hate ill-nature, that I hate vanity, that I hate dishonesty, but not that I hate or disapprove of falsehood. This is surely too evident to need enforcement; and, consequently, it appears, that the thorough-paced white liar is (I do not say that he will admit it—his favourite expedient may be resorted to) wholly devoid of the principle of truth.

Is there, then, an intrinsic value in truth? And is there, then, an essential criminality in falsehood, when it violates no other principle than that of simple truth? Most assuredly there is. On the grounds of expediency, indeed, the strictest adherence to truth in indifferent matters might be supported. Were falsehood admissible where no immediate ill consequences were anticipated, not only one of the great guards of virtue would be removed, but, in fact, the social compact would be dissolved: human conceits and fancies would supply the place of realities; conversation would lose its interest, and society its relish; and the most important concerns of human life would be at the mercy of every fool, who might thus scatter arrows, firebrands, and death, and say, Am not I in sport?

But truth has a deeper foundation than expediency or utility. The well-being of society is its consequence, and its effect; but not in any sense the occasion of its existence; though, as the great Hooker speaks of law, its voice be the "harmony of the world." Truth is, in fact, the reality of things; it is the light of the Eternal Sun shining on the universal system; it is the very essence of Him, who emphatically styles himself, "The Truth," communicated to all his works, and stamping on all things, in their various classes and kinds and natures, the image and superscription of their great First Cause. Truth, then, in man, is a conformity of his understanding and of his words to God's order, to his will, and to his voice, which speaks in every thing. It is by this truth, in his heart and in his mouth, that he lives in subordination to the divine government; that he moves within the track of the divine providence; that he resigns himself to the divine disposal; and makes God's will, and not his own, the rule and measure of his conduct.

Hence it follows, that falsehood is in its very nature criminal. Independently of consequences, or of wrong associations, it is sinful in its very essence; and in its simplest form bespeaks its original from him, who is the father of lies, and who was a liar from the beginning. If truth be the voice of God, shall we presume, in any instance, to extenuate a lie?—There may be, indeed, degrees of criminality in falsehood, as there are in blasphemy. It may not be the same offence to swear irreverently by the hairs of our head, as by heaven, or by the earth, or by the city of the great King: but, still, to falsehood, in every shape, we may most fairly accommodate the argument of which we are here reminded, and pronounce, beyond the possibility of contradiction, that if God has numbered the hairs of our heads; if his hand has formed them white, or black, and the truth of things has stamped them so; we cannot falsify even as to one of these, without lifting up our voice against (and shall I say, without in a certain sense denying?) the God that is above.

If these observations have any weight, the white lie (if we understand thereby an innocent falsehood) can have no existence in the nature of things; and thus the practice of saying "Not at home" is stripped of its last defence, and driven from this last "refuge of lies." It is time then, surely, Sir, for serious persons at least, to renounce it; to adopt other modes of repelling interruption or levity from their doors; or even, if they complain that this cannot otherwise be effected, rather to admit the occasional visits of intrusion, than to cherish falsehood in the very bosom of their domestic privacy.

ON

FALSELY SAYING,

"NOT AT HOME."

I TAKE the liberty of offering some further observations, as supplementary to the little paper on "Not at Home," which appeared in your publication of May last.

There is one imposing argument, by which the advocates for this practice endeavour to secure its permanency. They contend that this is but one of a large class of forms, all precisely of the same kind; and that if we reject it, we must, to be consistent, go a great deal farther; we must, in fact, renounce with it the use of terms, without which the common civilities of life could not be preserved. For instance, it is argued, that if we give up

"Not at Home," we cannot answer cards of invitation in the usual form; we cannot say, "We are sorry we cannot wait on" an acquaintance, unless we feel an unmixed desire for his society, and are prevented by some strictly insurmountable impediment. Now, I conceive, that this consequence by no means follows.

I will suppose myself invited to dine abroad, and my inclination to do so counteracted by a prior engagement. No one can, I presume, charge me with the slightest breach of truth, if I decline in the usual way, though there is surely no absolute or physical impossibility in the case. Why, then, if I have sufficient reasons of another nature for refusing an invitation, am I not at liberty to use the same courtesy? If I feel that my time may be more profitably spent at home, or if I have grounds for fearing that, in the company I expect to meet, such conversation or amusements may be introduced as are unsuitable to my sentiments, surely I may consider these obstacles at least as important as a prior engagement to another place. In such cases, then, I use the term "cannot," in its received import, as implying, not a strict impossibility, but an impediment sufficiently real to influence my conduct.

But is there no insincerity in professing that " I am sorry?" By no means. I may feel a decided disinclination to accept an invitation, and at the same time regret that I cannot oblige my acquaintance by compliance. I may experience, and should experience, real sorrow, if the impediment arises from any thing irregular in his mode of life. And with such sentiments I may, in perfect candour, accompany my refusal with an expression of sorrow; reserving to myself, as every wise man will, those secret reasons and motives, which it would be, perhaps, only mischievous to divulge.

But what if there be no serious motive, no moral consideration, nothing that can be called a reason in the case,—can I, in these circumstances, refuse an invitation in the usual form? Can I, in short, profess myself, with truth, " sorry" at not being able to accept it, when my own whim or fancy is the only obstacle? *In soberness, I do not think I can*,—I see no possible argument by which such expressions can in this case be reconciled with truth, unless we admit the ridiculous supposition that the writer is heartily sorry he is whimsical and capricious.

But, in fact, when we look for a high and delicate sense of truth, we naturally look for a great deal more. We expect to find a symmetry of character, an assemblage of those virtues, without which a mere insulated love of truth would be absolutely monstrous. And perhaps the advocates for truth have unintentionally betrayed its cause in nothing more than in even supposing it in association with depravity or folly, and in giving rules for cases where the sole intricacy arises from the impossibility of consistently preserving truth, where good sense and good nature are deliberately violated. In such an instance, then, were I asked how a man shall reconcile sincerity with caprice; how, where a courteous invitation is rejected from mere whim, that rejection shall be worded so as to accord with truth, my answer should be this: "Cease to be whimsical and capricious, and there will be no difficulty in the case." Leaving then such persons to the correction of their follies, we may safely pronounce, that no sober and consistently moral man is obliged to depart from established custom, in the particular we are now considering.

Let persons object as they please to thus gravely moralizing on the wording of a card; for my part, I conceive that no instance can be trivial in which the sincerely conscientious are disburdened of one needless scruple, or in which truth is vindicated from the charge of involving in its strictest exercise either coarseness or indecorum. If, in fact, this charge were founded, the whole symmetry of the christian character would be at an end, and that charity, which " rejoiceth in the truth," and which " behaveth itself not unseemly," would be self-contradictory, and, consequently, unattainable.

That sincerity and politeness are not indeed *always* reconcilable, we freely grant, and we have already noticed one instance in which they are not so. But whence does this arise? Not surely from the contrariety of the two, but from the intervention of counteracting causes: just as two pure and congenial liquids may refuse to blend, or, by their blending, may produce a noxious compound, if committed to an impure vessel. But is it, therefore, necessary, or wise, to throw both, or either of them, away? No, the fault is in the vessel, and not in the liquids, and you have only to cleanse the former to produce the effect you want. Let us then apply this principle to ourselves. The christian virtues are all harmonious and congenial; but christian virtues can live and centre only in a christian heart. If we find, then, in ourselves any obstruction to their kindly blending and harmonious exercise, shall we renounce them altogether? or shall we, if that were possible, be content with being virtuous by halves? Shall we not rather look to our own hearts, and purify the medium in which they refuse to blend?

But, in reality, truth and politeness are so far from inconsistent, that it is, perhaps, the union of these two virtues which gives the last finishing to the christian character. For let it be observed, that, reconcilable as we admit them to be, the sole principle on which they are so, is that which, in all ages, has been the acknowledged criterion of true goodness, namely, that we be inwardly what we would appear outwardly. What, in fact, can follow from a sincere desire to please, accompanied by a no less real hatred of all false pretences, but a constant endeavour to cultivate kind, and benevolent, and charitable affections; that, so as far as is possible, we may live in the habitual exercise of "love without dissimulation?" Nor is this mere speculation. I have myself known, in living persons, the united disinclination to falsify or to offend, produce a general softening of the character. I have seen it lead to the closest self-discipline, to the exclusion of hasty prejudice, of capricious dislike, of unnecessary singularity, and in constant daily action, as an influential, corrective, and governing principle.

One more observation, and I have done. Will it be thought visionary if I suggest, that a wise and delicate regard to truth naturally imparts a peculiar grace to polished conversation?—and that not merely by its native dignity and simplicity, but by a certain dexterity and felicity of address, which imperceptibly results from it. Blunt truth and blunt falsehood are at least agreed in one thing,—they are both straight forward; they require no choice of terms, no suitableness of manner, no fitness of occasion. Every animal endued with speech, can offend by truth, or flatter by a lie. But there is in intellectual things, as in corpóreal substances, a line of beauty: and this probably derives its claim to preference from the same source in both; the curbed or undulating line, or movement, bespeaking ease and softness: not, as it were, advancing to its destined point with a directness which implies necessity, nor with a defiance of obstruction which implies resistance; but (to exemplify what could not perhaps be otherwise described) flowing like a gentle river, which moves only where it can move with grace; which yields to every obstacle, but which still pursues its course, deriving from impediments themselves at once its extended utility and characteristic beauty.

This distinction between polished and vulgar intercourse consists, perhaps, in nothing more than in the *line* in which conversation runs; all that is elegant in the one, proceeding from the constant action of those restraints which check its right-forward movement; and all that is repulsive in the other, from those *home thrusts* and *random shots*, which no dexterity can escape, and no obstacle turn aside.

My meaning will be at once illustrated by two well-known instances: that of Sir James Melvil, who, being asked by Queen Elizabeth whether he esteemed herself or his mistress to have the fairest person, replied, that her Majesty was the fairest person in England, and his mistress in Scotland; and that of Cyrus, as related by Xenophon, who, being inquired of by his mother which he thought the handsomest, his father or his grandfather, answered, "Of the Persians, O mother, my father is much the handsomest; and of all the Medes I have seen, this, my grandfather, is the handsomest."

What was it, I would ask, which gave to these answers their value, or their perpetuity?

It was the impediment which the case presented to a direct reply, and the necessity which it imposed of evading, and, as it were, steering round those obstacles which forbid a right-forward movement.

Prudential caution, and not moral principle, was assuredly the obstacle, at least in the former of these instances; but still they both serve to illustrate my position; they both afford memorable examples of the effect of restraint upon conversation, and of the opportunities it furnishes for the exercise and exhibition of skill, of management, and of address.

But let these restraints be of a moral nature; let truth and genuine politeness be substituted for calculation and superficial polish; and surely the general operation of these principles on conversation cannot be questioned. Let it be tried by the acknowledged rules of taste, and it will be found, that conversation, thus regulated and disposed, possesses the very secret of elegance, proportion, and animation; that politeness is the graceful drapery which throws a veil over every unseemly part; and truth, the animating principle, which gives to whatever is disclosed, all the justness of symmetry, and all the expression and vividness of real life.

MEMOIR

OF

MRS. JARRATT.

HAVING experienced your kind attention to the short Memoirs which I successively sent you, of four of my departed children, and having reason to hope that those accounts were not void of utility, I transmit the following account of another departed daughter, whose conduct in life (if the testimony of friends may be admitted) was in many respects highly exemplary, and gave evidence of her love to God, and unfeigned faith in the Redeemer. I take this liberty also, at the request of some who were most intimately acquainted with her, and who have furnished me with such accounts as will convey a just idea of her character after she had ceased to be a member of my family.

Her natural disposition was frank, affectionate, generous, and cheerful. Religious impressions seem to have been made early upon her mind, and to have grown up gradually; but no particular period could be assigned for their commencement. In a familiar letter to her mother, when she had arrived at her twenty-fourth year, she thus expressed herself:—"It is a difficult thing for one surrounded by every comfort, to look upon this world as only a passage to the next. Indeed, the corruption of our hearts might be a sufficient reason for our wishing for a change, exclusively of all the joys that are promised to those who are so happy as to arrive at heaven: but the pain which the Christian feels on account of the corruption of his heart, is an *enviable* pain."

When about twenty-six years of age, she shewed great attention to her private devotions, usually retiring three times in the day for that purpose; a practice which she continued through life, though nothing of ostentation ever appeared on these occasions.

In 1797, she married the Rev. R. J——, with whom an union of sentiment and affection subsisted, which was increased and confirmed by their more intimate acquaintance with each other. She became the mother of eight children, of whom seven survive to deplore the loss of an affectionate, pious, and judicious parent.

In the education of her children, she evinced great firmness without harshness, and tenderness without indulgence. In this important branch of family duty her husband concurred, and properly took a leading part. The children were early brought to behave with decorum and submission to authority, even before their understandings were capable of receiving instruction. When they *were* capable, instruction was conveyed to them in an impressive, yet tender manner. She had a peculiar talent for reproving what she observed amiss in their conduct; of which the following little anecdote may be considered as a specimen:—Her youngest son, then six years of age, had one Sunday behaved in a careless, and somewhat irreverent, manner at church. She was at that time forbidden by her medical advisers to speak aloud, on account of a complaint at her chest; she therefore wrote down her reproof, and desired one of her sisters to read it to the offender. As he had expressed a wish to be a minister when he should arrive at a proper age, she put her reproof into the form of a sermon; and supposed the following address to be made by him to the children of his congregation. "I now address myself to little children.—You must go to church, but you may look about you; and if you have a book before you, you need never look at it; and you may move about all the time you are at church, and not remember one word that was said. This was the way I did when I was a little boy, and I do not remember ever feeling sorry for doing so." The boy felt the keenness of this irony, and seemed much ashamed of his conduct. This talent of faithful yet mild reproof, was not confined to her children; but was also extended to her friends, and to all that were about her.

The exercise of self-denial and mutual kindness was constantly and earnestly pressed upon the minds of her children; and as their understandings improved, the various duties of life were urged upon christian principles. The following extracts from a letter to one of her daughters will further shew her manner of conveying instruction to her family. While attentive to the least deviation in them from the path of *duty*, her constant aim was, to lead them to a right *faith* in the Redeemer, that they might not depend upon any righteousness of their own for pardon and acceptance with God.

"My dear ——, as it has pleased God to deprive me of the power to converse with you, I have determined to take up my pen, to point out one or two things that may be of use to you. You are now arriving at an age when religion should appear of the first consequence to you. If you do not begin now to be serious about your soul, there is a danger of your growing more and more indifferent to it. In Scripture this work which we have to do is called a warfare, which implies that we have enemies to fight against; but these enemies vary in different persons, so that I would have you set about an examination, what are the things in you which you know to be displeasing to God. There are some things which your friends can see; but there are more, I have no doubt, that are known only to God and yourself. By way of helping you to set about this duty of self-examination, as a kind mother, I will point out one or two things in you which I have observed, and which will be something to begin with in this good employment. It is said in the Bible, 'Be kindly affectioned one towards another;' and, 'Let brotherly love continue.' We should ask ourselves, Am I striving to keep this commandment? Do I ever give up my will, or any little self-indulgence, to make my brothers and sisters happy, and to please them? At one time I had very great pleasure in seeing you exercise this beautiful system of self-denial, more than you do at present. Now, to-day, you had a hassock which I observed you kept to yourself, while your sister was left without one. I cannot myself find out where the enjoyment was of doing this. You know that frequently on a Sunday, I have invited you to use part of mine; and it was more pleasure to me than having it all to myself. In little things which occur every day, the strife is,—'Let ME have it;' whereas it should be,—'I have more pleasure in gratifying you than myself.' This would be pleasing to God, and would also make you happier."

After giving some directions respecting the books she should read in the intervals of divine worship on the Lord's day, and recommending particularly the perusal of "Doddridge's Rise and Progress of Religion in the Soul," Mrs. J—— proceeded,—"I think also that you ought to take more time for your private devotions." She then earnestly advised her retiring to her room before bed-time, that she might have an opportunity of reading the Scriptures by herself, and thinking over what she had done in the day, and then added,—"It is not the length of your prayers that will recommend them to God, but faith in Christ, which alone can procure for us those things of which we stand in need. That is, it is Christ who procures them for us; but it is through faith that we receive them. Whatever we ask for, depending upon him, we shall receive. But as, on the one hand, we must not expect to recommend ourselves to God by our much speaking; so, on the other, we are to leave ourselves sufficient time, not to hurry over our prayers."

These little details may perhaps appear to some readers to possess scarcely interest sufficient to render them worthy of being so particularly recorded; yet I cannot but think that such familiar instances of religion, in quiet and domestic life, may oftentimes furnish a lesson of useful instruction, or a pattern for ordinary imitation, beyond what is derived from memoirs more replete with brilliant incidents or sentiments.

As it was her constant practice to speak evil of no one, so it was her delight to set before her children the example of any person with whose piety and good conduct she became acquainted. An instance appears in a letter to another of her daughters.

—"We are now at ——. Mrs. S—— is a pattern for all ladies to follow. If I and all my daughters were like her, we should be one of the best families in all ——shire. You can see by her conduct that the Bible is her guide. She has not the affectation of any grace, but the reality. *Self* seems in her to have no place. I believe she has habituated herself so long to act from higher principles, that it is very little self-denial to her to give up to others, and study their comfort rather than her own."

"I have looked into Miss Hamilton's work lately, and have been much pleased with her sentiments on self-denial. She points out very strikingly its beneficial effects, when it is exercised even in little daily occurences. It brings the mind into a state of subordination, which enables us to resist temptation, and prepares us for disappointments in life. I have myself frequently observed the different effects of disappointments on persons who are exercising themselves in this way, and those who are not. We can never be too young to begin this salutary employment. Indeed, I hope you do exercise it sometimes, for you have often had its advantages pointed out to you. I want it to be more a system with you. Had you omitted to take your meals, you would feel the want of them: let this principle then become more and more habitual to you, that so it may become one of your *pleasant* employments; and, in a manner, as needful as your meals.

"How happy should we all be, if we considered more how we might please God! He sees our hearts; and it is our motives by which he judges of our actions. Oh, my dear ——, let us pray God to give us the Spirit to *enable* us to do what is pleasing to Him; for without that Spirit we can do nothing."

It seems that the reproof contained in the former of these letters, had produced its proper effect; for, in a subsequent letter to one of her sons, she thus writes:—"There is one thing I ought to tell you in praise of your sisters, which gave me great pleasure. Mr. W. said, that they were very kind to each other. You know, my dear boys, what delight it would afford us to see *brotherly love* among you. I hope you have learned the one hundred and thirty-third Psalm, which I recommended to you. You recollect also, the fable of the bundle of sticks. I wish you all to remember it. When you return home at the next vacation, I hope we shall see a great improvement in this respect. *You* will be happier, as well as every one around you. Each one must determine to give up to others;

and you will find greater satisfaction in this, in the end, than if every one gave way to you. Indeed, it brings a present gratification with it. I hope you do not forget your promise to me, that you would read a portion of your Bible every day. This is a duty we should never forget. I hope also you will begin to think it a duty to improve your time, and strive against all *self-indulgent* habits. You will find it useful in future life."

In another letter to the same, written soon after the death of a pious woman, who died in the alms-house,—and with whom, notwithstanding the disparity of their circumstances, she had contracted an intimate friendship,—she thus endeavoured to impress upon him the example of that excellent woman, who was well known to all her children:—"When I saw Mary B—— before she died, she spake of the preciousness of a Saviour, and her own unworthiness. If we have not him for our help, we shall find it no where else. He is precious to them that believe. Let us then be in earnest to have the Holy Spirit to teach us to believe on Him. What a glorious change to Mary, who had lived in poverty all her life, and had many troubles of various kinds! We have lost a good woman's prayers. We know not but many of our mercies have been the fruits of her intercessions for us. We must now endeavour to improve them."

These extracts from her letters shew sufficiently the system of education which she, following the steps of her husband, pursued with her children; and, I trust, that system was not pursued in vain.

She was remarkable for punctuality in her engagements, and for method in her domestic arrangements; by which means she went through much business, and yet had leisure to pursue a course of reading for the improvement of herself and her daughters.

She was much interested in the concerns of the poor. Their wants were sought out, and judiciously relieved by her. She did not stand aloof from their company and conversation, but had usually two or three poor women to dine at her house on the Lord's day.

She had suffered much from the natural small-pox in infancy, which left a tendency to catarrh, that frequently affected her in the winter season, and at last terminated in a consumption, which proved fatal to her in the fiftieth year of her age. A visit which she paid to me the year preceding her death, had given me the opportunity of painfully observing the increase of her complaint: and the accounts which I received from time to time, after her return home, confirmed my apprehensions of her danger. I became solicitous, that her repeated recoveries from a dangerous situation should not induce, at this time, an unwarranted expectation of restoration to health, and therefore thought it my duty to lay before her my apprehensions respecting her real situation.* She received my letter about a month before her death, from which time her husband kept a journal of the most material circumstances relating to her; and during the last three weeks, another was kept by her eldest sister, who then went to visit her, and remained with her to the time of her departure. From these journals I have extracted the following accounts, which will further illustrate her character and conduct.

My communication of her danger was received by her with great calmness and composure, accompanied with strong expressions of her obligation to me for thus directly giving her my opinion of her situation. She observed, that many prayers had been offered to God for her recovery, which he had not thought good to answer: it was now, therefore, proper to leave that matter to him, and think only on the preparation for her removal.

* This letter has been printed in the Life of Mr. Hey. Part 2. Page 57.

She added, that her friends had also prayed that her illness might be sanctified: this she hoped and trusted would be granted to her, saying, "I desire to be resigned to God's will, knowing that he does all things well."

Her eyes being now turned from worldly affairs, and directed almost exclusively to the views of an eternal state, to which she saw herself hastening; she took a formal leave of her most intimate friends, as if about to proceed upon a journey whence she should not return. Though oppressed with difficult breathing, a harassing cough, and universal swelling of the body, she continued to ride out almost daily in an open carriage, and thus took the opportunity of visiting her more distant friends, to whom she communicated the letter which I had written to her, bidding them farewell with serious composure, and a placid cheerfulness that surprised and greatly affected those whom she visited on this occasion. Her husband, who accompanied her, gives this account of her behaviour: "I have beheld with astonishment her conduct during the last week. She has gone with the utmost composure and taken leave of different friends; and when we have met them on the road, with an unruffled mind, she has shaken hands with them with a view to a final farewell."

Her children being once collected in her room, she thus addressed them in a most kind and affectionate manner:—"You must, my dear children, read your Bible diligently. Do not neglect it. Enter into the spirit of it. Pray earnestly, not as if repeating a form of words, but understanding what you are praying for. Your hearts are naturally corrupt, and must be changed. Pray earnestly for new hearts. Watch against temptations. Keep apart from the world. There are means of grace, which God has appointed us to use. Seek an interest in Jesus Christ, and that will bring you peace at the last. You must be good, if you would be happy. The way of holiness is always a way of happiness. There must be an obedience unto holiness. Devote your youth to God."

She then particularly addressed her two eldest sons, who had expressed a desire to enter into the ministry. "If you wish to be ministers, consider the matter, that you may not be surprized," meaning with the difficulties which might occur in that office. "Weigh the matter well whether you will be on God's side or not. When you go to college, associate with none but those who are decidedly serious. Avoid evil company. Avoid the first approaches of temptation. The trials of your constancy will be many; and you will frequently have occasion to say, 'How can I do this great wickedness, and sin against God!' If you are ministers, may you be the means of turning many to righteousness. But it is not sufficient to preach merely morality, there must be something more. Preach the gospel: and what a blessing will it be, if you are made the instruments of good to your fellow-creatures!" She then added,—"I wish to leave you all my blessing, my dear children, and say this to you now, lest I should not have strength to say it at another time. May you all walk in the paths of holiness,—and may we all meet together in heaven!"

A deep humility was manifest in the whole of her conduct. This led her to maintain a constant jealousy over herself, and fear of self-deception. When her sister arrived, to whom she had been accustomed to open her mind freely, she took an early opportunity of requesting her assistance in the way of self-examination. "Deal *plainly*, and faithfully with me;—do not spare me. I think I meant what I said, when I prayed in the night, 'Search me, O Lord, and try my thoughts, and see if there be any way of wickedness in me; and lead me in the way everlasting:' but I am afraid of being hypocritical,—of acting a part,—of not being sincere." At another time, she expressed great fear of acting only under the impression of the immediate prospect of death, and the importance which such a situation would naturally give to those things which related to her eternal state, without being influenced by the *love* of God.

She was afraid of having greatly failed in the duty of self-examination; but to others, who were most intimately acquainted with her, every part of her conduct seemed to have passed in review before her. "I cannot describe," said one of her most intimate friends, "the humility expressed in her looks, while speaking of herself."

Of the rest which "remaineth for the people of God" she delighted to converse, saying at one time, "What a blessed employment it will be to praise God! I feel as if I could praise and love him to all eternity. Praising our Redeemer for his love to us will be sufficient to employ us to all eternity." At another time, when the conversation turned upon the happiness of heaven, she said she was much struck with that expression in the Psalms, as opposed to the unsatisfactory pleasures of this life,—"When I awake up after thy likeness, I shall be SATISFIED."

After a little pause, she repeated the word SATISFIED.

She often spoke with great pleasure of the hope of meeting her departed religious friends in heaven; at the same time expressing her desire to possess a greater meetness for that state of bliss and glory. Conversing with a pious minister upon the evidences of that meetness, she said she hoped she felt a strong abhorrence of sin, and also that she could repose her soul on the Saviour of sinners; but she felt distressed that she could not do both in a greater degree, adding, " but it is a great comfort that Christ changeth not. He is the same, yesterday, to-day, and for ever: *that* is my strongest encouragement,—if it were not so, I could have no hope."

She entertained a deep sense of the natural corruption of her heart; spoke of herself as having the seeds of all sin in her, which would, if unrestrained, have led her to all gross sin and wickedness; and said, there was a sufficiency of sin in her very best duties to condemn her. I am a sinful creature,—a *very* sinful creature." The subject of conversation one day being whether the sins of true believers would be mentioned at the last day, and what was implied in the expressions, "blotted out," and "cast into the depths of the sea," she remarked, that "she should have no objection to have her's made known, if it would add to the glory of the Redeemer."

She requested the prayers of her friends, that she might enjoy a more assured confidence of the love of God towards her. With respect to any happy feelings, she was exceedingly jealous of deception. She said that the goodness of God, as displayed in his word, had struck her exceedingly during the last year; but she wanted to have a more lively sense of the love of Christ in the work of redemption; and to feel what is implied in that expression of St. Peter, "Unto you that believe, He is precious."

She dreaded the thought of relapsing in the least from from the path of duty, and said one day to her husband, "If I must become worldly, I should not wish to be restored to health." Her constant aim was to grow in grace, and in the knowledge of Jesus Christ. She said, "I hope I shall advance more in meetness before I am taken away. I want an *entire* resignation to the will of God, and to know" (with more peaceful assurance) "that Jesus Christ is the propitiation for my sins." She admired the character of God as given in the Holy Scriptures; and studied the historical books as affording a display of that character. On the Sunday evening, a fortnight before her death, she expressed how much she had been struck with the exhibition of God's goodness in the one hundred and sixth Psalm, (read that afternoon in church,) even to those who were rebelling against him: "Our fathers regarded not thy wonders in Egypt," &c.; "nevertheless he helped them for his name's sake:" "and surely," she said, "He that was so ready to help them again and again, would not reject her prayers when she cried earnestly to him."

She possessed a deeply devotional spirit. The character given of her, by one who knew the most of her disposition and conduct, was, "She has been a woman of prayer." Her delight was in the ordinances of divine worship. In her extreme weakness she constantly attended both morning and evening prayer in the family: and was usually carried to church, either to the morning or evening service, (the latter of which she attended on the last Sunday of her life;) and when able she attended on both parts of the day. She often expressed the enjoyment which she experienced in these divine ordinances.

Her sufferings were considerable during the latter period of her life; so that she often seemed as if the least additional exertion would extinguish the lamp of life,—like a quivering flame, that any little blast would put out: yet her amiable, affectionate, hospitable feelings remained unimpaired: and her own sufferings never caused her to lose sight of the comfort of others, in the minutest instances. When reminded of her sufferings by the servant who waited on her, she would sometimes reply,—"My feelings are *very uneasy;* but I hope God will give me patience and submission, that I may not dishonour Him." Not a murmur or complaint ever escaped from her.

She was greatly beloved in the place where she resided; so that when, about a month before her death, the prayers of the congregation were desired for her, there was a loud sobbing heard from many in the church when her name was announced. This love was evinced in such a variety of ways, that one of her friends remarked, that it might be said, not only of the immediate circle which surrounded her, but of her more remote connexions also, "Behold, how they loved her!"

On the last day of her life she was carried into the garden adjoining the house: but her weakness was then so great, that she imagined she must have died there; yet, upon being brought in, she desired to sit at the table during dinner. After dinner she said to those about her,—"I feel my life a vapour; but though I say so, you are not to conclude that there are no stores for me in another world. I trust there are. I take nothing to myself. If I should even perish, I hope I shall not lay it to God's charge. I feel nothing whatever. The weakness of my body prevents me from feeling any thing. You have no idea what weakness is. Oh, that God would lift up the light of his countenance upon me!"

Her sister read to her some passages of Scripture; after which she desired that all would leave the room but one person, that she might pray. Having prayed, she was carried to bed, and dismissed her attendants after a hymn or two had been read to her. Her husband alone remained with her, and having given her a little refreshment about midnight, he lay down, and fell asleep. He awoke about four o'clock; but her happy spirit had departed, her countenance remaining unruffled, and her body in an easy reclined posture, as though she was in a sleep.

Thus graciously was the prayer answered, which she had once desired her friends to offer up for her, "That the last struggle might not be *very* painful."

The character given of her by the clergyman, who preached her funeral sermon, was summed up in the following manner.

"Though the nature of the malady with which the afflicted sufferer was visited for some time previous to her decease, prevented her from taking that part in colloquial intercourse which she had been accustomed to do in former years, to the delight and improvement of those who enjoyed her society, she still continued to be a source of much useful instruction to many of those who were about her. Though generally a silent, she was always a powerful, monitor. When she did occasionally engage in conversation, it was for the most part on topics connected with her most holy faith; and then she evidently breathed an element most congenial to the renewed constitution of her soul. To one of these occasions in particular, myself, in conjunction with others, am enabled to look back with mingled feelings of satisfaction and regret: an occasion, on which, if I mistake not, in the midst of her assembled family, the beauties of the christian character were strikingly displayed, in this depressed but wonderfully supported saint. The nature of that warfare, of which we have been speaking; the evidences of that faith, without which it cannot be carried on; and the glories of the eternal crown which is laid up in heaven, were then occupying the thoughts of her mind. Then indeed it was that unfeigned humility and self-abasement, a deep-rooted abhorrence of sin, a simple trust and reliance on the Saviour of sinners, a patient submission and pious resignation to the divine will, an earnest desire for an increase of faith, were too conspicuously exhibited not to arrest the attention of those around her. It was then evident to others, that while the outward man was daily and gradually decaying, the inward man was strengthened and renewed."

SUGGESTIONS

FOR RECONCILING THE

ARMINIAN AND CALVINIST.

I HAVE received much pleasure from the attempts which have been lately made by Mr. Cooper, in his excellent volume of Letters, as well as in your Review of that work, and by your Correspondent INGENUUS, to conciliate those pious persons, who, agreeing in the fundamental doctrines of Christianity, still maintain some degree of hostility as Calvinists and Arminians. That the Christians who choose to adopt these titles of distinction, should be brought to a uniformity of sentiment, respecting those doctrines on which they now differ, is not to be expected. But that the animosity, which has been too often excited by their difference, may be abated, or entirely removed, is not beyond the bounds of probability, where a moderate degree of christian candour possesses the heart of each.

Your Correspondent Ingenuus having invited any friend of the Christian Observer to point out terms of amity, that are " fair, easy, and practicable," I shall beg leave to offer a view of the subject, which has completely tranquillized my own mind, and which may tend to produce the same happy effect upon the minds of others.

The relief I have obtained with respect to the discordancy that appears in many passages of Scripture has been obtained, by considering the Bible in its doctrinal, no less than its preceptive part, as a PRACTICAL BOOK, and claiming for every doctrine it contains a corresponding state of heart and conduct in the receiver of that doctrine. And if we diligently attend to the instruction which each passage conveys, we shall find that those parts of Scripture which appear irreconcileable in theory, are yet perfectly reconcileable with respect to the practical effect which they are designed to produce upon our minds. Though often set in hostile array against each other by controversial combatants, it will not be denied by either party that an obedient regard to both becomes necessary to constitute the christian character.

The Scriptures abound with passages which represent religion as the effect of a divine agency upon the heart; yet, at the same time, command us to "*cleanse ourselves* from all filthiness of flesh and spirit." An exclusive attention to either of these representations, would produce in us erroneous sentiments as to doctrine, and defective conduct respecting our practice. Yet, as both are taught by the same authority, they have an equal claim upon our attention. Passages of the former kind teach us our depraved condition by nature, and urge us to implore the sanctifying influences of the Holy Spirit, to renew our hearts in righteousness and to strengthen every holy desire already wrought in us. They teach us also to give all the glory to God, for those holy desires or tempers of which we are conscious; and considering ourselves as mere recipients of his bounty, to arrogate nothing that is good to ourselves; while passages of the latter kind tend to produce a holy shame and deep remorse for the unholiness which yet remains in our hearts, and for which we are considered to be strictly responsible.

The sacred writers see no opposition in those passages which persons engaged in angry controversy on the subjects now under consideration have produced against each other: and whosoever seeks for the practical directions which the respective passages convey, will perceive that his religion would be defective, if either series of texts were suffered to produce a neglect of the others.

"Work out your own salvation," says the Apostle, "with fear and trembling: for it is God which worketh in you both to will and to do of his good pleasure." Philippians ii. 12, 13. How beautifully is the christian character described in the two distinct parts of this passage! The true believer in Christ labours with the most serious concern to avoid every thing that would endanger his salvation, and to perform every act of obedience with the same care that would be required if salvation were attainable merely by his own efforts; while at the same time he is conscious of his utter inability to maintain even a good thought, without the sanctifying operation of the Holy Spirit; and continually approaches the throne of grace, that he may be enabled to do those things which God has commanded.

When our Saviour says, (John vi. 37;) "All

that the Father giveth me shall come to me;" or, as it is expressed in verse 44, "No man can come to me, except the Father which hath sent me draw him;" and adds, (verse 37,) "And him that cometh to me I will in no wise cast out." How forcibly are we urged to supplicate those influences of the Holy Spirit, which, though absolutely necessary to our coming to the Redeemer, are represented as flowing only from the sovereign good pleasure of God; while at the same time all doubt is removed of a favourable reception, which there is no secret decree to prevent, if we truly come to Christ as the only Mediator betwixt God and man!

If difficulties remain in the Scriptures, as is certainly the case, they remain as tests of our humility, and demonstrations of our sincerity, whilst we pay a strict regard to all that is plainly revealed.

God hath declared in his holy word, that he "will have all men to be saved, and to come to the knowledge of the truth;" (1 Timothy ii. 4;) and also, "that there is none other name under heaven given among men whereby we must be saved, but the name of Jesus Christ." Acts iv. 12. Yet he hath not as yet seen fit to make this name known to all men. Millions of our fellow-creatures, to whom he *could* have sent the glad tidings of salvation as well as to us, have never heard of this saving name. Instead, then, of attempting to reconcile these apparently discordant passages of Scripture, we are constrained to cry out with the holy Apostle, " How unsearchable are his judgments, and his ways past finding out!" Romans xi. 33. These passages, however, convey to us most important instruction. They not only assure us of the good pleasure of God towards all who seek his favour in the way he has appointed; but call upon us to act as " workers together with him," in seeking the salvation of all men by every method in our power; and especially by communicating the gospel of Christ to those who are sitting in darkness and the shadow of death. The Scriptures assure us, as has been already observed, that it is God alone who can renew our hearts in righteousness, since it is he who worketh in us to *will*, as well as to *do*, of his good pleasure; so that if we are saved, our salvation must be ascribed to his free grace and sovereign good pleasure, " according as he hath chosen us in Christ before the foundation of the world, that we should be holy, and without blame before him in love; having predestinated us unto the adoption of children, by

Jesus Christ to himself, according to the good pleasure of his will." Ephesians i. 4, 5. Yet his predetermination of any event does in no wise lessen our obligation to promote it, if it be agreeable to his revealed will; nor diminish the wickedness of those who, in bringing that event to pass, transgress his moral commandments. Jesus Christ was "delivered by the determinate counsel and foreknowledge of God," to be offered as an atoning sacrifice for our sins; nevertheless, it was by "wicked hands" that he was "crucified and slain." Acts ii. 23. The Jews and Gentiles conspired to destroy this *anointed* of God; and in so doing were guilty of the greatest crime that ever was committed; yet in this they fulfilled what the "counsel" of God had "determined before to be done." Acts iv. 28.

How totally inexplicable are these mysteries in the providential government of God! yet they convey to us *practical instruction* of high importance. From them we learn the over-ruling power of the Almighty in every event. We are taught to consider our salvation as a work of free grace and mercy, yet without any excuse being afforded for our depravity and disobedience, which are wholly self-derived.

The purport of a passage may be obvious,

while some of the clauses which it contains are of difficult interpretation. The Calvinist and Arminian will annex a different meaning to the separate phrases in that awful caution against going back into sin, contained in Hebrews vi. 4—6: "For it is impossible for those who were once enlightened, and have tasted of the heavenly gift, and were made partakers of the Holy Ghost, and have tasted the good word of God, and the powers of the world to come; if they shall fall away, to renew them again to repentance," &c. Yet no one can doubt the general purport of the passage, as designed to guard us against the least approach to apostasy: and if we make this use of the caution, we need not be greatly distressed because we cannot satisfy ourselves about the exact meaning of its separate clauses.

St. Paul, in the eighth chapter of his Epistle to the Romans, expresses in strong language his persuasion of the final perseverance of God's elect; yet, in 1 Corianthians ix. 27, he informs us of the great caution which he himself used to "keep under his body, and bring it into subjection, lest by any means when he had preached to others, he himself should be a cast-away."

These passages are brought forward, by

the Calvinist and Arminian, as proofs of the truth of their respective tenets: and there is doubtless some difficulty in reconciling them as applied to the opposing systems. But, considered with regard to their practical effect, the opposition vanishes. The humble and cautious believer embraces both with equal regard, and finds no difficulty in their union. He cannot maintain too strong a confidence of his final perseverance, if that confidence does not diminish his fear of relapsing. Nor can his fear of relapsing be too great, if it does not diminish his confident hope of future glory.

If the pious Calvinist and Arminian would more confine their views to the practical instruction which every passage of Scripture is intended to convey, they would find a nearer approach to concord in their respective systems, than controversy has led them to expect. Experience happily proves the truth of this observation. I have often had much satisfaction in witnessing the harmony of religious persons of different sentiments respecting the Calvinistic controversy, when conversing on personal and practical religion; and when all idea of controversy was laid aside. And I am fully persuaded, that discord would give place to harmony in a very great degree, if personal and practical instruction were the grand object proposed to ourselves in our study of the Bible.

These observations might be carried on to a much greater extent: but enough has been said, I apprehend, to shew what I mean by considering the Bible as a *practical book*, and to point out the way in which Calvinists and Arminians may unite without any dereliction of their peculiar sentiments. Only let every passage of Scripture be regarded as teaching us individually what we are to be and to do, leaving the secret counsels of God towards others out of the question, and terms of amity will be afforded, which are "fair, easy, and practicable." Angry contentions among those who hold the fundamental doctrines of Scripture, will cease; and the faithful followers of the Redeemer will harmoniously join in the holy strife of shewing forth, by the obedience of their lives, their gratitude to Him who hath "loved them, and washed them from their sins in his own blood," and who will finally bring them to his heavenly kingdom, where, as kings and priests, they shall reign with him for ever and ever.

OBSERVATIONS

ON VARIOUS PASSAGES OF

SCRIPTURE.

OBSERVATIONS

ON THE

SIXTEENTH VERSE

OF THE

EIGHTH CHAPTER

OF THE

EPISTLE TO THE ROMANS.

The Spirit itself beareth witness with our spirits, that we are the children of God.

MANY have understood this passage of Scripture as implying that the Holy Ghost does produce in the mind of every true Christian a persuasion that his sins are forgiven, or in other words, that he is in a state of favour and acceptance with God; and, in consequence of this doctrine, have refused to acknowledge any one to be a child of God, who was void of this persuasion.

The following considerations may throw some light on this important subject.

1. If this belief of forgiveness, derived solely from an impulse of God's Spirit, be necessary to constitute a man a child of God, then there is a necessity for a new revelation from God, and the Holy Scriptures do not contain all the truths needful for our salvation. Such a persuasion, produced in this manner, is a new declaration from God, that I (William Hey, for instance) am forgiven, which is a fact no where declared in the Bible. The word of God declares, that all who believe in Christ are forgiven; and if I am conscious that I believe in Christ, I may *conclude* that I am forgiven: but if the Spirit of God tells me that I am forgiven, independently of any consciousness of my believing, then the Spirit of God makes a new revelation of something which the Bible does not contain. The supposed necessity of this impulse, which some have called the *direct witness of the Spirit*, certainly implies this conclusion, that the Holy Scriptures do not contain all the truths necessary to our salvation.

2. All that a man is *conscious* of with respect to this impulse, is, that he finds himself

persuaded that his sins are forgiven. He is not *conscious* that the Spirit of God works this persuasion; this is a fact he must *reason out*, or conclude from some circumstances attending the persuasion. If you ask a reasonable man why he believes that the persuasion which he feels of his forgiveness is the work of God's Spirit, he will tell you, that he finds this persuasion accompanied with love to God and all mankind, and a propensity to all holy obedience: and that he therefore *concludes* this persuasion to be the effect of a divine influence. He will acknowledge, likewise, that he should have just cause to think himself deceived, did he not find this persuasion accompanied with these holy affections.

These things being allowed, it follows, that this supposed impulse of the Spirit is not necessary to our assurance of being in the favour of God. For if I am conscious of holy tempers and affections, the Scriptures assure me that I am a child of God. "He that loveth is born of God, and knoweth God." I need nothing more than a consciousness of holy affections and actions, and a belief of the Bible to produce an assurance that I am a child of God. This supposed impulse of the Spirit is not therefore necessary for this purpose. If I am destitute of a consciousness of holy affections, it is the same with respect to any conclusions to be drawn by me, as if I were destitute of the affections themselves: and, if I were really destitute of these, I ought not to conclude myself to be a child of God, whatever impulse I may imagine myself to be the subject of.

3. To obviate the force of this reasoning, some have observed, that a Christian may be so oppressed with temptations, or the rising of corrupt inclinations, that he may not be able to maintain always a consciousness of holy affections sufficiently clear to produce assurance of his acceptance; and therefore, this operation of the Holy Spirit, which begets a persuasion of forgiveness independent of any consciousness of holy affections, is necessary for the comfort of the saints under such distressing circumstances.

But if this argument were of any force, it would establish delusion upon principle.

For if a man may, with propriety, maintain a persuasion of his acceptance with God when he is not conscious of possessing holy affections towards Him; then he may with propriety maintain such a persuasion when he has no such affections; that is, when he is a child of the devil. Because, if a man is not conscious of holy affections, it is the same thing to him with respect to any sentiments which he ought to maintain, as if he were destitute of such affections; and to be destitute of holy affections is to be under the divine displeasure.

Supposing a man possessed of a persuasion of his acceptance from some diabolical impulse, which is but supposing a possible case, and you are obliged to apply this reasoning to rescue such an one from his delusion. You must remind him that his false assurance is not accompanied with the fruits of the Spirit, and that every one is deluding himself who supposes himself to be in the divine favour without partaking of the divine image. And if a man has those gracious affections, which are the fruits of the Spirit's sanctifying influences, he has the strongest ground of assurance which he can possibly have, namely, the infallible authority of God's holy word, which is the most indubitable testimony that can be given.

4. The Scripture under consideration speaks of an *evidence* being given of our acceptance, and if we suppose the operations of the Spirit, which we call his *witness*, to consist of the

production of holy affections in the mind, together with an illumination of the understanding to discern those holy affections, we then suppose the Holy Spirit in this work to give us a real *evidence* or *proof* of our being in the divine favour, whereas, a mere *persuasion* gives no *proof* of this, but leaves a man still under the necessity of seeking for a proof elsewhere, if he would maintain an assurance on rational and scriptural principles.

The passage under consideration will admit of a translation somewhat different from that in our English Bible, full as consonant (to say the least) with the original, and the context. It might, with great propriety, be translated, "The same spirit" (viz. the spirit of adoption, mentioned in the preceding verse) "beareth witness with our spirits, that we are the children of God."—The Apostle is evidently enumerating several marks of God's children, and among others he mentions that of their having received the spirit of adoption, which he opposes to the spirit of bondage that formerly possessed their minds. The most natural interpretation of which passage seems to be this;—"Ye are not now actuated by a slavish disposition, which formerly extorted an unwilling service from you; as a slave serves his master to whom he is in bondage, merely through fear of punishment; but ye are now governed by a nobler principle, and ye serve God with the disposition of an obedient child, who performs a willing service to his kind parent:" and this, says the Apostle, proves that ye are the children of God.

5. This method of founding our assurance of God's favour on a consciousness of holy affections and actions is expressly taught in other passages of Scripture, particularly in St. John's First Epistle, where the subject is repeatedly mentioned, and explicitly treated of. There we are commanded to make our sanctification the foundation of our assurance, and are pointed to this as the grand distinguishing mark of our being in the divine favour. " Hereby we do *know* that we know him, if we *keep his commandments*." chapter ii. verse 3. " Whoso *keepeth his word*, in him verily is the love of God perfected:" " *hereby know we* that we know him;" verse 5. " Ye *know* that every one that *doth righteousness* is born of him;" verse 29. " In *this*" (the committing or not committing sin) " the children of God are manifest, and the children of the devil;" chapter iii. verse 10. " We *know* that we have passed from death to life,

because we *love the brethren;*" verse 14. "Let us not love in word, neither in tongue, but in deed, and in truth. And *hereby* we know that we are of the truth, and shall *assure* our hearts before him;" verses 19 and 20. "If our hearts condemn us not, *then* have we confidence towards God;" verse 21. "Every one that loveth is born of God, and knoweth God;" chapter iv. verse 7, &c.

In these passages we are told, in the plainest manner, that if we have renounced the commission of sin, and do find in ourselves a sincere love to God and the brethren, leading us into the practice of all righteousness; that thereby we know that we have the true saving knowledge of God, that we are born of him, and may assure ourselves of his favour. Here is taught the scriptural ground of *assurance* in terms so clear, that it is a wonder how this subject can admit of the least debate among Christians.

OBSERVATIONS

ON THE

ELEVENTH AND TWELFTH VERSES

OF THE

FIRST CHAPTER OF THE GOSPEL ACCORDING TO ST. JOHN.

He came to his own, and his own received him not: but as many as received him, to them gave he power (right or privilege) to become the sons of God, even to them that believe on his name.

1. It is of great importance to have just notions of that faith which God has appointed to be the medium of our acceptance with him; and this passage of Scripture gives us a very plain and explicit description of it: it is *to receive Christ* under the various characters which he sustains.

2. This is evidently more than merely to believe that what is written in the Bible is true. The devils believe thus, as St. James assures us, but they do not receive or submit to the Lord Jesus Christ; on the contrary, they oppose his authority and government with the utmost malignity. An assent to the truth of what Christ hath spoken, is undoubtedly included in the notion of true faith; but it does not fully express what the Scriptures intend by *believing* ON *the name of the Son of God.* I may believe that the writings of Julius Cæsar, called his "Commentaries," are true; but, as the Church of England justly argues, I have no dependance *on* Julius Cæsar, nor do I expect any thing from him. I *believe* Julius Cæsar, but I cannot, with any propriety of language, be said to *believe* ON him.

3. Neither is faith in Christ, as some suppose, a persuasion that my sins are forgiven: for this notion is a manifest absurdity. The Scripture promises that if I believe in Christ my sins shall be forgiven: my faith must therefore precede my forgiveness. But if faith is a persuasion that my sins are forgiven, then my forgiveness is prior to my faith, or I believe a lie. It would be a dreadful thing indeed to

suppose, that the Most Holy should command me to believe what is not true; and it is adding folly to wickedness to imagine, that my belief of a falsehood should make it true. Far be it from us to attribute such impious absurdity to the Almighty.

4. To conceive rightly of that faith of which so great things are spoken in Scripture, and which is appointed to be the instrument, or condition, of our acceptance with God; let us consider what are the characters which he bears on whom we are to believe; for to believe *on* him is only to have affections correspondent with those characters. He on whom we are to believe is the Son of God, who is become our Prophet, Priest, and King. To believe on him, is to receive him in these characters; to submit to him in each of these capacities; and to have those sentiments and affections towards him which these characters and offices demand from us. It is heartily to acquiesce in the truth of every thing that he hath spoken, to depend on the merit of his death as the atonement for our sins, and to submit in every thing to his government and authority.

5. To believe in Christ is evidently opposed

to rejecting him, in the passage under consideration. And as opposites often illustrate each other, let us consider what they did in rejecting Christ, who are here condemned for not receiving him. Their rejection of Christ plainly consisted in their refusing to believe him to be the Son of God, and to pay that regard to him which the characters he sustained demanded. They did not acquiesce in the truths he delivered; they refused to depend on him as the Lamb of God slain for their sins; and they would not have him to reign over them. This rejection of Christ was their crime, and the ground of their condemnation. The reverse of this is faith in Christ, in that sense of the word in which it is declared to be the condition of our acceptance.

6. This notion of faith is not only natural, simple, and easy to be understood by the meanest capacity; but it likewise comprehends, and reconciles all the various descriptions of faith which are given in the New Testament. Whether faith be represented as a belief that Jesus is the Christ, (as in 1 John v. 1;) as receiving his testimony, (John iii. 33;) as duly regarding his propitiation, (Romans iii. 25;) or as obeying him, (Hebrews v. 9;)

they are all included in the expression *receiving* him, and are shewn to be parts of that whole whereof the true justifying faith in Christ consists.

7. Would we, therefore, make a rational inquiry into the soundness of our faith, so as to lay a just foundation for assurance of being in the divine favour; we must examine whether we really believe that Jesus is the Son of God; whether we firmly assent to the truth of every thing he has revealed in his holy word; whether we depend solely on his death as the propitiation for our sins; and are determined, through his grace, to yield ourselves up to his guidance and direction. If this is our case, we believe in Christ, and have the strongest evidence that can be given, that we are reconciled to God, and that we are heirs of eternal glory.

8. To this account of faith it may be objected, that if obedience to Christ be included in the idea of faith itself, this were to suppose, that we are justified by works, in part at least, whereas the Scripture is very express in asserting that we are not justified by works. But upon maturely considering this matter it will be found, that the notion of faith above

defended is not contrary to the declarations of Scripture, that we are not justified by the works of the law, but by faith in Christ. For let it be considered in the first place, that whatever be our description of faith, it must be allowed to be an act of the mind, which is strictly speaking *a work:* for acts of the mind are as much our *works* as acts of the body, in a religious sense of the word. "Then said they unto him, What shall we do that we might work the works of God? Jesus answered, and said unto them, This is the *work* of God, that ye *believe* on him whom he hath sent." John vi. 28, 29. So that justification by faith could never be opposed to justification by any thing that is a work, for faith itself is a work. Again, neither can faith be opposed to every act of obedience; for faith itself is an act of obedience. We are as much commanded to believe in Christ, as to love God; "This is his *commandment*, that we should *believe* on the name of his Son Jesus Christ, and love one another, as he gave us commandment." 1 John iii. 23. And, therefore, to believe is as much an act of obedience as to love God.

When, therefore, it is asserted in Scripture that we are not justified by the works of the law, it must mean, that we are not justified in consequence of that obedience to the law to which justification is promised independent of the merits of Christ; namely, a complete, unsinning obedience; and that no obedience of ours is the meritorious cause of our justification. The duty required by such scriptural declarations is, that we do not consider ourselves as having merited favour at the hands of God, but look upon ourselves as wholly indebted to the mercy of God in Christ for our pardon and reception to eternal glory.

THOUGHTS

ON

CHRISTIAN PERFECTION.

---

1. The Scriptures repeatedly declare, in express terms, that there is no man who does not fall short of that obedience to God, which the moral law requires. There is not a just man upon earth that doeth good, and sinneth not." Ecclesiastes vii. 20. " There is no man that sinneth not." 1 Kings viii. 46. " Who can say, I have made my heart clean, I am pure from my sin?" Proverbs xx. 9. " Who can tell how oft he offendeth?" Psalm xix. 12. &c.

What reason is there to think, that these texts, which are found in the Old Testament, do not relate to mankind in all ages?

2. The Scriptures speak of a more abundant effusion of the Holy Spirit under the gospel dispensation; and the New Testament affords us a clearer display of our duty, and more abundant motives to the practice of it than the Jewish dispensation did. Supposing then, that the measure of christian holiness is not to be taken from that of the Jews; it will not follow, that there are any Christians to whom the above cited passages of Scripture may not be applied.

To illustrate this matter, let us suppose it to be asserted in the Old Testament, that there was no man living who did not remain ignorant of many things. Let us suppose, likewise, the New Testament to declare, that Christians had better opportunities of obtaining knowledge than the Jews, and that, in fact, Christians did advance to greater degrees of it than the Jews; and that the knowledge of the former was not to be measured by that of the latter. Every man of common sense must discern that this did not amount to a contradiction of the general assertions in the Old Testament respecting man's knowledge. Notwithstanding all these declarations in the New Testament, it might still be true, that there was no man who was not defective in knowledge.

This is precisely the case with respect to what is said concerning the holiness of mankind. The Old Testament asserts that there is no man who does not fall short of his duty to God; and the New Testament does not contradict this assertion, though it represents the Christian dispensation as affording greater advantages for growth in holiness, than the Jewish; and speaks of a more abundant effusion of the Holy Spirit under the latter, than took place under the former. We are therefore bound to believe the general assertions of the Old Testament with respect to all mankind, unless the Scriptures had left us as express declarations that these passages were only intended to point out the state of mankind in one period of the world.

3. But upon what ground is it believed, that there are Christians who do live without sin, and who are not defective in their duty to God? The foundation of such an opinion is this,—That there are found in the New Testament, *commands* and exhortations to perfect

obedience; *promises* from God of bestowing it; and *prayers* of inspired persons for it. A sufficient answer to these arguments is found in this consideration, that the same commands, promises, and prayers, are found in the Old Testament as in the New. And if these do not prove the sinless state of any pious Jew, neither will they prove it of any pious Christian. In the Old Testament, God commanded the Jews to love Him with all their heart, which is the sum of perfect obedience to the moral law; and added, by way of promise, "The Lord thy God shall circumcise thy heart, and the heart of thy seed to love the Lord thy God with all thine heart," &c. Holy men likewise prayed, under divine inspiration, that God would create in them a clean heart and renew a right spirit within them: yet there was not a just man who did not sin. No argument, therefore, can be drawn from such commands, promises, and prayers in the New Testament, which will set aside the truth of these general assertions respecting man's sinfulness.

5. Besides, in our interpretations of Scripture, we are not to take every expression we meet with, in a sense which it would bear in any other connexion; nor to understand every

sentence of Scripture in its most obvious and literal sense. But we are to discover the meaning of the inspired writers, by considering the scope and context of each passage, and by comparing it with other passages which may serve to determine the real design of the writers. For instance, St. John says, that "as Christ is, so are we in this world." Now Christ is perfectly free from the least degree of ignorance or unholiness;—he is superior to angels, and equal with the Father. But it would be blasphemy to apply this literal meaning of the sentence to any man. Other passages of Scripture then must direct us to the true meaning of this. The Evangelist says, that Zachariah and Elizabeth lived in all the ordinances and commandments of the Lord *blameless*; and at the same time informed us, that the former so far disbelieved the promise of God, as to bring down upon himself the punishment of a temporary dumbness. Holy men under the Jewish as well as the Christian dispensation, are frequently styled *perfect*, though their failures in obedience are sometimes recorded in the same passages. St. John, who frequently uses the word *perfect*, tells us, that "if we love one another, the love of God is perfected in us." So that we have the greatest reason to believe, that the inspired writers used this and such like terms in a qualified sense; and that the meaning of such expressions in the New Testament is similar to those in the Old Testament.

REFLECTIONS

ON THE

TWELFTH VERSE, &c.

OF THE

FIFTH CHAPTER OF ST. PAUL'S EPISTLE TO THE ROMANS.

Wherefore, as by one man, sin entered into the world; and death by sin; and (even) *so death passed upon all men, for that all have sinned.*

The entrance of sin into the world, and the consequences of man's first disobedience, are subjects of the highest importance. They involve some of the greatest mysteries of the divine conduct in the government of the world; and ought to be considered with the most profound reverence and humility.

In this passage of Scripture the Apostle shows both the relation in which mankind stand towards their first parent, and the penalty incurred by the first transgression.

The following reflections on these important topics are submitted to the consideration of the christian reader.

I. 1. It is plain, from the whole scope of the passage, that Adam did not act merely in his individual capacity; but that the effects of his conduct extended to all his posterity. " By one man sin entered into the world, and death by sin; and so death passed upon all men." verse 12.

2. The sufferings brought upon us by the sin of our first parent were not accidental, but by design. They were the effects of the sentence pronounced by the Judge of all. " The *judgment* was by one to *condemnation*;" verse 16. " By the offence of one *judgment* came upon all men to *condemnation*;" verse 18. " By one man's disobedience *many were made* (*κατεσταθησαν*, constituted) sinners;" verse 19.

3. If judgment passed upon all men in consequence of Adam's disobedience, then

Adam was the representative of mankind. In that covenant made with Adam, the effects of which were designed to extend to his posterity, Adam acted as the federal head of his posterity.

Mankind were treated in their first parent in their *aggregate* capacity; so that his disobedience was considered as the sin of the species. "Death passed upon *all* men, for that all have sinned;" verse 12. Whether the words ἐφ' ᾧ be translated, as in our text, "for that;" or as they are in the marginal reading, "in whom;" or, as Dr. Taylor translates them, "unto which;" this truth is still taught by the passage, that all mankind partake of the consequences of Adam's sin, because all have sinned. The original transgression being the sin of the species, the whole human race are exposed to the punishment of it. Infants, who have not sinned "after the similitude of Adam's transgression," that is, in their own persons, are in the number of those who have sinned unto death, in that original transgression by which death entered into the world.

4. This method of treating mankind in their aggregate capacity, by an express covenant made with our first parents, is analo-

gous to the constitution of nature, and to the method of God's dealing with the Jews during the theocratical government. It is adopted also by nations and other bodies of men, in their transactions with each other.

5. (1.) It is analogous to the constitution of nature. Our birth subjects us to partake of the same treatment with our parents. And we cannot enter into society without making ourselves liable to be dealt with in an aggregate capacity. The case of families and nations is clear in point. How often does God visit the iniquity of the father even upon those children who detest his crimes? And how often are subjects of a kingdom involved in the general distress accruing on account of the sins, which, in their individual capacity, they abhorred and resisted? Men are daily affected in their most important concerns, by the conduct of others with whom they are connected; and this by the appointment of Him who governs the world with wisdom and justice.

(2.) It is analogous to the mode of God's dealings with the Jews during the theocracy under which they lived. The Jews had often reason to complain, in the language of the prophet, " Our fathers have sinned, and are not; and we have borne their iniquities." The temporal blessings and curses, which were the peculiar sanctions of the Sinai-covenant, were often sent, or withheld, as consequences of the behaviour of their predecessors or governors. Sometimes the greatest judgments came upon the congregation on account of the crimes of individuals, who held no extraordinary rank in the community. The story of Achan (Joshua vii.) affords one of the most striking proofs of the divine procedure above mentioned.

God had expressly commanded the Israelites to destroy every thing belonging to the city of Jericho, except the " silver and gold, and vessels of brass and iron;" which were to be " consecrated to the Lord;" chapter vi. verse 18 and 19. Achan, an individual of no great note among the Israelites, concealed in his tent some part of the devoted things; and God treated this crime as the crime of the people at large; and punished the people for it as he had threatened; verse 18. The sacred historian gives this account of the transgression, (chapter vii.) " But the *children of Israel* committed a trespass in the accursed thing; for Achan took of the accursed thing, and the anger of the Lord was kindled against the *children of Israel.*"

When Joshua fell down before the Lord, astonished at the repulse which the people had met with before Ai, in which thirty-six of them were slain; he receives this account of the cause of that repulse. "*Israel* hath sinned, and *they* also have transgressed my covenant: for *they* have taken of the accursed thing, and *they* have put it among their own stuff. Therefore the *children of Israel* could not stand before their enemies, because *they* were accursed." verse 11, 12.

The men who lost their lives before Ai for this crime, were, in their individual capacity, totally innocent with respect to the crime for which they fell, as appears by the whole story; but the offence was considered as the sin of the people in their aggregate capacity; and, therefore, as *Israel* had sinned, *Israel* must suffer till the people at large had purged themselves by the destruction of Achan, and of all that belonged to him.

The total destruction of Achan's household, when Achan was discovered to be the perpetrator of the crime for which the nation had suffered, is an instance of the judgment of

God coming upon *families* in their aggregate capacity.

(3.) It is analogous to the procedure which the laws of nations have established among mankind. Distinct kingdoms must act towards each other in their aggregate capacity; and, on this account, individuals may, without injustice, suffer for crimes to which they had not personally consented.

All arguments against the propriety of treating mankind in an aggregate capacity must, therefore, be precluded; and we must cease to consider the world as under the righteous government of God, before we can allow that such treatment is universally unjust.

II. 1. If we consult the Scriptures we shall find, that *death*, when spoken of as the wages of sin, means eternal misery. " Sin, when it is finished, bringeth forth *death*." James i. 15. " If a man keep my saying," (saith Christ,) " he shall never see *death*." John viii. 51. " Whosoever liveth, and believeth in me, shall never *die*;" chapter xi. 26. When, therefore, the Almighty threatened death as the punishment of Adam's disobedience, we must understand the expression as explained by the concurrent testimony of the Old and New Testament, to mean the proper "wages of sin," eternal misery. Temporal death, with all the pains and diseases which bring it on and accompany it, was undoubtedly included in this threatening. So, also, was *spiritual* death, or that loss of righteousness and true holiness which chiefly constituted the image of God in which Adam was created.

2. Adam being constituted the representative of the human race, his whole posterity became liable to the same punishment which he incurred by his transgression. On this account we are exposed to sickness and death. On this account we come into the world with a moral depravity; and on this account we are "by nature children of wrath." Ephesians ii. 3.

The mode of expression used in the fifth chapter of the Romans plainly intimates, that the whole species of mankind are involved in the same sufferings, and exposed to the same condemnation by the one original offence. "By the offence of one" (or as it may with equal propriety be translated, *by one offence*) "judgment came upon *all men* to condemnation. By one man's disobedience many" (or, *the many*) "were made *sinners*." There is a remarkable repetition of this doctrine in the passage, as of a truth of great importance and unpleasant nature.

3. The doctrine of our redemption by Jesus Christ throws great light upon this of our fall in Adam. They are counterparts to each other. It is strongly insisted on in the Scriptures, that none can obtain salvation, but through that one Mediator between God and man, who "came to seek and to save that which was lost." If infants, therefore, partake of the benefits of Christ's death, they must be involved in the general condemnation.

Adored be the goodness of God, that he has appointed an ordinance to assure us of his favourable regard to them, before they are capable of acting in their individual capacity; as he has likewise appointed another ordinance for assuring all penitent and believing adults, of their acceptance, after numberless additional offences, through the prevailing atonement of our adorable Redeemer.

4. If it be thought an objection to this

doctrine, that God hath declared by the prophet Ezekiel, (chapter xviii. verse 20,) "The son shall not bear the iniquity of the father;" it should be remembered, that this passage, if taken in its most extensive sense, would contradict the sanction of the second commandment, which assures us, that God does "visit the iniquity of the fathers upon the children." It would likewise contradict many other Scriptures and facts which confirm the reality of this procedure. But if the passage in Ezekiel be expounded by its context, the meaning is plainly this;—That if a wicked man beget a son who abhors his father's impiety, and truly turns to God in righteousness, this son shall find favour with God, notwithstanding the iniquity of his father. This passage does not contradict the doctrine of the universal exposure of mankind to condemnation by the one original offence, because we are not connected with our immediate parents in such a covenant as that by which we stood connected with our first parent. But notwithstanding our condemnation on this account, every man will find acceptance with God who truly turns to him in the way He has appointed.

5. Upon the whole;—Two objections only

can be brought from reason against that original constitution which the chapter under consideration plainly teaches.

(1.) That moral conduct being a personal thing, the consequences of it, in reward or punishment, can only be personal.

(2.) That, allowing the justice of treating men upon some occasions, in an aggregate capacity; the punishment, in the case now considered, is too great for the offence.

The former objection is clearly invalidated by the authentic facts which have been adduced. And it is impossible to pay any regard to divine revelation, however corrupt men's ideas of Christianity may be, without allowing what must overturn this objection.

If it be an unrighteous proceeding to treat men in an aggregate capacity with respect to punishments for immoral conduct; then the righteous Judge of all can never treat men so. He will no more inflict the least punishment on this account, than he will inflict the greatest: because he is as far from doing a small act of injustice, as a great one. But the most violent opposers of the doctrine of original sin have been obliged to acknowledge that temporal death comes upon mankind in consequence of Adam's disobedience, which was the threatened punishment of his offence; and in allowing this they grant, that the punishment of immoral conduct may justly be extended further than to the person immediately offending.

The second objection amounts to no more than this; that, in the judgment of the criminal or sufferer, the degree of punishment exceeds the magnitude of the crime. But was this ever considered in human judgments as a sufficient objection to the propriety of any judicial proceeding? This objection may powerfully strike our imagination; but it can have no force upon our unbiassed reason. The universal Judge knows perfectly the nature of every offence; and adapts the punishment in every case with the most exact justice, for " true and righteous are his judgments."

This most important doctrine of Scripture loudly proclaims the exceeding sinfulness of sin; and should lead us to admire and value the unsearchable riches of divine grace in our redemption by Jesus Christ.

ON THE DOCTRINE OF FINAL PERSEVERANCE.

In discussing the doctrine of the final perseverance of the saints, two points must be previously determined.

1. What is meant by the term saints.
2. What by their perseverance.

By the term saint or holy person, is to be understood one, who is thoroughly convinced of the odious nature of sin; and, in consequence of this, has the most sincere abhorrence of it, and an unfeigned regret that he has ever offended God in thought, word, or deed. He not only fears to offend God, but he has also a true love of the divine character as revealed in the Holy Scriptures. He esteems the justice of God as well as his mercy. He thinks the ways of God, concerning all things, to be right. With sincerity he renews his baptismal covenant, determining, by the aid of divine grace, to be the faithful soldier and servant of Christ to the end of life. Yet, conscious of his numerous defects and deviations from the purity of God's most holy law; he daily looks up to the atoning sacrifice of his Redeemer, in whom alone he confides for pardon and acceptance with God.

This is the person of whose perseverance the doctrine in question maintains a confident hope. They who believe the doctrine to be scriptural, apprehend, that there is ground from various promises of holy writ, to think, that such an one will persevere in the holy course upon which he has entered, as they consider him to be now partaker of a new nature, which renders obedience his determined choice. This they judge to be the meaning of the Apostle, when he says: "If any man be in Christ, he is a new creature. Old things are passed away; behold, all things are become new."

The perseverance, then, of which they

speak, is a perseverance in holiness, a continuance in well-doing.

Yet, surrounded as we are by temptations of various kinds, and not entirely freed from the corruption of nature, derived from our first parents, a contest is maintained within; the flesh still lusting against the spirit. Hence occasional deviations arise, even in the best of men; but sin does not habitually prevail.

The practical use which any good man can rationally make of the doctrine is, the maintenance of a lively hope, that "neither death, nor life, nor angels, nor principalities, nor powers, nor things present, nor things to come, shall be able to separate him from the love of God which is in Christ Jesus our Lord." But this hope can no longer be maintained than while he retains the above marks of a saint, or holy person; for to such only is the promise of perseverance made. "My sheep hear my voice," saith Christ, "and I know them, and they follow me; and they shall never perish, neither shall any pluck them out of my hand." No one, therefore, can maintain a well-founded confidence that he shall never perish, but he who hearkens to the voice of Christ, and follows him.

The doctrine, then, cannot be legitimately employed to support any man in a course of sin, as such a course destroys its foundation.

It is allowed, with sorrow, that this doctrine may be abused; that an unlawful and unscriptural use may be made of it; but this concession affords no proof of the falsity of the doctrine, since the most clear and incontrovertible doctrines of the gospel are liable to the same abuse. Other Scriptures, besides those more difficult ones to be found in St. Paul's writings, are wrested by some persons to their own destruction. Nay, the gospel in general, which, to the pious mind, is a "savour of life unto life," to the heart fraught with deceit, proves a "savour of death unto death."

OBJECTIONS

TO SOME OF THE

CAPITAL DOCTRINES OF CHRISTIANITY,

ANSWERED UPON THE

PRINCIPLES OF COMMON SENSE.

TO SOME OF THE

CAPITAL DOCTRINES OF CHRISTIANITY,

ANSWERED UPON THE

PRINCIPLES OF COMMON SENSE.

THE Scriptures address themselves to the common sense of mankind, and speak, as far as the nature of the subjects will admit, in such terms as are commonly made use of. We ought, therefore, to make use of our common sense in interpreting the Scriptures: not to teach the Almighty what it is fit for him to reveal, but to understand the meaning of what he has revealed: and a proper application of the maxims which common sense dictates will, I think, remove some of the principal difficulties contained in the system of Christianity.

The chief objections which lie against the christian scheme, according to the best observation I have been able to make, are those which the doctrines of original sin, and the sanctifying influences of the Holy Spirit, give rise to.

It seems, at first sight, contrary to reason, that men should be depraved or holy in consequence of some exterior influence, something which does not originate from themselves. It seems, in such a case, as if men could not help being sinful or righteous; whereas, common sense dictates, that nothing is good or bad in a man which is involuntary, or has no connexion with his own choice.

These appear to me to be the fundamental objections against the christian religion. The rest are either raised against other doctrines connected with these, chiefly on account of that connexion; or are the effect of antipathy to the purity of its moral precepts.

The following propositions contain a plain answer to these objections.

Proposition I. No man can justly be required to do what is, properly speaking, out of his power; that is, what he cannot do, though he were ever so well inclined, and used ever such efforts to effect.

This maxim is so plain a dictate of common sense, that it may seem needless to add any thing by way of illustrating or confirming it. But as I shall have occasion to make much use of it, and as the force of the terms in which it is expressed, may not be obvious to every reader; I shall add a few words to confirm its truth, and shall endeavour to remove all ambiguity from the expressions.

The Apostle St. Paul, speaking to the Corinthians concerning the measure of their liberality, builds his reasoning upon this maxim. "If there be a willing mind," says he, "it is accepted according to that a man hath, and not according to that he hath not." 2 Corinthians viii. 12. There is no man, I believe, who can doubt of the reasonableness of this determination; and I would beg of any one who entertains the least scruple with respect to the proposition I have above laid down, to ask himself, why this determination is reasonable. Is it not because no one can justly be required to do what is out his power? Suppose, for a moment, that the Apostle had made a contrary determination, and had required of every one to give away twice as much as he was possessed of. Would the common sense of any man have suffered him to look upon this as a reasonable command? By no means.

The maxim, then, is indubitable: but let us carefully attend to the meaning of the expression, *out of our power*, and words of like import, as *cannot*, *unable*, *unavoidable*, *impossible*, *incapable*, *irresistible*, *necessary*, *&c*. The words which I have added, as explanatory in the proposition, exactly point out the meaning of such terms, which have always a relation to a contrary desire and endeavour, that either *is*, or *may be*, supposed in the case. A thing is *necessary*, in the original and proper sense of the word, when it is, or will be, notwithstanding all supposable opposition. Or it is necessary, with respect to us, when we cannot help it, let us do what we will. The word *impossible* has manifestly a reference to some supposed power exerted to bring a thing to pass, which is insufficient for that effect, or a thing is impossible to us, when the utmost exertion of our powers is ineffectual to accomplish it. That is properly *irresistible*, which overcomes all our opposition, resistance, and endeavours to the contrary. A man cannot properly be said to be *unable* to do any thing which he could do if he would; and, therefore, the terms *cannot*, and the like, are never used in their proper sense, unless such words may be added, as imply the existence of an inability, notwithstanding a contrary will and endeavour.*

It is the more needful to settle the meaning of such relative terms, because we frequently use them in a sense different from that which is their primary and proper one. In common language we often apply the terms, where no such contrary will and endeavour can be supposed; and this sense of the words, I shall, by way of distinction, call their *improper* sense.† When we say, for example, of a generous man, that he cannot do a base action, we do not mean that such an one could not do it if he would, which is implied in the proper sense of the word *cannot;* we only mean to assert, in a strong manner,

* These relative terms are always used in their primary and strict sense, in the following pages, unless where the contrary is intimated to the reader.

† It is not meant to be asserted, that it is improper to use these terms in any sense except their primary one; but the different meaning of words ought to be clearly pointed out, when the force of the reasoning depends upon that difference.

that such a generous person *will* not act basely. It is in this sense that divines make use of these relative terms, when they say, that God is *necessarily* holy, that he *cannot* mistake, or that it is *impossible* he should act unjustly; for the case will not allow us to suppose the existence of a contrary will and endeavour; no more is meant than that God *is certainly* holy, and *will always* act justly and wisely.

The reason of our adopting these terms on such occasions seems to be this; that, the certainty of an event being one of the most striking circumstances relating to *necessity*, when we would express in the strongest manner the certainty of any event, we use terms borrowed from necessity, though the event has nothing else in common with necessity, but the certainty implied in it.* And, as the terms borrowed from necessity are most commonly used in their improper sense upon mo-

* Every *necessary* event is *certain*, but a *certain* event is not always *necessary*. It may be said with propriety, "All men must *necessarily* die;" because they must die whether they will or not. But we cannot properly say; "A good man *necessarily* does good actions;" because we cannot add, that he does them whether he will or not: in strict propriety of speech it can only be said; "A good man *certainly* does good actions."

ral subjects, the certainty of an event is often called its *moral necessity:* but this expression is very apt to mislead us, as *morality* and *necessity*, in the proper sense of the words, are incompatible.

The greatest care should be taken to distinguish the *proper* from the *improper* sense of the words *cannot*, *unable*, *impossible*, *unavoidable*, *incapable*, *necessary*, &c. as these senses are not only different, but, in some respects, diametrically opposite. If a man *cannot* do a thing, in the proper sense of the word, he is perfectly free from blame, provided that want of power is the only hinderance: but we often intend the highest degree of blame by the expression, when we use it in the improper sense; as when we say of a very covetous man, "He is such a wretch, he *cannot* do a generous action." Or, when a person, stimulated by the ill treatment of his opponent, says, "I thank God, I have in me a soul *incapable* of treating an adversary with contempt," he means to assert his own good disposition as something worthy of praise: whereas, was he really *incapable* of a base passion, in the proper sense of the word, this incapacity would be no more virtuous in him than it is in a stone; or than the incapacity of flying is in mankind.

Proposition II. **There are only two things which can prevent our compliance with any known command that is laid upon us; and these are *inability* and *unwillingness* to obey.**

I say, any *known* command, as otherwise *ignorance* might be reckoned a third source of disobedience: though, since this is always either voluntary or involuntary, it might not unjustly have been ranked with one or other of the two causes I have mentioned, had I omitted this restriction. But to pass by this, it is a plain maxim of common sense, that a man either *cannot*, or *will not*, do what he is bidden: and since it has been already shown that a man is so far excusable as he is truly and properly unable to obey what is commanded, this consequence will certainly follow, that *unwillingness* is the only source of criminal disobedience.* Supposing a man

* It is not meant to be denied, that the understanding is darkened by sin; but the assertion in this passage only implies, that criminal ignorance always arises from the blindness or hardness of the *heart*, as the Apostle informs us. Ephesians iv. 18.

If we suppose a man perfectly desirous of knowing the will of God, in order that he may practise it, and using every method which God has appointed to obtain that should, by his own voluntary act, render himself incapable, in any instance, of future obedience; the guilt of this voluntary act would be justly imputed to him, and might be greater or less in proportion to the bad consequences flowing from it: yet what he was unable to do, notwithstanding he should be ever so well inclined to do it, could not be accounted sinful in him.

Proposition III. All that we suppose necessary to constitute a man's actions virtuous or vicious, i. e. of a moral nature, is *voluntariness*, provided the man be of sound intellects.

We do not at all consider how a man came to choose what is good or bad, in order to judge of his responsibility; but we conclude that a man's actions are of a moral nature, and that, of consequence, he is perfectly responsible when he does what is agreeable to him, or acts from his own choice. In most

knowledge; we cannot imagine such a person to be under any degree of criminal ignorance. But this might consistently be supposed, if *unwillingness* were not the only source of criminal disobedience.

instances we suppose a man's choice to depend, in some measure, upon something exterior to himself, as the advice, persuasion, or example of others ; but a man is entirely free, and answerable for his conduct, when he acts from his own inclination, whatever were the means of producing that inclination.

Should any one imagine, that more than *voluntariness* is necessary to perfect responsibility, it must be this, that a man's choice should flow from himself as well as the voluntary act ; and this objection must mean, either that every choice must proceed from a prior choice, which is absurd, because the first choice can have none before it ; or that every thing exterior to man, which biasses the mind and produces choice, is destructive of his moral agency and responsibility. If the latter sense of the objection be true, then men can never become good or bad from example, precept, persuasion, or any other means possible to be used for those purposes. The effect of all these means is to bias the mind so as to produce a good or bad choice ; and if our choice should cease to be good or bad, when produced by these exterior means, then they are no longer the means of virtue or vice ; and counsel, persuasion, or example, are totally useless, and unavailable to any moral purposes. But this is a conclusion so wild and contrary to the common sense of mankind, that the objection, from whence it certainly flows, must fall to the ground. *

* The excellency or odiousness of every external act is derived from the internal disposition from whence it flows, in the nature of which disposition consists the virtue or vice which we ascribe to outward actions. A good disposition or affection of the mind is virtuous and commendable, from its *own nature;* and the deformity of a vicious disposition or affection resides in the nature of that affection, and not in any circumstance or appendage of it. As for example, we justly condemn *ingratitude for benefits received* as a bad disposition, without considering how the subject of that odious temper came to be ungrateful. If the temper actually exists, and is exercised, it is justly esteemed detestable. And indeed, the viciousness of every bad disposition must reside in its own nature, or it would be impossible to determine any disposition to be odious.

That mankind do consider the good or evil of a disposition as resident in its own nature, is further evident from hence, that they universally allow there are good and bad *natural* dispositions. But if the virtue or vice of a disposition did not reside in its own nature, there could not possibly subsist in the human mind any such idea as that of a good or bad *natural* disposition.

It may be considered as an objection to this sentiment, that we often conceive of a person as less culpable in a vicious action, when we know him to have been urged to it by the bad advice or example of others. But if we trace the reasonings of our minds in these extenuations, we shall discover that they do not contradict, but are rather founded

Before I proceed to point out the consequences which flow from these propositions, I would intreat the reader to satisfy himself with respect to their validity. They appear to me to be some of the plainest maxims of common sense; but I would advise him to follow me no further, if they are not perfectly clear to him. If my reader is satisfied with regard to the premises, I must then request that he will reject no conclusion which may fairly be deduced from them, merely because it may appear to him somewhat disagreeable.

upon this sentiment, which is a plain dictate of the common sense of mankind. For when we are disposed to extenuate the guilt of any vicious action, to which a person has been led by the bad advice or example of others; we suppose that from these causes he may have committed the action under consideration, with a less evil disposition than would otherwise have attended it. We suppose that bad instruction and example either prevented him from discerning so clearly the evil of the action, or urged him to commit it with some degree of unwillingness.

These are real alleviations of guilt, because they imply a less evil disposition exerted in any action; but they are founded on this supposition, that the morality of every action is determined by the nature of its internal correspondent affection. A man's guilt is greater when he acts alone, or against advice and persuasion, or with a clear view of the evil of his crime, because it argues a worse disposition so to act.

Let us follow truth wherever she may lead us.

Corollary I. From what has been said, it clearly follows, that if there are any divine influences exerted in order to the production of holiness in men, they must, in some way or other, operate upon the will, since the want of a proper inclination or disposition is the only source of criminal disobedience.

If these influences be supposed only to communicate a *capacity* of obedience, they are unnecessary, as well as ineffectual: unnecessary, since nothing can be our duty which we are incapable of performing; and ineffectual, since holy acts consist in the right *use* of our powers. The sum of our duty to God is, to serve him with all our power or capacity; but a man can always do what is in his power; whatever increases his power or capacity, increases the matter of his duty, but brings him no nearer to the fulfilment of it.

Corollary II. If obedience is the certain effect of these divine influences, this argues no necessity in the case; for *necessity*, in the proper sense of the word, is always opposed to *volunta-riness;* but true obedience is always voluntary. A right will, or disposition, is the certain source of obedience, with respect to external acts; and, with regard to those that are internal, it is the very thing required.

If a man acts aright of choice, or chooses what is good, he therein fulfils his duty; his actions are praiseworthy. If he acts amiss of choice, his actions are punishable. We can go no higher in our ideas of responsibility, than to the voluntary acts of a man in his senses.

So, likewise, if disobedience is the certain effect of some kind of influence derived from our first parents, this does not alter the criminality of such disobedience, if we disobey freely, or of choice.

Corollary III. The scriptural doctrines of *divine grace*, and *native depravity*, are not in the least opposed to the common sense of mankind.

We know not, indeed, how the Spirit of God influences men's minds so as to produce holy dispositions; neither do we know how persuasion or example influences men's volitions. We see that these do so, and the fact being very common, we are not surprised at it; but we have no more reason, *à priori*, to think this would be case, than the man who first found a loadstone had reason to think that it was capable of guiding the adventurous mariner across the trackless ocean.

We know not how it comes to pass, that mankind have universally a propensity to moral evil. The Scriptures concur with experience in asserting the fact; and the former teach us, that it is, in some way, the consequence of the transgression of our first parents: but how this happens we know not, any more than we know how it happens, that certain sounds, striking upon the ear, have a connexion with our future volitions and actions.

They who would account for the wickedness which experience shows to be general in the world, by supposing it to be solely the effect of example and persuasion; and deny the existence of a native propensity to evil, on account of the necessity which this doctrine is supposed to imply, are very inconsistent with themselves.* Nor is there any

* For there is no more necessity in the dispositions or

more necessity in volitions excited by the divine influence of grace, than by the human influence of persuasion. They are causes of volition equally exterior to a man; and the manner in which they produce their effects is, in all the cases, unknown; so that if the one implies any necessity, the other does the same. If any one should suppose, that these sources of volition differ from each other in this respect, that the one sort *certainly* produces volition, and not the other; this argues no difference with regard to the thing objected: for to say that divine grace certainly produces holy volitions or affections, is only saying, that it produces them, or that it succeeds in the production of the designed effect oftener than human persuasion: but when the effect is produced by either, the necessity would be the same, if it were possible that there could be any necessity in the case.

The opposers of the above-mentioned doctrines are, therefore, premature in their triumph, when they suppose the absurdity of them demonstrated on account of the necessity which they infer. "If men are naturally

voluntary acts of men, which originate from our connexion with our first parents, than in those dispositions or voluntary acts which arise from our connexion with one another.

depraved," say they, " then they cannot help sinning; and if they cannot help doing what is forbidden, disobedience is not their fault." The objection is entirely founded on the ambiguous use of the terms *cannot help*, &c. which, in their most common acceptation, are expressive of necessity, but which cannot, in that sense, be justly applied to the present case: for every man may obey God if he will, since obedience is included in choosing what is commanded. The fault of mankind is, that they choose wrong, and therefore it cannot properly be said of them, that they cannot avoid sinning, because they can avoid it if they will; that is, if their dispositions perfectly coincide with the commandment: but true necessity implies the certainty of a thing, notwithstanding all possible dispositions, desires, and endeavours to the contrary.

The same reasoning is applicable to the doctrine of *divine grace*.

Corollary IV. When the Scriptures declare, that men *cannot* love and serve God without the inspiration of his Holy Spirit, they make use of this term, and such like, in their *improper* sense, to express merely the *certainty* of the event; they mean that men *will* not love God without this inspiration or influence, as they sometimes express it. In the use of such language they adapt themselves to the common forms of speech among men. There are indeed some passages in which, at first sight, more seems to be intended: but when we consider how frequently these relative terms, which are strictly and primarily expressive of necessity, are used in their improper sense, and how much the Scriptures are accommodated to the ordinary modes of speaking, common sense obliges us to explain them with that latitude which we use in other similar cases.

One of the most remarkable of these passages is that contained in the seventh chapter of the Romans, where the Apostle says, "To will is present with me, but how to perform that which is good, I find not: for what I would, I do not; but what I hate, that do I. The good which I would, I do not; but the evil which I would not, that I do."

We cannot suppose the Apostle to mean

(whether we consider him as speaking of himself, or personating another) that there was no defect in his desire to do the will of God; or that, although he perfectly chose the will of God at all times, and to the most steady disposition to good, added his utmost endeavours to accomplish what was commanded, yet obedience would not follow: for the nature of the commandments contradicts such a notion, since they are all summed up in this, "Thou shalt love God with all thy heart, and thy neighbour as thyself." Now, if there had been nothing amiss in his disposition, but a perfectly right will had been always present with him, it is plain the commandments would have been performed, as they are all included in a right will or disposition. The Apostle's words are, therefore, to be understood with that latitude which common usage allows in such like expressions, and may be explained in some such way as this: that he desired, upon the whole, to do the will of God, this disposition being predominant, governing the general tenour of his conduct; but that through the existence of a contrary disposition, called by him *the flesh*, he was defective in his obedience, and often failed of that conformity to God's will which suited the general bent of his inclination.

Corollary V. The preceding maxims of common sense tend to give us just ideas of the doctrines of *original sin* and *divine grace*.

Mankind are not, by nature, void of a *capacity* of serving God, in the proper sense of the word; because, as hath been observed, the divine law only requires them to use their powers to his glory. If men were truly incapable of obeying the moral law, that law, with respect to them, would be unreasonable. But men are *unwilling* to serve God; they choose what is forbidden; their voluntary acts, when they are left to themselves, are evil. This state of mankind is sinful, and punishable; for we cannot possibly require any thing more than voluntariness in men's actions to constitute them punishable or rewardable, without setting aside the use of all means whatever of rendering men good or evil.

Some who have professed to believe and defend the doctrine of man's natural depravity, have represented it rather as a state of weakness, than of wickedness; rather as an affliction, than a fault. But such representations destroy the very notion of depravity: they lead men to throw the blame of their crimes upon their Maker, and to make that an excuse which is, in fact, an aggravation of their wickedness. It would be considered a very strange excuse for any bad action, if the accused person were to say in his own defence, " It is true, I have done the bad action with which I am charged; but then this ought to be said in my favour, that I did it from a bad disposition; and, consequently, I am much less blamable, than if I had had no bad inclination to prompt me to it."

Those influences of the Holy Spirit, which we call *divine grace*,* are often incautiously represented as communicating merely a capacity of obedience, even by those writers who strenuously assert that nothing can be matter of duty to any one which he is incapable of performing. We do not, indeed, understand how the Spirit of God influences the minds of men in the production of ho-

* By this expression, and other synonymous ones in this tract, those operations of the Holy Spirit alone are intended, which are immediately productive of holy dispositions in us, which the Scriptures call the " Sanctification of the Spirit," and " renewing of the Holy Ghost;" and which we implore when we pray that God would " incline our hearts" to keep his laws.

liness; but we know that the effect of his sanctifying influences is similar to the effect of good advice and example, so far as they prevail; and, for aught we know to the contrary, the mode of operation may in both cases be the same. Men are not, therefore, any more to be considered as *machines* in being the subjects of divine influences, than in being the subjects of those which are human. Neither of these kinds of operation deprives a man of his choice, yet both of them influence his choice. If a preacher sets forth the amiableness of virtue with such clearness of argument and power of persuasion, as to dispose any of his audience to choose what is virtuous, we are far from thinking that this exterior influence has lessened the excellency of that virtuous choice, or turned the sincere convert into a mere machine. And should we suppose the argumentation of a preacher to be so just, and his persuasiveness so great, as *certainly* to influence the minds of all who heard him to a virtuous choice, we should never imagine that the certainty of this good effect did at all lessen the moral agency of those who were so happy as to be the subjects of it. Common sense requires us to use the same reasoning with respect to the sanctifying influence of the

Holy Spirit; the certain effect of whose operations can never alter their nature.

The Holy Scriptures speak largely of the sanctifying influences of the Spirit of God; and of the influences of that malignant spirit who "walketh about as a roaring lion seeking whom he may devour," and who "worketh" powerfully "in the children of disobedience." They likewise insist frequently upon the good and bad effects of instruction, persuasion, and example: yet they always represent men as perfectly responsible for their voluntary acts, notwithstanding any influence whatever.

THE OBJECTION TREATED OF IN THE NOTE, PAGE 537, FURTHER CONSIDERED.

"THOUGH it be allowed, that in considering the virtuousness or viciousness of men's actions, we only take into our estimate the *nature* of the dispositions from whence they arise, and do not hesitate to determine upon the quality of any action, when the disposition which produced it is known, without staying to inquire how the disposition itself was produced: yet this procedure," it is said, "does not remove the difficulty of our allowing the real morality of such dispositions as are supposed to be produced by some external influence, as by the corruption of nature derived from our first parents, or the sanctifying influences of God's Holy Spirit. For, in our reasonings on this subject, we always suppose, that men's moral dispositions do ultimately originate from themselves, and are not *certainly* connected with any external influence."

"To prove this," it is said, "let us appeal to the sentiments of any thinking and sensible person, and ask whether he would judge a man to be responsible for those dispositions which are immediately produced in him by some external influence." The answer, it is supposed, would certainly be in the negative, and would therefore show, that the doctrine of the certain efficacy of divine influences is not agreeable to the common sense of mankind.

In answer to this, it may be observed, that the resolution of this question, when thus formally proposed, does not determine the matter in debate.

For, 1. It is extremely difficult to state the question in such a manner as shall not convey the idea of necessity, which certainly excludes morality so far as it operates. When we think of the efficacy of divine influences, we can scarcely forbear considering them as operating, *whether we will or not*, and producing an *unavoidable* compliance. These ideas, secretly conveyed in the terms made use of, determine the answer.

2. We know how extremely apt men are to deny the plainest principles, when they are urged as premises to some disagreeable conclusion. We begin to discover difficulties in the most simple truths, when we are aware of some consequences being deduced from them which we do not choose to allow. We should, therefore, see if the matter cannot be determined by some unexceptionable evidence; and consider whether there are not some circumstances in which mankind universally agree to use such a mode of reasoning as is here controverted. If there is *any* case in which mankind universally agree to allow the morality of dispositions produced by external influence, the question is decided.

Many cases might be produced, in which the moral dispositions and actions of mankind are considered as arising from external influence. One instance will suffice. It is universally allowed that a man's moral conduct frequently depends upon his education; and in allowing this, we grant that moral dispositions may be produced by external influence. There is nothing less subject to a man's choice than the mode of his education; it is, in most cases, as independent of his own choice as the circumstances of his birth. We have no concern in determining the situation, understanding, condition, or disposition of our parents. The first principles instilled into our minds could not be weighed by us before they were admitted. Our tempers and dispositions were forming when we could neither understand the effect of the influence to which we were exposed, nor guard against its consequences. Yet who doubts the moral influence of education?

It does not lessen the force of this reasoning, to observe, that education does not *always* determine our moral conduct in life; but that many persons act in a manner directly contrary to what might have been expected, considering the manner of their education. For if the moral conduct of some men is the effect of their education, it is the same thing, with respect to this argument, as if all men acted agreeably to their education. If education *ever* determines a man's moral conduct, then morality may be produced by external influence. If moral dispositions and conduct cannot be the effect of extrinsic influence, then so far as education produces any disposition or conduct, in the same degree the morality of that disposition or conduct is destroyed; and education can have no influence in producing what is morally good or evil.

The expectation which arises in our minds with regard to the future moral conduct of any one, of whose education we are witnesses, proves, that we allow there is a tendency in education to produce moral effects: but education can have no tendency to determine our moral conduct, but by its influence in producing moral dispositions. The universal belief of this tendency proves, that mankind universally allow the possibility of producing moral dispositions by external influence; and, consequently, that such external influence as operates only by the production of moral dispositions, does not destroy our moral agency and responsibility.*

* No one who considers and believes the history of St. Paul's conversion can doubt, that good moral dispositions may be the effect of an influence that originates from without us. For this remarkable man was changed (in a moment as it were) by the influence of God's Holy Spirit, from being a blasphemer, a persecutor, and an injurious person, to be an humble disciple of the holy Jesus. His rage was turned into meekness, his threatenings into prayer, and his fury into holy zeal.

CONCLUSION.

The doctrines of the innate moral depravity of mankind, and of the sanctifying influences of the Holy Spirit, are attended with inexplicable difficulties; yet these difficulties are of such a nature, that they do not afford even a presumption against the truth of the doctrines which they accompany.

For no one can reject these doctrines on account of the difficulties which attend them, and which have been already stated, but he must involve himself in the most palpable absurdities. He must reject the universal experience of mankind; and combat the plainest dictates of common sense.

The introduction of moral evil into the world, and its prevalence in all ages, cannot be accounted for upon any scheme unincumbered with difficulties.

Let any person capable of close reflection inquire, how it comes to pass that the generality of mankind in all ages have not been truly virtuous, since virtue is acknowledged to have an intrinsic amiableness.*

To say, that mankind have been led away by their passions contrary to their better judgment, is only to allow the fact, but to give no reason for it. It is to say, that mankind have not followed the will of God so far as they have known it.

If you say, they have followed bad examples, I ask, why they followed these rather than good ones.

If you tell me they received bad instructions, you do but remove the difficulty one step backwards, without giving any solution of it. For it may be asked, how did it happen that bad instructions were given, or bad examples afforded, instead of good ones. Or, if good and evil were equally set before them

* By *virtue*, I here mean a temper and conduct in all things conformed to the will of God, as far as that will has been made known.

by instruction or example, why did they prefer the evil. Remove the difficulty as often as you please, it still recurs, and must remain unanswered upon the hypothesis here adopted.

The Scriptures inform us how sin entered into the world; and profane history concurs with sacred in exhibiting the general depravity of mankind. These accounts must be admitted as indubitable facts, though attended with difficulties which we cannot solve.

The universal concurrence of mankind annexes responsibility to all the voluntary acts of every man who retains his understanding. Yet we daily see, that these acts are influenced by a great variety of circumstances. But all laws, both human and divine, must be given up as irrational, if we are resolved to withhold our approbation or dislike, until we know why a man chooses one mode of conduct rather than another. No general answer can possibly be invented to solve that famous question,—"What determines the will?" Let ingenuity be racked for the solution, the answer will always be an identical proposition. Mr. Locke's solution is manifestly absurd, as it puts the effect for the cause. If the mind is in perfect equilibrium, (as must be the case previously to any *choice*, which is a mental preponderation,) it cannot be uneasy: if it is uneasy, it has willed, or is inclined one way.

Since the manner in which the mind is influenced by that variety of causes continually operating in the common affairs of life, cannot be discovered, we should not wonder 'that the manner in which the Holy Spirit of God influences the mind, is equally unknown. We perceive that men are often directed in their choice by the arguments and persuasions of others; and why may not the Divine Agent produce good volitions, by suggesting suitable arguments, either directly, or by the instrumentality of others? But I pretend to assert nothing concerning the mode of operation in any case where volition and subsequent conduct are produced. I only know that if a man acts voluntarily, he acts responsibly, unless he be deprived of his understanding.

If a certain number of children were educated in the most proper manner by parents of the most virtuous character; and an equal number of children were educated by parents hardened in vice;—would the chance be equal, whether the greater number of good men would be found among the virtuous or the vicious? No one can entertain a doubt on this subject. But let us attempt to give a reason for our expectation in such a case, and we must be constrained to resolve the question into a matter of mere experience. Yet the virtue and the vice produced by these means respectively, most certainly are not destroyed by their cause. Virtue and vice do not cease to be such, because they have originated from good or bad education.

The *certainty* of the event in the case of moral influence, creates no additional difficulty in our attempts to explain that influence. For the difficulty resides in the nature of the event, and not in its frequency. If argument, persuasion, or example, produce good or bad moral conduct in men, the nature of the connexion between the cause and the effect, in this case, is not altered by the frequency of the event. If any objection can be made to the cause, it must arise from the *nature* of that cause, and not from the frequency of the effect produced.

Whatever difficulties attend the doctrines of innate moral depravity, and divine grace; the same attend the constitution and course of nature, as they lie against all influence whatever.

Let us then bow down before the great

Author of our nature, whose revealed will contains no greater difficulties than are contained in the order and government which he has established in the world.

Let us make a due practical use of the truths which He has made known to us, either by His providential dispensations, or His more immediate interpositions. Convinced that He hath not been pleased to gratify our curiosity in our researches into the hidden causes of things, let us improve our knowledge of their manifest properties and effects. Let us revere and obey His revealed will. The speculative mariner, or the fastidious philosopher, would not act with greater absurdity in refusing the use of the magnet, till he could understand the nature of the hidden influence of magnetism, than might be imputed to us, if we should refuse to oppose the evil propensities of which we are conscious, or to implore the assistance of God's grace, of which we feel our need, until we could comprehend how the one or the other operates upon our minds.

Let us check such curiosity as would only mislead us, and improve the facts which we know to the advantage of human life; though we must still remain in the state of children, who are taught to obey the directions of their parents, before they can comprehend the reasons of those commands, which are given for the regulation of their conduct.

ADDITIONAL OBSERVATIONS RESPECTING THE SUBJECT OF THE PRECEDING PROPOSITIONS AND COROLLARIES.

THE case of *madmen* has been thought, by some, to be an unanswerable objection to that notion of moral liberty and responsibility asserted in the preceding observations.

"Madmen," say they, "act voluntarily; their conduct is the effect of their own choice; and, therefore, according to the foregoing notion of responsibility, they are equally responsible for their conduct with other men, and ought to be treated with respect to reward or punishment as moral agents; but this conclusion being universally allowed to be absurd, the premises from whence it clearly follows, must be false."

Although I have obviated this objection in the preceding propositions, by asserting that they are the voluntary acts of men in their senses, which we determine to be of a moral nature, yet a consideration of the real state respecting moral agency into which insanity brings a man, will throw greater light upon this subject, and tend to evince the truth of the preceding assertions respecting the common notion of responsibility.

The state of madmen, with respect to their actions, is similar to that of men who are dreaming in their sleep. In both cases, a distempered imagination causes a wrong conception in them with regard to their situation and actions; so that a by-stander can never certainly determine, from appearances, what such persons are doing according to their own apprehensions of things. Supposing a man who is dreaming, who is in a febrile delirium, or who is insane, to throw himself out of his chamber window and to be dashed in pieces in the street, we can never determine this to be an act of suicide, because for aught we know, the man might mistake every thing relating to this action, so as to imagine he was plunging himself into some cooling stream of water, with a view to take the pleasure of swimming. Under such a disturbance of the understanding, a man may cut the throat of a brother, whom he dearly loves, and imagine he is saving that brother from the devouring jaws of some wild beast.

In such cases, we cannot question a man with respect to any action, because we have properly no action to fix upon him. Whereas, when a man has a sound understanding, we can have no doubt about the nature of any action in question, provided it be certain that such an action was done by that person. Being certain of the action itself, we have then only to inquire what was the disposition, temper of mind, or volition, which gave rise to that action. And it is owing to the connexion between the external act and the internal volition, that the man becomes responsible for his conduct.

Neither sleep, nor insanity, annihilate a man's dispositions, nor do they prevent the exercise of them in his actions; but they prevent us from knowing what such a man was doing according to his own conceptions; and therefore prevent our forming any notion of the goodness or badness of the disposition which gave rise to any action under consideration.

It does not at all appear, that a state of insanity makes a man less the subject of divine jurisdiction; because our omniscient Judge perfectly understands the nature of every action. He knows how far it arose from a good or bad disposition, and what were the views and conceptions of the agent. But since we can only collect our knowledge of these things from the action itself, considered with all its circumstances, and as our judgment is formed upon the supposition, that the action was the same in our view and in that of the agent, we are obliged, in charity, to suspend our judgment, when a diseased understanding may hinder a man from knowing what he does.

These observations show, that no just objection can be made to the preceding notion of responsibility from the case of madmen; but that in this, as well as other cases, we suppose the morality of an action to lie in the nature of the volition that produces it.

This further appears from considering, that even in human judicatories, where only overt acts are cognizable, the criminality of an action rests upon the disposition with which the action appears from the circumstances to have been connected. Where one man is put to death by another, it is from the apparent disposition that the action is denominated murder, manslaughter, or mere accident. Nay, the very same action may be either criminal in the highest degree, simply indifferent, or highly praiseworthy. Thus, a man may inflict a fatal wound upon his fellow-creature as his murderer, as his executioner, or by the appointment of the Creator and Proprietor of all, as a victim in sacrifice, as in the case of Abraham and Isaac.

External acts may be useful or hurtful to others, and so may the rays of the sun, or the agitation of the air: yet no rational being will blame the sun or the air when they prove detrimental, because the agents act not from choice; being incapable of good or bad dispositions, they are not moral agents. We pass the same judgment upon the involuntary actions of mankind: if a man, when convulsed, happens to strike his neighbour on the face, no one regards the action as an injurious assault: but if a bad disposition, as malice, hatred, or wantonness, directed the blow, every one would esteem the act to be a criminal injury.

A little reflection may therefore fully satisfy us, that virtue and vice have their proper residence in our dispositions or volitions: and that it is the *nature* of these, and not their *cause*, which truly denominates them good or bad; rewardable or punishable.

DEFENCE

OF

EPISCOPACY,

DERIVED FROM THE

NEW TESTAMENT.

DEFENCE

OF

EPISCOPACY,

DERIVED FROM THE

NEW TESTAMENT.

To the Rev. Thomas Dunham Whitaker.

Reverend and Dear Sir;

As obedience to the will of God in all particulars, concerning which the Scriptures have given us instruction, is the duty of every professor of Christianity; I have considered it as a branch of that regard which I owe to those sacred records, to inquire whether they contain any instructions relative to the formation and order of that society, which constitutes the visible church of Christ on earth.

I was aware that this subject had been a fruitful source of controversy among Christians of different denominations. But having neither leisure nor inclination to peruse many massy folios, which might perhaps have perplexed, rather than instructed me; I determined to apply to the fountain-head of knowledge; and, without inquiring after the opinions of others, to attempt the settling of my own, by a careful perusal of the New Testament.

Sensible of the effect which education has, in fixing a firm prepossession in our minds, I strove to lay aside all pre-conceived opinions; and endeavoured to find out the meaning of the inspired writers, by comparing those passages which treat upon the subject that I had in contemplation.

In pursuance of this design, I wrote down on one page every passage, or, at least, the principal passages of Scripture, which had a relation to my subject; and, on the opposite page I remarked what appeared to me to be the plain meaning of, or obvious conclusion from, the several passages which I had transcribed. Having finished this task, I examined the result, and drew up a general view of the subject. From this investigation, I obtained more satisfaction than I expected to find, when I set out upon my inquiry.

My papers have lain by me for many years, having been compiled for the guidance of my own conduct, and the instruction of my children. They have, indeed, occasionally, though rarely, been shown to a serious friend, with whom I might happen to converse upon the subject.

About three years ago, happening to read in a periodical publication a paper upon church government, which seemed to me to contain some unwarrantable assertions, I drew up the following observations on the orders of ministers in the christian church, which you were pleased to think might be of use to some, whose minds are wavering upon the subject. I send them to you in consequence of the request, which, perhaps, the partiality of your friendship has led you to make, and commit them to your disposal. If you should incorporate them into any work of your own, designed for public view, I have only to intreat the candour of your readers, that they would not try them by the writings of polemical divines, but by the New Testament, whence I have endeavoured faithfully to extract them. I have prefixed a few general reflections on church government; but my principal observations are confined to the orders of ministers, and the manner of their appointment, as being that branch of church government, which is, perhaps, the most clearly laid down in the New Testament, and that which involves in it some of the principal questions on which Christians of different denominations are at variance.

I am, Reverend Sir,

With much respect,

Your Friend, and humble Servant,

W. H.

GENERAL REFLECTIONS ON CHURCH GOVERNMENT.*

---

1. It appears, from various declarations of our Saviour and his Apostles, that the christian church shall never cease to exist in the world; we may, therefore, fairly conclude, that the directions which are given in Holy Writ for the formation of the church in the time of the Apostles, are to be applied to the same society in all ages; allowance being made for the cessation of those miraculous powers which were granted to the first Christians, and for the unavoidable disturbance to which the regular order of the church may be exposed in times of persecution. What the inspired Apostles considered as important in the formation of the church, ought not to be

* Written about the year 1798.

considered by us as of little import. The church must be formed after some model; and we have no authority to deviate from that model which inspiration dictated, unless it be in such things as are, by a change of circumstances, rendered impracticable. It is not a sufficient objection to say,—The Apostles did not declare, that this order was to be perpetual. Such a declaration was unnecessary. A regulation appointed by divine authority, in a society that was designed to continue to the end of time, bears the stamp of perpetuity upon the face of it. It should become impracticable, before it should cease to be practised by those who take the Word of God for their guide. All laws which are not expressly made for a limited time, are of course perpetual, until they are abrogated by an authority equal to that by which they were enacted. Christians of all persuasions seem to agree in these sentiments; for they either profess to form their church government on what they conceive to be the primitive model, or attempt to support, by the authority of Scripture, that order which they have adopted from accidental circumstances.

2. The commands relative to church government, like those which relate to many

other duties, are partly positive, and partly discretional.

In this case we are as much bound by the positive declarations, as if nothing had been left to our discretion. General directions are also given for the regulation of those circumstances which are committed to our discretion. We stand in the same predicament with relation to other duties. Alms deeds, for instance, are positively enjoined, but no specific proportion of our wealth is directed to be set apart for this purpose. Yet we have general directions to guide our conduct in this discretional circumstance. It is our duty to collect those particulars which the Apostles clearly enjoined, by precept or example, in the formation of the christian church, as far as they are applicable to a settled state of the church. Such injunctions we are bound to follow. No private opinions of what is best, can authorize us to depart from them. In all matters left to our discretion, we must conduct ourselves by those general rules which the Scriptures afford for the guidance of that discretion. If it should appear, for instance, that the Apostles appointed different orders of ministers in the church, but did not appoint a particular mode of conducting public worship; the christian church is bound to retain those orders of ministers, but may exercise its discretion with respect to the mode of worship, provided the general rules given for the guidance of that discretion are observed. Or, if the Apostles have marked out with precision the duties of an officer of great consequence in the christian church, whose continuance in the church was necessary for the execution of that plan of church government which they, by divine inspiration, had appointed; and yet have left no directions how this officer should be elected in future ages; we are bound to consider the office as perpetual, but the mode of election to that office as discretional.

3. Some persons have imagined, that if matters relative to church government had been of importance, they would have been more clearly revealed. Such imaginations are highly improper, if divine revelation has given any directions relative to this subject. We must not pretend to dictate to the all-wise God, how he shall reveal his will to us. If he has revealed it in any way, this ought to be considered as sufficient to command our obedience.

That excellent writer, Bishop Butler, has observed, that a preponderance of argument in favour of any duty requires our obedience, as well as a more clear and explicit revelation. Let it be granted, for the sake of argument, that no particular form of church government is *commanded* in Scripture; yet, we cannot thence conclude, that all christian churches have equally the support of divine authority. For the inspired Apostles formed the first christian church after a particular model; and if any modern church has the example of the Apostles on its side, all other things, being by the supposition equal, this church has a preponderance of argument in its favour.

4. But the example of persons acting by divine authority, not only affords a preponderance of argument in favour of any branch of conduct, in which they may be imitated; but it is expressly proposed in Holy Scripture, as a model of our conduct. The Apostle Paul says, "Walk so as ye have us for an example;" and no good reason can be given why his example should be followed only in things pertaining to private life. His example, as a superintendent of the christian church, calls for imitation. We may, therefore, rank among the number of divine precepts, such rules as he prescribed for the formation and government of the christian church, as far as they

relate to it in a settled state, in which no miraculous powers were to exist, nor special inspiration to directs its governors.

5. Though the Scriptures are our only sure guide with respect to christian doctrines and practice; yet, if it should appear, that the Scriptures are silent with respect to a matter of fact, well known to those whom the Apostles addressed in their Epistles; we seem to be directed in this particular to the first writers in the christian church, who have mentioned the fact concerning which we are inquiring. If, for instance, an officer of some consequence in the christian church is frequently mentioned in the New Testament, in the choice of whom great care was to be observed, and yet the sacred writings are silent with respect to the duties of his office; we are evidently led to inquire of the first christian writers, what these duties were, and to acknowledge them to be the proper duties of the office.

6. It has been considered by many as a sufficient proof of the rectitude of the government subsisting in any church, that the labours of its ministers have been beneficial to mankind. If these have turned sinners unto righ-

teousness, they are regarded as possessing a sure testimony of the divine approbation of their conduct. The conversion of sinners has perhaps never been effected by any who have opposed, or neglected, the fundamental doctrines of the gospel; but success in this important concern will not prove that a minister is altogether right in his sentiments or conduct. The differences which subsist among pious and successful ministers of different persuasions must convince us, that errors to a certain degree are not inconsistent with success. Yet we should always keep in mind, that a wilful neglect of any divine command can admit no apology. We must not argue, that, because our obedience is strict in matters of great concern, we may allow ourselves to depart from the gospel rule in matters of inferior moment. We should always keep in mind the declaration of our Saviour when comparing the tithing of mint, anise, and cummin, with the weightier matters of the law; "These ought ye to have done, and not to leave the others undone." We may not be aware of the injury which religion, in a course of time, may sustain, by a departure from that order in the church which divine authority has established: nor are we allowed to weigh the consequences of disobedience, with the view to satisfy ourselves in the neglect of any divine command.

One general command respecting church government is, "Let all things be done decently and in order;" and if success is to be considered universally as a proof of right conduct, then no one was ever instrumental in turning a sinner from the error of his way, who, in that part of his conduct which proved beneficial, was guilty of a breach of this command. I will not at present consider what decency and order require, but will, in this argument, leave every one to his own judgment. I will only appeal to the conscience of every reader, whether he is persuaded, that the spiritual good above-mentioned was never effected by any one, while departing from such conduct as decency and order required.

Again; the same conduct may do good in one respect, and mischief in another. If we are to regulate ourselves by events, and not by divine commands, we must first know whether the conduct in question will do more good or harm. This rule is very uncertain, and must always be superseded by the authority of a divine command. It can only be called in aid in matters of which the consequences are doubtful, and of such as are left entirely to our own discretion.

If even greater good should appear to be done, for a time, by following our own plans; yet a conduct not regulated by divine authority, may bring on a course of events attended with irreparable mischief, far out-weighing the present temporary advantage.

Further, when we allow ourselves to break through the order of divine appointment, with the prospect of doing a greater good; we depart from that subordinate station in which Divine Providence has placed us. We take upon ourselves to direct, where we ought to obey. We disregard that express divine prohibition of doing evil that good may come; and forget that sentence which the Apostle has pronounced upon all who conduct themselves by such a principle, "Whose damnation is just."

7. The charge of uncharitableness seems to deter many from entering upon the inquiry, whether any mode of church government has exclusively the stamp of divine authority. They see good men of all persuasions, and therefore think it needless to inquire, which form of church government is most conformable to the plan laid down in Holy Scripture. They are also deterred from this investigation by the idea, that a claim to divine

authority in an affair concerning which good people are so much divided, would imply an uncharitable censure upon all who differ from ourselves.

True christian charity will never deter us from the most strict inquiry into our duty. We are not to guide ourselves by the conduct of others, who have no greater claim to inspiration than ourselves. The unerring word of God, the Bible, is our rule of faith and practice. "Let God be true, and every man a liar." It is our duty to examine the word of God carefully, that we may regulate our conduct aright in every particular. We shall not be excused in any neglect or error, concerning which divine authority would set us right, by pleading the example of others. Nor does it necessarily follow, that we must condemn others, who profess to follow the same guide as ourselves, because we may differ in our interpretation of some things contained in divine revelation.

ON THE ORDERS OF MINISTERS IN THE CHRISTIAN CHURCH, AND THE MANNER OF THEIR APPOINTMENT.

WHEN our blessed Redeemer took leave of "the eleven disciples," he commanded them to teach all nations, and promised to be with them "always, even to the end of the world:"* but He gave no instructions respecting the different orders of ministers in his church, nor the manner of their appointment. This promise, however, implied that there should be a succession of ministers in the christian church to the end of the world. And as our Saviour also promised to instruct his Apostles by his Holy Spirit, and to guide them into all truth; we must look into the Acts of the Apostles, and their Epistles, to discover the will of our Lord on this subject.

* Matthew xxviii. 20.

The question to be investigated in these observations is this,—What instructions have the Apostles given, either by example or precept, respecting the different orders of ministers, in a settled state of the church, after their departure? I say, in a *settled* state of the church, after the departure of the Apostles: because its first state was so extraordinary, and so fraught with miraculous powers, that a perfect imitation of it cannot be adopted. This original state of the church is thus described by the Apostle Paul. "God hath set some in the church, first apostles, secondarily prophets, thirdly teachers; after that miracles, then gifts of healing, helps, governments, diversities of tongues."* Apostles and prophets are gone: gifts of healing, and diversities of tongues have ceased. We must be content with teachers and governors. Let us inquire what the Scripture has said concerning these.

This list is a little varied in the Epistle to the Ephesians, where it is said, "He gave, some, apostles; and some, prophets; and some, evangelists; and some, pastors and teachers."† What the word *evangelist* means,

* 1 Corinthians xii. 28.

† Ephesians iv. 11.

Prophets are so clearly distinguished in both these pasif it implied a distinct order, cannot be collected from Scripture. It is but mentioned in two other places, viz. Acts xxi. 28. "We entered into the house of Philip the evangelist." And 2 Timothy iv. 5. "Watch thou in all things, endure afflictions, do the work of an evangelist, make full proof of thy ministry." The word literally means a preacher of the gospel. The use of it in any other sense must be conjectural.

The titles appropriated to ordinary teachers in the church of Christ, are bishops, presbyters or elders, and deacons. Perhaps we shall discover another order to which the Scriptures have given no title, except in the Book of the Revelations. It may be proper to remark, for the sake of those readers who are not acquainted with the original language of the New Testament, that the terms of *presbyter* and *elder* are strictly synonymous; the former being only a Greek word with an English termination, and the latter, a translation of that Greek word into pure English. To avoid confusion, I shall only use the word presbyter, as having less ambiguity.

sages, from *pastors* and *teachers*, that we cannot, by any just reasoning, consider the conduct of the former as conveying a direction for that of the latter.

It seems that presbyters were the ordinary ministers of the church. Paul and Barnabas, in their first tour from Antioch, *ordained them* presbyters in every church.* Paul being in haste to be at Jerusalem on the day of Pentecost, determined to sail by Ephesus, and called the "presbyters of the church," † giving them his parting advice, as to ordinary ministers of the church. Paul left Titus in Crete, to "ordain presbyters in every city."‡ The business of ruling and teaching the flock belongs to them. Let the presbyters that rule well be counted worthy of double honour, especially they who labour in the word and doctrine." ||

The terms, *bishop* and *presbyter*, are used in the New Testament for the same kind of minister. There are five passages from which this appears to be the case. When St. Paul sent from Miletus for the presbyters of Ephesus, he commanded them "to take heed to all the flock, over which the Holy Ghost had made them overseers, (it is the same word in the original, which is elsewhere translated *bishops*,) to feed the church of God, which He hath purchased with his own blood." § St. Paul

* Acts xiv. 23. † Acts xx. 17. ‡ Titus i. 5.
|| 1 Timothy v. 17. § Acts xx. 28.

says to Titus, "For this cause left I thee in Crete, that thou shouldest ordain presbyters in every city, as I had appointed thee. If any be blameless, the husband of one wife, having faithful children, not accused of riot or unruly; for a bishop must be blameless,"* &c. In these two passages, the terms are clearly synonymous.

The same Apostle addresses his Epistle to the Philippians, "To all the saints in Christ Jesus, which are at Philippi, with the bishops and deacons. Can we suppose, that there were many bishops, and no presbyters at Philippi; or that St. Paul would omit mentioning these, while he addresses the deacons? These suppositions are so improbable, that I can entertain no doubt of the term *bishop* being here used for *presbyter*.

Again; the Apostle, in his first Epistle to Timothy, chapter iii, gives particular directions respecting the character of those who were to be admitted to the offices of *bishop* and *deacon*, but does not, in that chapter, make mention of *presbyters*. The passage is natural and void of difficulty, if, by the term *bishop*, we understand *presbyter*; in any other sense, the omission of the term *presbyter* is unaccountable;

* Titus i. 5, 6, 7.

since Timothy was left at Ephesus, as Titus was in Crete, for this purpose (among others) of ordaining presbyters.

Lastly; St. Peter, in his first Epistle, chapter v., says, "The presbyters, who are among you, I exhort, who am also a presbyter," (for though the Apostles were superintendents of other ministers, they still fulfilled the office of ordinary preachers of the gospel,) "feed the flock of God which is among you, *taking the oversight* thereof," (or, as it might be rendered, "executing the office of a bishop,") "not by constraint, but willingly,"* &c. From these passages it is plain, that the terms *bishops* and *presbyter* were used as synonymous by the writers of the New Testament.†

* 1 Peter v. 1, 2.

† No difficulty can arise from the application of the term *bishop*, to ordinary presbyters, if we take into consideration the original meaning of the word, and the manner in which it is applied in the Scriptures. The word in the original signifies an *overlooker* or *overseer*, and is thus properly translated in the English Testament. Acts xx. 28. For the presbyters were the overseers of the flock of Christ; and it is with relation to the *flock*, and not to other ministers, that the presbyters are called bishops: as in the passage last quoted; "Take heed to the *flock*, over which the Holy Ghost hath made you overseers" or bishops. So also in 1 Peter, chapter v. "Feed the *flock* of God which is among you, taking the *oversight* thereof," &c. Whereas,

Before I proceed to inquire whether the Scriptures have given us any intimation of a church officer, superior in rank to that of a presbyter, let us hear what is said respecting deacons. No instructions are given to Titus respecting this office; but in the first Epistle to Timothy, the same character for piety and good conduct is required in deacons as in presbyters. Nay, it is added, "Let these also first be proved, then let them use the office of a deacon, being found blameless;" chapter iii. 10. Yet this office seems to have been probationary with respect to a higher office, for it is said, "They that use the office of a deacon well, purchase to themselves a *good degree*." *Ib*. 13. But wherein did the office of a deacon consist? The Scriptures have not informed us. Some readers may be surprised at this assertion, and ask, Were not seven deacons appointed to take care of the public stock in the church?* It is true, that "seven men of honest report, full of the Holy Ghost and wisdom," were chosen by the people, and

superintendents, as the Apostles, and by delegation from them, Timothy and Titus, were overseers or bishops of other pastors, as the Epistles to Timothy and Titus abundantly prove.

* Acts vi.

appointed by the Apostles to take care that no partiality should be shown in favour of the Hebrew women, in distributing the daily portion of food provided by the church; but these men are not called *deacons*, except in the running title of our Bibles. The text does not give them that name. Indeed, if it did, we should gain but little information as to the perpetual office of a deacon; for the employment imposed upon them was local and temporary, and has long since ceased to exist. In no part of the New Testament, that I recollect, is the office of a deacon described.

Though the office of a deacon is not described in the New Testament, it must have been perfectly understood, not only by Timothy to whom minute directions were given for the choice of proper persons to fill that office; but also by the Christians of that period, among whom the duties of the office were daily exercised. The christian church of modern times ought, therefore, to search out the nature of the office in those ecclesiastical writings which approach the nearest to the times of the Apostles.

Two properties of the office may be collected from the Scriptures. First, that it was an office, which, in point of importance, was similar to that of presbyter; for the same marks are laid down for the guidance of Timothy in the choice of deacons, as in the choice of presbyters. They were to be men of similar piety and good conduct in every relation of life. And, secondly, the office is described as probationary. It was designed to be a step to something higher. The rest must be supplied from the stores of ecclesiastical history.

We proceed then to inquire, whether the Apostles did appoint any officer in the church, of a degree superior to that of presbyter; such an officer as would now be called a bishop.* That we may, with greater certainty, discover the truth in this investigation, let us first state what is the peculiar office of a bishop, considered as superior to a presbyter; and then inquire, whether the Apostles appointed any such officer in the church.

The peculiar office of a bishop consists in these four particulars.

* The reader must not understand me as hinting, that this appropriate use of the word *bishop* is of modern date. By consulting ecclesiastical history he will find, that it was used in this appropriate sense by those who had been contemporary with the Apostle John, and that the christian church continued to use it in this sense after the death of the Apostles. But my observations are confined to the account which is given of the christian church in the New Testament.

1. In ordaining presbyters and deacons.

2. In superintending the doctrine of these ministers.

3. In superintending their conduct.

4. In regulating those matters in the church, which are not settled by divine authority.

Now these duties of a superintendent or bishop, were committed by the Apostle Paul to Timothy and Titus.

1. They were appointed to ordain other ministers, as the Apostles had done before them. "For this cause," says the Apostle to Titus, "left I thee in Crete, that thou shouldest ordain presbyters in every city, as I had appointed thee;" chapter i. 5. So, likewise, special directions were given to Timothy respecting the choice of those whom he should ordain presbyters or deacons.* Of these directions I shall have occasion to speak hereafter.

2. They were appointed to superintend the doctrine of these ministers. So says the Apostle to Timothy: "I besought thee to abide still at Ephesus, when I went into Macedonia,

* 1 Timothy iii.

that thou mightest charge some that they teach no other doctrine.*

3. They were appointed to superintend the conduct of other ministers. "Against a presbyter receive not an accusation, but before two or three witnesses."† He who is authorized to receive accusations, and hear witnesses against any person, is authorized to be the judge of that person.

4. They were appointed to regulate such matters in the church, as were not settled by express divine command. "For this cause left I thee in Crete, that thou shouldest set in order the things that are wanting;" that are left *undone*, as the margin expresses it.‡ This was a branch of apostolic authority which is here delegated to Titus, as appears from 1 Corinthians ii. 34. For, when the Apostle Paul had rectified the erroneous manner of receiving the Lord's Supper, into which the Corinthians had fallen, by stating to them the nature of that ordinance according to its original institution, he adds, that he would regulate inferior matters when he should be pre-

* 1 Timothy i. 3. † 1 Timothy v. 19.
‡ Titus i. 5.

sent with them. "And the rest will I set in order when I come."

Some other peculiarities of the office of superintendent might perhaps be collected from the New Testament; but these will suffice to show, that there was an office in the church, superior to that of presbyter; but (including it) though no name is given in the New Testament, except in the Revelations, to the persons who were to fill that office by delegation from the Apostles. The office itself, however, is described with great clearness; and two persons are mentioned to whom that office was delegated by the Apostle Paul.

We will now consider what was the mode of appointing presbyters and deacons; and to whom was the choice of persons, to fill those offices, committed.

The persons chosen were solemnly set apart by prayer and imposition of hands, in which (if we may form a judgment from one instance) the presbytery joined with the Apostle. In the first Epistle to Timothy, the Apostle Paul says, "Neglect not the gift that is in thee, which was given thee by prophecy, with the laying on of the hands of the presbytery;" chapter iv. 14. In the second Epistle, speaking, as it seems, of the same transaction, the

Apostle says, "I put thee in remembrance, that thou stir up the gift of God, which is in thee, by the putting on of *my hands*;" chapter i. 6. These passages are of equal authority, and therefore prove, that the presbytery joined with the Apostle in the imposition of hands, when Timothy received the gift of God, whatever that gift implied. Supposing the expression to refer to the ordination of Timothy, and supposing this ordination to be a specimen of all other ordinations, it will then follow, that the presbytery joined with the Apostle, or some delegated superintendent, in the imposition of hands; but no mention is made in the New Testament of any ordination to the ministry by presbyters, without the presence of an apostle, or some superintendent delegated by an apostle.

But to whom was the choice committed of persons who were to fill the office of presbyter or deacon? To the persons who were delegated by the Apostles to execute the office of superintendent or bishop; for thus runs the apostolic injunction respecting ordination: "The things that thou hast heard of me among many witnesses, the same *commit thou* to faithful men, who shall be able to teach others also."*

* 2 Timothy ii. 2.

When the "daily ministration" of the food provided for the widows was conducted with partiality, the Apostles desired the people "to look out among themselves, seven men of honest report, whom they appointed to serve the tables." Or when the charitable contribution of the Corinthians was to be carried to Jerusalem, St. Paul tells them, "that whomsoever they should appoint, them would he send to bring their liberality to Jerusalem.* But I recollect no instance of the people choosing either presbyter or deacon. The seven men chosen to serve the widows, as I have already observed, are not called deacons in the Acts of the Apostles.

After the traitor Judas had destroyed himself, the disciples, by the direction of Peter, appointed two persons out of the number of those who had accompanied our Lord through the whole of his ministry, that one might "be ordained to be a witness," with the other Apostles, "of his resurrection." The choice of this person was submitted to the Almighty, by the intervention of the lot. "They prayed, and said, Thou, Lord, who knowest the hearts of all men, shew whether of these two *thou hast chosen.*" This was a singular case,

* 1 Corinthians xvi. 3.

and was not considered by the Apostles, or their delegates, as a precedent for future ordinations.

Some persons have been of opinion, that the original word, used to express the ordination of presbyters by Paul and Barnabas,* implies, that it was done with the suffrage, or voting, of the people. As this word has been thus paraphrased by an excellent writer on the New Testament,† I shall subjoin a remark or two on this paraphrase. The word in this passage, translated *ordained*, does undoubtedly imply a choice or election, and did in its primary sense, I believe, express the election by lifting up of hands. But every person conversant in the original language of the New Testament must know, that it often signifies choice or election, simply, without voting.‡ Now since this is the case, as is allowed by the author to whom I allude, it is impossible to prove that the votes of the people had any thing to do with these ordinations, merely from the use of that Greek word, unless the context had given some intimation, that the

* Χειροτονησαντες δε αυτοις πρεσβυτερους. Acts xiv. 23.

† Dr. Doddridge. "Family Expositor," vol. iii. page 228.

‡ The reader may see many instances of this collected by Dr. Hammond, in his note on the text in question.

votes of the people directed the choice of the Apostles. But no such hint is given in the context. The most fair method of discovering the meaning of an author in any doubtful word, is to examine how he uses that word in other parts of his writings. Now the word here supposed to imply the votes of the people, is used but once besides, I think, by St. Luke; and there it could not imply any voting, or other interference of the people, for it is used to express the choice of God himself. "God shewed him openly; not to all the people, but unto witnesses *chosen before* of God."* St. Paul does not use this Greek word when he commands Titus to *ordain* presbyters; chapter i. 5. but another word,† which has no relation to the suffrage, or other interference of the people; and which is properly translated *ordain* (*i. e.* constitute or appoint) presbyters.

There is abundant proof, that the election of the presbyters and deacons was to be made by the superintendents who were appointed to ordain them. For what end does the Apostle Paul give Timothy and Titus such minute directions respecting the character of persons

* Προκεχειροτονημενοις υπο τȣ Θεȣ. Acts x. 41.

† Καταςησης κατα πολιν πρεσβυτερȣς.

to be ordained by them, if these directions were not to guide their choice? After all these directions, Timothy is commanded to use great caution in his choice; in scriptural language, to "lay hands suddenly on no man." If the choice was not committed to him, and his business was only to lay hands upon those whom the votes of the people presented to him, it was no matter how suddenly he laid his hands upon them. Though these considerations seem quite sufficient to produce conviction, yet the evidence is not exhausted; for the Apostle expressly says, that the directions which he gave to Timothy concerning the character of the persons to be ordained, were designed to guide *his* conduct. "These things write I unto thee, hoping to come unto thee shortly; but if I tarry long, that thou mayest know how thou oughtest to behave thyself in the house of God, which is the church of the living God." *

As the persons who filled the office of superintendent or bishop, were chosen by the Apostles themselves; and as no delegation of their power to choose successors in this office, is mentioned in the New Testament; the church

* 1 Timothy iii. 14, 15.

of Christ is necessarily left to its own discretion with respect to the manner of continuing this office in the church. The superintendent was clearly the next in station to the Apostle, as far as related to the ordinary and permanent state of the church. And, with respect to the ordination of presbyters and deacons, and the regulation of inferior matters in the church, he was manifestly endowed with apostolic power. The christian church will, therefore, make the nearest approach to the primitive model, by continuing a succession of superintendents through the intervention of their predecessors of the same order. At any rate, a succession of these officers must be continued, if the primitive model of church government is to be pursued; for there is no instance in the New Testament of any ordination of presbyter or deacon, either by the peoplê, or by the presbytery alone.

The importance of the episcopal office will more clearly appear, if we sum up and reduce into one view, those passages in the Epistles to Timothy and Titus, which exhibit its peculiar duties; at least, those which relate to the four branches of the office which I have already mentioned.

Let us then suppose the Apostle Paul to

have given the following commission to one who was already a presbyter.*

"My dear son;

"As my affairs have called me out of Asia into Greece, and I have 'besought thee to abide at Ephesus when I went into Macedonia;' I think it proper to give thee in writing such instructions as are necessary for the guidance of thy conduct. There are many presbyters at Ephesus, and these require some one to superintend them, as they superintend 'the flock over which the Holy Ghost hath made them overseers.'† I have observed with sorrow, that there are some of them in danger of 'giving heed to fables;' nay, who *have* already 'turned aside unto vain jangling; desiring to be teachers of the law; understanding neither what they say, nor whereof they affirm.' Now, I beseech thee, look well to the doctrine of these ministers. If it be

* To prevent interruption by quoting the chapter and verse of each text as it occurs, I shall only give the text between inverted commas. The reader may easily find the passages, as they are all contained in the Epistles to Timothy and Titus, unless where it is otherwise noted.

† Acts xx. 28.

possible, prevent error from spreading in the church. Remember, that for this purpose I left thee at Ephesus, 'that thou mightest charge some that they teach no other doctrine,' than that which they have received from me. 'Of these things put them in remembrance, charging them before the Lord, that they strive not about words to no profit, but to the subverting of the hearers.' Be diligent both in government and instruction; and what thou hast learned from me, 'these things command and teach.' Exert the authority with which I have invested thee, and put to silence improper teachers. 'For there are many unruly and vain talkers, whose mouths must be stopped, who subvert whole houses, teaching things which they ought not.' And as heresy is destructive to the purity of the church, suffer not a person tainted with this contagious disease to remain in the communion of the faithful, when repeated advice and counsel have failed to reclaim him. 'A man that is an heretic, after the first and second admonition, reject.'

"I also command thee, that thou look well to the conduct of the ministers over whom I have placed thee. But execute this delicate business with discretion. The character of ministers is of great consequence. And, although I have appointed thee to be the judge of their conduct, yet be not hasty to condemn any one without a fair hearing. 'Against a presbyter do not *even* receive an accusation, but before two or three witnesses.'

"See that the ordinances appointed by Christ are observed in the church according to his appointment. Yet there are many inferior matters which thou must regulate as *decency* and 'good order shall require.'* 'For this cause left I thee' at Ephesus, 'that thou shouldest set in order the things that are wanting, and that have hitherto been left undone.'

"Use the utmost caution in the choice of persons who are to execute the office of ministers. I do not consider all as forward, who seek to be overseers of the flock of Christ; for, 'if a man desire the office of a bishop, he desireth a good work.' But accept no candidate for this office, unless he 'be blameless, vigilant, sober, of good behaviour,' and 'have a good report of them that are without' the christian church, 'lest he fall into reproach.' Do not ordain 'a novice, lest, being lifted up with pride, he fall into the condemnation of the devil.' Be not hasty in forming thy judgment of men's characters, however fair they

* 1 Corinthians xiv. 40.

may appear; 'lay hands suddenly on no man. Stir up the gift of God which is in thee, by the putting on of my hands, with the laying on of the hands of the presbytery.' And in the solemn act of ordination, let the presbytery join with thee in the imposition of hands, seeing thou canst not follow a better example than that which was shown at thine own ordination.*

"Finally, my son, 'be strong in the grace that is in Christ Jesus. And the things that thou hast heard of me among many witnesses, the same *commit thou* to faithful men, who shall be able to teach others also.'"

These passages of Scripture, (which, I hope, have not been in any degree perverted by my paraphrase,) with others of the same import, have satisfied my mind, that in the primitive church there were *superintendents*, answering to the officers now called *bishops*. By what name these should be distinguished in after ages, is of no consequence. Whether they should be itinerant, or stationary; whether they should exercise their functions over a small or a large district; whether they should

* This is the method enjoined by the Church of England in her ordination service for presbyters.

stand totally unconnected with the government under which they might live, or be called to give their advice in matters of public concern; would depend on a variety of circumstances, which we are not at all concerned to inquire after, and enumerate.

OBSERVATIONS ON THE GOVERNMENT OF THE CHRISTIAN CHURCH, DURING THE LAST PERIOD OF THE SACRED HISTORY CONTAINED IN THE NEW TESTAMENT.

If we are desirous of knowing what kind of government was established by divine authority in the primitive church of Christ, we must not look for it in those passages of Scripture which represent the Apostles and other ministers as engaged in the exercise of the miraculous powers with which they were endowed; nor in those passages which describe the disturbed state of the church, through the violence of persecution. We must look for it in those appointments which have an evident respect to futurity; and fix our regard on those passages of Scripture which describe the church in its most settled and ordinary state.

My inquiries have hitherto been confined to the formation of the christian church during the life of the Apostle Paul. But the sacred history carries us somewhat further, and exhibits the government of the church at a later period. The Epistles which St. John was commanded to write to the seven churches in Asia, will throw further light on this subject.

St. John is supposed to have out-lived the rest of the Apostles,* and the churches to which he wrote seem to have been for some time in a settled state. We have, therefore, a good opportunity of learning from these Epistles, what was the true apostolic form of church government.

Our information will chiefly arise from considering what kind of minister was designed by the term, "angels of the churches." I take for granted, that the term implies a minister of some description. The strain of the Epistles, and the distinction made between

* "Domitian banished him into the solitary Isle of Patmos, where he was favoured with the visions of the Apocalypse. After Domitian's death, he returned from Patmos, and governed the Asiatic churches. There he remained till the time of Trajan."

Milner's Ecclesiastical History, vol. i. edit. 2. page 138.

the *angel* and the people of which the church consisted, point out this so clearly, that no doubt can arise in the mind of any one who is content to take the Scriptures in their most obvious meaning.

It seems also sufficiently plain, that the *angel* was an individual person. He is always addressed as such by the inspired writers. And as it is expressly said, that there were *seven* angels, and one in each church, there can be no ground for contest on this subject. I shall not dwell, therefore, on the absurdity of a contrary supposition, though that is manifest from the minute description which is given of each of the angels.

By the term *angel* must then be meant, either the sole presbyter presiding over the congregation of christians at Ephesus, Smyrna, &c. respectively; or a *superintendent* in each church, presiding over the presbyters as well as over the flock.

In order that we may form our ideas on this subject in exact conformity to the Scripture history, let us consider the state of the first of these churches addressed by the Apostle John, concerning which we have the most ample information, and apply our conclusions to the rest of the churches; in doing which, we shall find ourselves supported by the instructions addressed to the angels of the other churches.

The labours of St. Paul had been abundant in the Lesser Asia. He had at one time preached in the Jewish synagogue at Ephesus "for the space of three months;" and, "when divers were hardened, and believed not, but spake evil of that way before the multitude, he departed from them, and separated the disciples, disputing daily in the school of one Tyrannus. And this continued by the space of two years; so that all they which dwelt in Asia heard the word of the Lord Jesus, both Jews and Greeks. So that not alone at Ephesus, but almost throughout all Asia, this Paul" (in the language of Demetrius) had "persuaded and turned away much people."*

It is probable, therefore, that by the "church of Ephesus" was meant, not only the christians in that city, but those also in the adjacent country; a great number of whom must have been converted to the truth during this long residence of the Apostle. If this was the meaning of the term used by St. John, the "angel of the church of Ephesus," must have been a minister presiding over a considerable

* Acts xix. 8—10, 26.

district. But omitting this reasonable supposition, it is clear, that the number of christians residing in the city of Ephesus was so great, as to require the care of several presbyters. For, when St. Paul passed by this city in his way from Greece to Jerusalem, he summoned these presbyters to meet him at Miletus. "From Miletus he sent to Ephesus, and called the *presbyters* of the church."*

It is certain, therefore, by the term "angel of the church of Ephesus," could not be meant the sole presbyter, or minister of the congregation of christians at Ephesus.

The *angel* of the church must, of consequence, have been the *superintendent* presiding over the presbyters, as well as over the flock.

This establishment was not new. It had subsisted for some time in the church of Ephesus, as I have already shown, when describing from the Scriptures the authority which St. Paul had delegated to Timothy. He had been left by the Apostle at Ephesus, to superintend the teaching and the conduct of the presbyters in that part; and to ordain others, as the state of the church might require.

The Epistle of St. John to the church of

* Acts xx. 17.

Ephesus shows, that the same authority which St. Paul had delegated to Timothy, was possessed by the *angel* of the church who resided at Ephesus when the Apocalypse was written.

When St. Paul appointed Timothy and Titus to be superintendents, or bishops, over other presbyters, he gave them minute directions for the regulation of their conduct in that important office. It was not necessary that such directions should be given to the angels of the seven churches in Asia, as they were already settled officers in the christian church, and were in the actual exercise of those powers which St. Paul committed to Timothy and Titus. We must not, therefore, expect to find the duties of a superintendent amply displayed in these short epistles to the angels of the seven churches, as this had been already executed in the Epistles to Timothy and Titus. St. John was led to mention the duties of the office only incidentally, as the persons who now held it required praise or reproof, according to their respective conduct in the execution of that office. But the incidental mention of the peculiar functions of the office, affords as clear a proof that it was held by the persons addressed, as is afforded by the more minute description contained in the Epistles to Timothy and Titus.

Nothing can prove more clearly that, the *angel* of the church of Ephesus was the superintendent of other ministers, than the notice which is taken of his authority to try the pretensions of those who laid a claim to the highest office in the christian church. "*Thou* hast tried them which say they are *Apostles*, and are not; and hast found them liars."* The angel of this church had exercised his superintending authority with zeal and discretion, and now receives the approbation of his conduct from the great Head of the church, through the hands of the Apostle.

The same authority is recognised with respect to the *angel* of the church at Thyatira, but in a way of reproof, instead of commendation. For, after the Apostle had expressed our Lord's approbation of his faith and patience, &c. it is added, "Notwithstanding I have a few things against thee, because thou sufferest that woman Jezebel, who calleth herself a prophetess, to teach," &c. Now it could not have been the subject of blame in the angel of the church in Thyatira, that he

* Revelations ii. 2.

suffered this pretended prophetess to exercise her talents among the christians in that city, or district, unless he had possessed the authority of examining the pretensions of those who laid claim to the extraordinary gifts of the Holy Spirit, and of silencing improper teachers; which, as hath been already shown, were the functions of a *superintendent*; that is, of a minister in the christian church, who, ever since the apostolic age, has received the title of bishop.

From these passages of Scripture I am convinced, that *Diocesan Episcopacy* * was established by divine authority in the christian churches in Asia, before the death of the Apostle John; and I can find no reason from Scripture to think that, the government of the churches in Asia differed from that of other christian churches. They were all under the care of the same persons;† matters of great concern, respecting them universally, were determined by a synod of the Apostles and

* By *Diocesan Episcopacy*, I mean the government of the church by *superintendents* or bishops, each presiding over his own district, though subject to a general synod of bishops and presbyters. Acts xv. 6. xvi. 4.

† "That which cometh upon me daily, the care of *all* the churches." 2 Corinthians xi. 28.

presbyters at Jerusalem;* and the decrees made for the government of the churches were distributed by Paul and Silas, as they went about preaching the gospel.†

My duty to the great Head of the church compels me to respect that authority which appears to me so clearly to have been established by his direction; and I pray God, that this authority may always be exercised for the benefit of his "church, which he hath purchased with his own blood;" that it may be presented to Him at length, "a glorious church, not having spot or wrinkle, or any such thing; but holy and without blemish."‡

* Acts xv. 6.

† "And as they went through the cities, they delivered them the *decrees* for to keep, that were ordained of the Apostles and presbyters which were at Jerusalem."
Acts xvi. 4.

‡ Ephesians v. 27.

THE END.

J S Hughes, Printer, 66, Paternoster Row, London.

Lightning Source UK Ltd.
Milton Keynes UK
UKHW011455160119
335572UK00010B/543/P